OBJECT ORIENTED PROGRAMMING AND C++

OBJECT ORIENTED PROGRAMMING AND C++

(Second Edition)

R. Rajaram

PUBLISHING FOR ONE WORLD

NEW AGE INTERNATIONAL (P) LIMITED, PUBLISHERS

New Delhi • Bangalore • Chennai • Guwahati • Hyderabad
Jalandhar • Kolkata • Lucknow • Mumbai • Ranchi

Visit us at **www.newagepublishers.com**

Published by New Age International (P) Ltd., Publishers
First Edition:1997
Second Edition: 2007
Reprint: 2009

Branches:

- 36, Malikarjuna Temple Street, Opp. ICWA, Basavanagudi, **Bangalore**. ✆ (080) 26677815
- 26, Damodaran Street, T. Nagar, **Chennai**. ✆ (044) 24353401
- Hemsen Complex, Mohd. Shah Road, Paltan Bazar, Near Starline Hotel, **Guwahati**. ✆ (0361) 2543669
- No. 105, 1st Floor, Madhiray Kaveri Tower, 3-2-19, Azam Jahi Road, Nimboliadda, **Hyderabad**. ✆ (040) 24652456
- RDB Chambers (Formerly Lotus Cinema) 106A, Ist Floor, S.N. Banerjee Road, **Kolkata**. ✆ (033) 22275247
- 16-A, Jopling Road, **Lucknow**. ✆ (0522) 2209578
- 142C, Victor House, Ground Floor, N.M. Joshi Marg, Lower Parel, **Mumbai**. ✆ (022) 24927869
- 22, Golden House, Daryaganj, **New Delhi**. ✆ (011) 23262370, 23262368

ISBN (10): 81-224-1964-X
ISBN (13): 978-81-224-1964-1

Rs. 195.00

C-09-03-3542

Printed in India at Mohan Lal Printers, Delhi.
Typeset at Goswami Associates, Delhi.

PUBLISHING FOR ONE WORLD
NEW AGE INTERNATIONAL (P) LIMITED, PUBLISHERS
4835/24, Ansari Road, Daryaganj, New Delhi-110002
Visit us at **www.newagepublishers.com**

PREFACE TO THE SECOND EDITION

Object Oriented Programming and C++ has stood the test of time. The book has been in circulation among students since its first edition appeared in 1997.

With the advances in OOP concept, necessity arose to include two chapters on Exception Handling and Template and Standard Template Library. Twenty additional programs have been included with outputs, to enable the student to test them.

Most programs up to Chapter 13 will run on Turbo or Borland C++ environment. The programs in Chapters 14 and 15, and the additional programs were tested in Debian Linux. The student is encouraged to try them on Linux or UNIX environment.

The book has a new face and a different setting. In the course of the transition, some errors might have set in. Readers finding such errors are requested to send in their response to the author at mdu_rajaram@yahoo.com. Suggestions for improvement are most welcome.

The author expresses his gratitude to the most benevolent Dr. (Mrs.) Radha Thiagarajan, Chairperson of Thiagarajar College of Engineering, Madurai, for affording the conducive environment to undertake this project. His thanks are due to Mr. Karumuttu T. Kannan, Vice Chairman and Correspondent, and Dr. V. Abhai Kumar, Principal of the college for their support and encouragement. The author also thanks his research scholars who helped in proof reading the manuscript.

Madurai **R. Rajaram**

PREFACE TO THE FIRST EDITION

This book is designed with the Indian reader in mind. The author has cautiously avoided verbosity and circumlocution as they add fat to the book and make it bulky and unwieldy. Conforming to the slogan "Small is Beautiful" the book has been deliberately kept thin. It is crisp, precise and brief.

The book has been revised from its original form offered to the students of the Computer Course in Computer Programming of Thiagarajar College of Engineering, Madurai, on the suggestion of a anonymous reviewer. It is now fit for the general reader and students, particularly of the B.Sc., B.E., PGDCA, MCA, M.Sc., Degree courses of most Indian Universities and training institutes offering C++ as a course.

The author places on record his gratitude to Dr. (Mrs) Radha Thiagarajan, former Vice-Chancellor of Alagappa University, Karaikudi, and Chairman of the Governing Council of Thiagarajar College of Engineering and Mr. Karumuttu T.Kannan, Correspondent of the college for their encouragement and support. Dr. M.V. Ramamoorthy, Former Principal, and Dr. R. Srinivasan, Principal, extended all facilities of the college to undertake the work and the author extends his thanks to them.

The author is grateful to Mr. Siya, Lecturer in Electronics Communication Engineering for thoroughly editing the manuscript in the light of the reviewers suggestions. He also thanks his other colleagues in the CSE department: Dr. N. Ramaraj, Mrs. R.R. Shyamala, Mr.C. Sridharan, Miss G.Andal Jayalakshmi, Mr. N. Murali, Mrs. P.Sharmila Kanna, Mr. R.Pandiarajan, Mr. R.Hariharan, Mr.N.Pungazhendi, Miss. S.Sivagami, Sivabalan and Veerabadran.

R. Rajaram

PREFACE TO THE FIRST EDITION

This book is designed with the Indian reader in mind. The author has cautiously avoided verbosity and gimmicks as they add fat to the book and make it bulky and unwieldy. Conforming to the slogan "Small is beautiful" the book has been deliberately kept thin. It is crisp, precise and brief.

The book has been revised from its original form offered to the students of the Computer Course in Computer Programming of Thiagarajar College of Engineering, Madurai, on the suggestion of an anonymous reviewer. It is now fit for the general reader and students, particularly of the B.Sc., B.E., PGDCA, MCA, M.Sc., Degree courses of most Indian Universities and training institutes offering C++ as a course.

The author places on record his gratitude to Dr. (Mrs.) Radha Thiagarajan, former Vice Chancellor of Alagappa University, Karaikudi, and Chairman of the Governing Council of Thiagarajar College of Engineering and Mr. Karumuttu T. Kannan, Correspondent of the college for their encouragement and support. Dr. M.V. Ramamoorthy, Former Principal, and Dr. R. Srinivasan, Principal, extended all facilities of the college to undertake the work and the author extends his thanks to them.

The author is grateful to Mr. Siva, Lecturer in Electronics Communication Engineering for thoroughly editing the manuscript in the light of the reviewers suggestions. He also thanks his other colleagues in the CSE department: Dr. M. Pamaraj, Mrs. R.R. Shyamala, Mr. G. Sudharsan, Miss G. Angel Jayalakshmi, Mr. N. Murali, Mrs. P. Sharmila Kanna, Mr. R. Pandiarajan, Mr. R. Harihar, Mr. N. Poongazhendi, Miss S. Sivagami, Sivabalan and Venkatram.

R. Rajaram

CONTENTS

Chapter 1

Introduction to OOPS and C++

Chapter 1

Introduction to OOPS and C++

Object Oriented Programming is considered as important as the development of the first high level language at the early days of the computer age. Why Object Oriented Programming when we were just about to settle down comfortably with good old procedural languages like Pascal, Basic, Fortran, Cobol?

One of the chief weaknesses of Procedural languages is its complexity which OOPS is able to cope with easily. The objectives of OOPS is clear, reliable and easy-to-understand programs.

C++ which supports OOPS is very popular. There are two versions: Borland's Turbo C++ and Borland C++. Some vital features about them are data hiding, encapsulation and polymorphism. Does this sound Greek and Latin to you? Don't bother, you will understand these terms as you study programs using these concepts.

Does one need any prior knowledge in programming languages? Yes. It would be good if you have some background in Pascal or C, particularly in the Turbo environment. Others like Basic, Fortran or any one of them would be an added advantage. A fair knowledge about the use of MS-DOS is also expected.

Can't an absolute novice to computers learn OOPS and C++ ? Why not! You only need enthusiasm like in any other activity. The very fact that you possess this book and have started reading it, shows that you have necessary enthusiasm to learn C++. Therefore do not hesitate, take the plunge now.

What is the minimum system requirement?

1. Borland's Turbo C++: good for beginners.
2. Borland's C++: good for the experienced users. It includes assembler, debugger, utilities to develop MS window programs.
3. PC XT, AT or PS/2 or compatibles.
4. Turbo C++ (tc) requires MS-DOS 2 or higher versions.

5. Borland C++ (bc) requires MS-DOS 3 or higher versions.
6. 640 kilo bytes RAM, 6MB Hard Disk or Floppy Disk drive.
7. 80 column monochrome or colour monitor.
8. Mouse - optional.
9. MS - windows - optional.

Would knowledge of C help learning C++? Yes and No. A knowledge of C would help understanding pointers, structures of C++. But a lack of knowledge in C need not be a deterrent. Actually C and C++ are two different languages, though they have similar syntax. You'll find that you may have to unlearn many things in C, while learning C++. The transformation is going to be exciting and thrilling.

As we said C++ supports OOPS. OOPS have objects and classes. What do these imply? Now recall that in a procedural language, a program gets the data, processes it and gives the result as an output. This is done by a sequence of instructions called a program. Here data has a second class status. Whereas in OOPS data is considered the most important factor and given a prime status.

In procedural language we have subroutines, subprograms or procedures. Whereas in C++ these are considered to be functions. Functions are also known as modules. A module does a specific task.

The module or function is regarded as the cornerstone of structured programming. The function do things that any one program statement does.

C++ will liberally use concepts like global variable and local variable. A global variable is defined outside a function and is accessible by all functions. But allowing such free access is liable to corrupt the data. Whereas in C++ such free access to data and consequent mutilation of data is prevented by the concept of data hiding.

A local variable is defined within a function. It is accessed only by the particular function in which it is defined.

Other characteristics of C++ are its extensibility, which means it is able to create new data types. OOP languages are able to combine data and functions that operate on these data, called objects. The functions that access and operate on objects is called member functions. Therefore we say data is hidden, thereby preventing accidental alterations.

When data and functions are combined into one entity, we call it as encapsulation. In Small Talk OOP language member functions are called methods.

We say that objects are members of classes. We have the liberty to include any data type and functions as objects of a class. However, defining class does not create objects.

Now what is a class? It is a collection of similar objects. One of the unique characteristics of class is inheritance. To understand class and inheritance consider a class called Business.

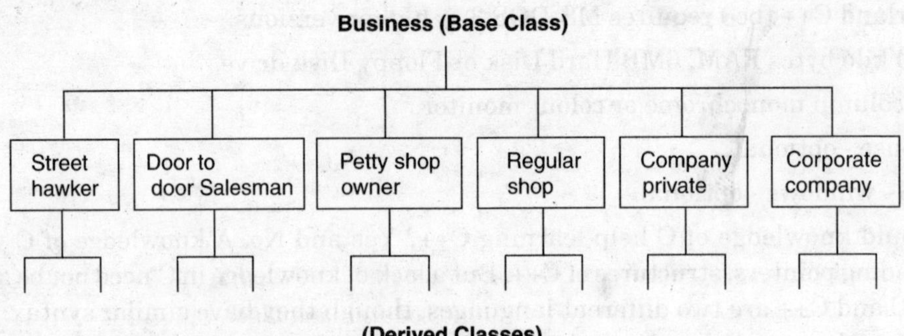

Thus you find that Business is the base class and from it several classes can be derived. Each has its own peculiarities and traits. Each subclass may again be divided into further subclasses. Thus we say that the derived class inherits some features of the base class, but add new features of their own.

To extend this discussion further, assume that several different sections of a procedural program perform the same action. Then examine them and pull out the common elements and organize them into one function. Thereafter the different sections can invoke this common functions to perform the common action, besides performing individual processing as well.

Another useful feature of C++ is its reusability. You have known library functions in procedural languages. In C++ you can create classes, which can be used by other programmers, just like invoking any library functions. Further inheritance enables a programmer to adopt an existing class and add new features and capabilities to it.

Other peculiarities of C++ are creation of new data types, polymorphism and overloading. We'll see how new data types are created during the programming studies. Polymorphism means using operators and functions in different ways, depending on what they are operating on.

An overloaded operator implies giving the capability to an existing operator to operate on new data.

Thus you are now aware of the power and potentialities of this new language of the future.

Of course the best way to learn any computer language is to sit with the terminal and sweat it out. As the famous author Fowler of Oxford English Dictionary said, "There is no royal way to learning". In case you do not have free access to a terminal, you need not be bogged down. You may use this book to familiarize with the syntax of C + + and equip yourself so that when a terminal is available, you can put it to the best use.

REVIEW QUESTIONS

1.1 What is the chief weakness of procedural language?

1.2 Which version of Borland C++ is sufficient for a beginner?

1.3 What are the 3 most important features of C++?

1.4 Does working in Turbo environment require a knowledge about using MS-DOS?

1.5 What additional features are built into Borland C++?
1.6 Which version of MS-DOS would suffice for Turbo C++?
1.7 Which version of MS-DOS is required for Borland C++?
1.8 What minimum capacity of RAM is needed to run C++?
1.9 What minimum capacity of Hard Disk is required for C++?
1.10 Is a mouse an absolute necessity?
1.11 What is common about C and C++?
1.12 Do procedural languages give prime status to data?
1.13 What two factors distinguish OOPS from procedural language?
1.14 How are subroutines, subprogram or procedures branded in C++?
1.15 What is considered the cornerstone of structured programming?
1.16 What do you consider the major drawback of global variable?
1.17 How can mutilation of data due to global definition be prevented?
1.18 What is the ability to create new data types in C++ called?
1.19 What do you call data when member functions operate on these data?
1.20 What is the name of such functions that operate on objects?
1.21 How do you brand combination of data and functions into one entity?
1.22 Does defining a class create objects?
1.23 What is the collection of similar objects called?
1.24 What will you say is the unique characteristics of class?
1.25 Suppose you create a class which can be used by other programmers like a library function, what is it called?
1.26 What do you call it when operators and functions are used in different ways?
1.27 What do you call an existing operator that is given capability to operate on new data?

Answer

1.1 Complexity
1.2 Turbo C++
1.3 Data hiding, encapsulation and polymorphism
1.4 Yes
1.5 Assembler, debugger, utilities to develop window programs
1.6 2 or higher
1.7 3 or higher
1.8 640 KB
1.9 6 MB
1.10 Only Optional
1.11 Same syntax
1.12 No
1.13 Objects and classes.
1.14 Functions or modules
1.15 Functions or modules
1.16 Data corruption
1.17 Data hiding
1.18 Extensibility
1.19 Objects
1.20 Member functions
1.21 Encapsulation
1.22 No
1.23 A class
1.24 Inheritance
1.25 Reusability
1.26 Polymorphism
1.27 Overloaded operator

Chapter 2

Programming Concepts in C++

Chapter 2

Programming Concepts in C++

OBJECTIVE

The chapter discusses basic programming constructs, variables, input/output statements, comment statement, arithmetic operators, increment operators, data conversions and library functions.

C ++ KEYWORDS

void	int	break	switch	case
char	const	float	unsigned	double
signed	short			

2.1 ORGANISATION OF A C++ PROGRAM

Let us straight away study a simple C++ program and learn its organisation.

```
//Demo.CPP
//Illustrates organisation of C++ program
#include <iostream.h>
void main( )
   {
   cout <<"Welcome to C++ IDE";
   }
```

Analysis

1. Comment is started with two slashes. The name of the program is DEMO.CPP. Another comment tells about the task of the program. Using double backslash can contain a comment in one line only.

2. #include < iostream.h> is a preprocessor directive. It tells the compiler to substitute the header file "iostream" at this point of the program . The header file is needed to use objects such as cout and cin.

   Preprocessor directive is a command to the compiler to do certain action, like including a file.

   Header file is a name of a predefined file.

3. "void" is a C++ keyword, which implies that no value is returned by this program.
4. main( ) is a function which tells the compiler where to start control from. It is a function as indicated by the empty parentheses.
5. The body of the main function is put within curly braces { }.
6. "cout" is an object which directs the string enclosed within the double quotation marks to the screen for display.
7. Each C++ program statement must be terminated by a semicolon.

   The output of the above program is:

```
Welcome to C++ IDE.
```

Aside:

The function may be part of a class or independent or stand alone. The main ( ) function may call member functions in various objects or call other independent or stand-alone functions.

Each C++ statement is terminated by a semicolon. You may have any number of statements in one line separated by semicolons. But for sake of clarity and readability it is good to have only one statement in one line. Generally in a statement white space, *i.e.*, spaces, carriage return, linefeed, tabs, vertical tabs, formfeed, are ignored by the compiler.

For example the following is perfectly acceptable.

```
#include <iostream.h>
void main ( )
   {
   cout <<"welcome to C++ IDE.";
   }
```

So also the following is OK.

```
void main ( ) { cout << " welcome to C++ IDE." ; }
```

Very long string constants may be broken up with backslashes (\) as shown:

```
cout <<"welcome to the\
integrated Development\
Environment";
```

cout is called an object, which is predefined in Turbo C++ to correspond to standard output stream.

< < is called the insertion or "put to" operator. It directs the string on the right of the object to the left. ie. string to cout.

Actually "< <" is the left shift operator. However it is made to perform a different task here, and hence it is called an "over loaded" operator. Overloading implies it does a task in addition to its predefined one.

There is no real string variable type in C++. It is treated as an array of characters. Comments may also be written using /*.*/

This permits multiline comment such as;

```
/* this is a
comment statement
of the
multiline type */
```

But is preferable in C++ to use double slash (//).

The following program illustrates liberal use of comments:

```
// comments.CPP
// shows liberal use of comment statements
#include <iostream.h> // preprocessor
                      //directive
void main ( )              // main function
   {                  //body of main begins
   cout <<"Integrated development environment,.";
                      // Output statement
   }                  //end of main function
```

2.2 VARIABLE TYPES

C++ has integers, floating point numbers and characters as variables.

An integer occupies 2 bytes of storage in machines operating on MS-DOS. The range of values handled by any integer is — 32768 to 32767.

The following program shows how integers are handled.

```
// integer.CPP
// use of integer variables shown
#include <iostream.h>
void main( )
   {
```

```
int int1; int int2;
int1 = 34;
int2 = int1 + 66;
cout << "int1 + 66 = ";
cout << int2;
}
```

Analysis

1. This source program is called "integer. CPP".
2. "int1" , "int2" are declared as int or integer type variables. "int" is a C++ keyword.
3. int1 is assigned value 34 using the assignment operator " = ".
4. int2; is computed by an expression where int1 is added to 66.
5. The first object cout outputs the string within double quotes.
6. The second object cout displays contents of int2.

Aside

All declarations and definitions must be terminated with semicolons. A declaration sets up a variable name and specifies its type. A definition assigns memory for such variables. Definitions may be placed anywhere in the program even after an executable statement.

This point is obvious from the following program.

```
// centfar.CPP
// celcius to fahrenheit conversion
#include <iostream.h>
void main( )
  {
  int c;
  cout <<"Enter temp in C:";        // prompt
  cin >> c; // standard input stream
  int f = c * 9 / 5 + 32;      //expression
  cout << c <<" celcius is" <<f<<"fahr." <<' \n';
```

Analysis

1. "cin" is an object of standard input stream. It accepts input through a keyboard and assigns it to "c". "iostream" header files enable the use of this object. The operator >> assigns it to c.
2. In the expression "int f = c* 9/5 + 32;" type of "f" is a declared after two executable statements. Here we say "f" is a purely auto (automatic or temporary) variable. "auto" is a C++ keyword. We'll be discussing about auto storage class in a later chapter.

The output of this program is :

```
Enter temp in C : 30        <ret>
30 celsius is 86 fahr.
```

The number 30 is typed through the keyboard and entered.

3. Note the '\n' control character in the last cout. It is known as the escape sequence for new line, and causes the cursor to move down by one line.

2.3 VARIABLE NAMES

For naming variables the following rules apply.

(*a*) lower case, uppercase or both alphabets maybe used.

(*b*) digits 0 – 9.

(*c*) underscore (–) as beginning or intermediate character.

(*d*) 32 significant characters are recognized.

Valid variable names:

```
tce Tce _tce _madurai
name_of_the_student pay123
```

Invalid : (Explain why invalid)

#madurai 5street int char

float

Keywords cannot be used as variables names. Class and function names follow the same rules. Lowercase and uppercase alphabets are distinguished as different names.

```
(eg)   tce Tce tCe tcE TCE TCe TcE tCE
```

2.4 CHARACTER VARIABLES AND STRINGS

"char" is the keyword to declare and define a character variable. It needs one byte of memory and can handle integers from - 128 to 127.

char variables generally store only ASCII characters, which range from 0 to 127 or 0 to 255 (MS-DOS).

A character constant is enclosed within single quotes. A string constant is enclosed within double quotes.

'a'   '*'   '9'   'A'   '+' are char constant

"madurai" "development" "tce" are string constants

Now study this program:

```
// character.CPP
// handling character variables
```

```
#include <iostream.h>
void main( )
   {
   char ch1='T';    // defined & initialized
   char ch2='\t';   // esc seq for tab
   cout <<ch1; cout << ch2;
   ch1 ='c';        // assignment
   cout << ch1;
   cout << '\n' ;   // cursor goes to new line
   }
```

Analysis

1. "ch1" is defined as char type and assigned const T.
2. ch2 is defined as char type and assigned the tab character \t . It is called the escape sequence for horizontal tab. This will cause the cursor to move over to the next tab stop.
3. In the assignment statement ch1 is assigned new value 'c' replacing the original 'T".
4. The '\n' is another escape sequence which causes the cursor to move over to a newline.

   The output of this program is:

```
T    c
```

2.5 ESCAPE SEQUENCES

Escape sequences are cryptic commands included with standard output object cout, to perform specific actions. The complete list is given in Table 2.1

Esc sequence	*character*	*Action*
\a	bell or beep	sounds a bell
\b	backspace	moves cursor back 1 space
\f	formfeed	next line
\n	newline	next line
\r	carriage ret	carriage return
\t	tab	horizontal tab
\\	backslash	for comment statements
\'	single quote	
\ "	double quotes	
\xdd	hexadecimal	base of 16 numbers

'\xdd', is used for graphic character representation. For example '\xE3' could display pi (π). Here E3 is hex notation for 227.

2.6 FLOAT TYPE VARIABLES

Float type variables can store real numbers. There are 4 types called float, long, double and long double. Float occupies 4 bytes of memory and has a range of 3.4E - 38 to 3. 4E38 and can be represented to 7 digit precision.

Floating point constants may be written in exponential form with E for the exponent.

The following program shows how to handle floating point constants.

```
// float pt.CPP.
// floating point variables and constants
#include <iostream.h>
void main( )
    {
    float R, r:
    const float PI = 3.14154;
    cout << "Enter R of circle:";
    cin >>R;
    cout << "Enter r of circle:";
    cin >> r;
    float annarea = PI * ( R + r) * ( R - r) ;
    cout << "Annular area is "<< annarea << endl;
    }
```

When compiled and executed the output was:

Enter R of circle: 2.35	<ret>
Enter r of circle: 1.75	<ret>
Annular area is 7.728187	

Analysis

1. Variables R and r are declared as type float. Each variable would occupy 4 bytes in memory.
2. The statement

   `const float PI = 3.14154;`

   does several tasks. It is declared a "const" (constant) thereby PI remains unalterable throughout this program. Any occurrence of PI is automatically substituted by the value 3.14154. "const" is a C++ keyword.
3. In the expression for computing the area of the circular ring, a variable called "annarea" is set up as type float. This is another example where definition is done only when required; and not at the beginning itself.

4. In the last standard output object cout, "endl" is another way of moving the cursor to newline. It has the effect of the escape sequence '\n'.
5. Note the output is given default 6 decimal places accuracy. We shall see later on how to restrict the desired number of digits by use of "set precision" manipulator.

Aside

Instead of "const" qualifier, a preprocessor directive could be used to associate a constant value to PI, such as

```
#define PI 3.14154
```

But in C++ this procedure is dissuaded. Wholly uppercase letters are used in such definitions only as a matter of style.

2.7 USE OF MANIPULATORS

We'll see how two manipulators "setw" and "endl" are used. "endl" is alternate for '\n' or newline or linefeed character. "setw" organises output right justified and fixes the width of the output. To use "setw" operator the "iomanip.h" header file must be included as a preprocessor directive. "endl" works even without the header file.

```
// manipulator.CPP
// demo on use of setw
#include <iostream.h>
#include <iomanip.h>    // setw( )
void main( )
   {
   int mdu=12, mad=35, tri=7, coim=11;
   cout<<"Name of city"<<"Population"<<endl
       <<"Madurai   "<<mdu<<endl
       <<"Madras    "<<mad<<endl
       <<"Trichy    "<<tri<<endl
       <<"Coimbatore "<<coim<<endl
       <<"          "<< endl;   //without setw de
                                //fault setting
   cout<<setw(12) <<"Name of city" <<setw(12)
       <<"Population"<<endl
       <<setw(12) << "Madurai "<<setw(12) << mdu <<endl
       <<setw(12) <<"Madras" <<setw(12) << mad <<
   endl
       <<setw(12) <<"Trichy" <<setw(12) << tri <<
```

```
    endl
        <<setw(12)<<"Coimbatore "<<setw(12)<<
    coim<< endl;
                //with setw manipulator
        }
```

The output is:

```
Name of city        Population
Madurai             12
Madras              35
Trichy              7
Coimbatore          11


Name of city        Population
     Madurai                12
      Madras                35
      Trichy                 7
  Coimbatore                11
```

Analysis

1. Header file "iomanip" is needed to use "setw" manipulator.
2. The "int" declaration sets up 4 variables ""mdu", "mad", "tri" and "coim" and also initializes them. This sort of multiple definition helps to save space.
3. The first object "cout" uses the default setting. The strings are left justified during the display. Subsequent strings are made of equal length for sake of uniformity.
4. "endl" manipulator at end of each line causes cursor movement to newline. This is the same as the escape sequence '\n'.
5. The empty double quotes introduces a blank line, so also the "endl" manipulator, so that 2 blank lines appear between first and the second outputs.
6. In the second object cout, "setw" manipulators are used. The argument 12 allows a 12-space width to contain the first string, and another 12 space width for the second variable.
7. Note that in the output city names and numbers are right justified giving a neat appearance.

2.8 A TINGE ABOUT OTHER DATA TYPES

An integer is considered to be signed. It occupies 2 bytes of memory space and has a range of values of – 32768 to 32767. An unsigned integer can handle a range of value from 0 to 65536.

What if an integer is greater than 65536?

We can define a "long" integer. A long integer occupies 4 bytes in memory and has a range of – 2,147,483,648 to 2,147,483,647.

The letter "L" maybe used with long integer constants, such as 45676L to denote that this is a long integer, it is automatically treated as long. If a program uses long, double or long double indiscriminately, more memory space is occupied and execution is slowed down drastically. Therefore these should be used sparingly.

Does C++ tolerate mixed mode arithmetic expression? Yes it does. It converts a lower type precision variable into a higher precision variable during the course of the computation. What do we mean by this?

```
   x    =        y    +   Z    *    a
double      unsigned    int     float
```

In this expression z is converted into float, and then the multiplication "z * a" is done. The unsigned y is converted to float and added to z * a. The result of the computation is converted to double before storing in x.

It is good practice to avoid mixed mode. This is done by using cast operators. Here we force or coerce one variable type to become another variable type. The above expression could have been written as:

```
x = double(Y) + double( Z) * double(a)
```

This is the preferred syntax for cast operator, though the other representation as shown will also work.

```
(double) y
```

Let's see the havoc that results due to improper use of data definitions.

```
/ / improper.CPP
// wrong definition causes memory run out
#include <iostream.h>
void main( )
   {
   int integer=32000;       //range-32768 to 32767
   unsigned int integ=32000; //range 0 to 65536
   integer=(integer * 2)/5;
   integ =( integ * 2)/5:
   cout<<"signed integer= " <<integer<<endl;
   cout<< "unsigned integer= " <<integ<<endl;
   integer=(integer*10)/10;
   cout<< "signed integer = " <<integer<<endl;
   integ=32000;
   integ=(long(integ)*10)/10;
   cout<<"long integer ="<<integ<<endl;
   }
```

The output is:

signed integer	**= – 307**
unsigned integer	**= 12800**
signed integer	**= – 307**
long integer	**= 32000**

Analysis

1. In the expression

   integer = (integer * 2) /5;

   32000 × 2 = 64000 exceeds the range of "int" . Therefore the result – 307 is erroneous.
2. Whereas in the expression.

   integ = (integ * 2)/5

   32000 × 2 = 64000 is within the range of unsigned int, and so the result is correct.
3. Similarly the result is bound to be incorrect for computing (integer * 10)/10.
4. However we have used cast operator long with integ, therefore the computation of (long(integ) * 10)/10 is correct.

   The table summarises different types of variables

Keyword	*Range of values*	*Byte of memory*
char	– 128 to 127	1
int	– 32768 to 32767	2
long	– 2147483648 to 2147483647	4
float	3. 4E – 38 to 3. 4E 38	4
double	1.7E – 308 to 1. 7E308	8
long double	3.4E – 4932 to 1.1E4932	10
unsigned char	0 to 255	1
unsigned int	0 to 65536	2
unsigned long	0 to 4294967295	4
'E' here stands for	10	

2.9 A DABBLE ON ARITHMETIC OPERATORS

Arithmetic operators in C++ are * / + –. The modulus operator (%) gives the remainder of an integer division. The % has a higher precedence than the redirection operator (< <). Use of parentheses can always override precedence.

There are arithmetic assignment operators which help to write an expression compactly. For example x = x + y can be written as x + = y. Others in this series are – =, / = , % = ,* = .

Further on we have the increment operators x + + , + + x. One is post increment and the other is preincrement. Similarly we have post decrement and pre - decrement operators: x – –, – – x.

The following program illustrates use of these operators.

```
// operators.CPP
// arithmetic assignment operators
#include <iostream.h>
void main( )
   {
   int value= 45;
   value +=15;            //value = value+45=60
   cout<<endl<<value;
   value -=13';           //value = value- 13=32
   cout<<endl<<value;
   value *=5;             //value = value*5=225
   cout<<endl <<value;
   value /=7;             //value = value/7=6
   cout<<endl<<value;
   value %=4;             //value = value%4=1
   cout<<endl<<value
   }
```

Analysis

The "end1" manipulator in each object causes the result to be displayed on new line.

```
//incdec.CPP
//increment and decrement operators
#include <iostream.h>
void main( )
   {
   int numb=15;
   cout<<"numb = "<<numb<<endl;
   cout<<"numb = "<<++numb<<endl;
   cout<<"numb = "<<numb<<endl;
   cout<<"numb = "<<numb-- <<endl;
   cout<<"numb = "<<numb<<endl;
   }
```

The output is:

```
numb = 15
numb = 16
numb = 16
numb = 16
numb = 15
```

The reader is encouraged to figure out how this output was obtained.

2.10 MUSINGS ON FUNCTIONS

Built-in Library functions are available in C++. They are of different types such as mathematics, graphics, memory management and data conversion. They can also be called pre-defined functions.

A function, be it user-defined or built-in library function, is furnished an argument. The function is processed using the argument and returns a value.

For using pre-defined functions, appropriate header files must be included in preprocessor directive. Say, to use the sqrt( ) function, the preprocessor directive is as follows:

```
#include <math.h> //searches standard include dir
#include "math.h" //searches current directory
```

All library functions are included in CS.LIB library header file. This library file is linked to the object file during linking process.

Suppose we invoke a library function without including its header file, then an error message appears as follows:

Function 'sqrt' should have a prototype in function main ( )

We shall know the different header files as we progress. Now let us examine a program that uses a "math.h" function sqrt ( ).

```
// sqrtfunc.cpp
//Invoking function through header files
#include <iostream.h>
#include <math.h> //for sqrt function
void main( )
   {
   double n, a;          // floating pt 8 bytes
   cout <<"Enter a +ve number:";
   cin>>n;
```

```
a = sqrt(n);
cout<<"Square root of "<<n<<" is "<<a<<endl;
}
```

Analysis

The sqrt( ) function accepts and returns a floating point value of type double.

The output is:

```
Enter a +ve number: 7890                              <ret>
Square root of 7890.000000 is 88.825672
```

REVIEW QUESTIONS

2.1 What symbol designates a comment?
2.2 Using the // can the comment spill over to next line?
2.3 What does the # symbol denote?
2.4 What objects are included in header file iostream.h?
2.5 What keyword implied a function does not return any value?
2.6 How do you tell the compiler from where control starts?
2.7 How do you recognize the body of a function?
2.8 Is cout an object or a function?
2.9 How should a C++ program statement be terminated?
2.10 How many statements may be accommodated in one line?
2.11 What do you understand by white space?
2.12 Is it necessary that one C++ statement be accommodated in one line only?
2.13 How can long string constants be punctuated so as to be put in several lines?
2.14 What is the symbol for insertion or "put to" operator?
2.15 Can you brand < < as an over loaded operator?
2.16 Does C ++ have real string variable?
2.17 Then how are strings treated?
2.18 How can you contain multiline comments?
2.19 What are the 3 prime variable types in C++?
2.20 How many bytes of memory is assigned to an integer in MS-DOS?
2.21 What is merely setting up of a variable called?
2.22 What do you call a variable that is set up and also assigned space in memory?
2.23 Is it necessary that all data types be defined before the first executable statement?
2.24 What object belong to standard input stream?
2.25 What is the escape sequence for newline character?
2.26 Can underscore be used as first character in a variable?
2.27 Is "char" a variable name or keyword?

2.28 Can lowercase and uppercase alphabets be mixed in variable names?
2.29 How many bytes of memory is requred for char type constant?
2.30 How is a character constant recognized?
2.31 What is the escape sequence for tab character?
2.32 What escape sequence enables you to represent graphic characters?
2.33 Name the 3 different types of floating point variables or constants.
2.34 To what digit precision is a float type constant represented?
2:35 How else can the following statement be replaced: const float PI=3.14154?
2.36 What does the manipulator end1 imply?
2.37 How many places of decimal are displayed by default?
2.38 Which header file must be included to use setw?
2.39 What range of values does an unsigned integer have?
2.40 How many spaces in memory does a long integer occupy?
2.41 How can you indicate a long integer?
2.42 Does C++ tolerate mixed made expression?
2.43 Suppose you have unsigned integer added to float variable in an expression, in which mode is the computation done?
2.44 What type of operator coerces a variable to become another type?
2.45 Which has the higher precedence: % or < < ?
2.46 What is the name of the operator which associates an arithmetic expression to a storage location?
2.47 How can you compactly rewrite the expression x = x + 1 using the preincrement operator?
2.48 What header file must be included to use the sqrt( ) function?
2.49 In which directory is the search made to locate a header file if it is enclosed within angles brackets < > ?
2.50 Where is the search made for a header file which is enclosed within double quotation marks?
2.51 Which header file includes all library functions?
2.52 What happens if a built-in library function is invoked without its header file being included?

Answers

2.1 //
2.2 No
2.3 Preprocessor directive
2.4 cin, cout
2.5 void
2.6 main( )
2.7 curly braces
2.8 object
2.9 semicolon
2.10 any number
2.11 spaces, CR, LF, Tab, formfeed
2.12 No
2.13 backslash
2.14 < <
2.15 Yes
2.16 No
2.17 array of characters
2.18 /* .... */
2.19 integer, float, char
2.20 2 bytes
2.21 declaration
2.22 definition
2.23 No
2.24 cin
2.25 '\n'
2.26 Yes

2.27 Keyword

2.28 Yes

2.29 One

2.30 Single quotes

2.31 ' \t'

2.32 'xdd'

2.33 float, double, long double

2.34 7

2.35 #define PI 3.14154

2.36 Newline character

2.37 6

2.38 iomanip.h

2.39 0 to 65536

2.40 4 bytes

2.41 L

2.42 Yes

2.43 float

2.44 cast operator

2.45 %

2.46 arithmetic assignment operator

2.47 ++x

2.48 math.h

2.49 standard include file

2.50 current directory

2.51 CS.LIB

2.52 error message

Chapter 3

Looping and Branching

Chapter 3

Looping and Branching

OBJECTIVE

Looping and branching control statements are discussed. Values compared in an expression maybe data types such as char, int, float or user-defined classes. The hierarchy among various operators as arithmetic, relational and logical is established. The concept of structured programming is emphasized through proper indentation, which is a visual aid to show beginning and end of a loop.

Keywords:

for	while	long	if
else	do	default	continue
goto			

3.1 RELATIONAL OPERATORS

There are 6 relational operators in C++ .

Symbol for operator	Meaning
>	greater than
<	less than
= =	equal to
! =	not equal to
>=	greater than or equal to
<=	less than or equal to

Any of these operators used in an expression may yield a value true (1) or false (0). Unlike other languages, C+ + does not have special boolean variables to represent true or false values. The following program shows use of some operators.

```
// relation.cpp
// shows use of relational operators
#include <iostream.h>
void main( )
   {
   int n;
   cout << "Type in value n: ";
   cin >> n;
   cout << n <<"!= 8 has logic value ="<< (n! = 8)
       << endl;
   cout << n << " == 15 has logic value = "<< (n ==
       15) << endl;
   cout << n <<" <=27 has logic value ="<< (n<= 27)
       << endl ;
   }
```

The output is:

Type in value n : 13 <ret>
13 ! = 8 has logic value = 1
13= = 15 has logic value = 0
13 < = 27 has logic value = 1

As no new point is involved in this program no elaborate explanations are offered.

As we shall be using these relational operators in our programs to come hereafter, this brief introduction would suffice for the present.

3.2 THE FOR LOOP

The syntax of the for statement is

```
for (int k = 0 ; k < 100 ; k ++)
    body of the for loop;
```

"for" is a C++, keyword. Within the parentheses it contains expressions separated by semicolons.

The first k = 0 is the initialization expression.

The second k < 100 is the test expression.

The third k + + is the modifying expression.

Here we have shown a postincrement. The following program shows the use of "for" statement.

```
// forstat. CPP
// shows use of for statement
# include <iostream.h>
void main( )
   {
   for ( int k = 0; k <5; k++)
       cout << " Madurai Meenakshi" << endl;
   }
```

The output is:

Madurai Meenakshi
Madurai Meenakshi
Madurai Meenakshi
Madurai Meenakshi
Madurai Meenakshi

Analysis

1. The index k has initial value 0.
2. This value is compared with 5, and since the test expression is true, the string "Madurai Meenakshi" redirected by the object cout is displayed.
3. The "end1" causes cursor to move to a new line.
4. The index k is incremented by 1 and then tested. Thus the "for" loop is executed 5 times in this case, for k = 0, 1,2,3,4.
5. After the 5th looping k becomes 5, and the test gives false. Therefore execution stops.

Aside

The body of the "for" loop is a single statement. The semicolon is used at the end of the object cout and not at the end of the for statement. This is a simple illustration of the for loop.

What if it has a body of several statements? This is handled as shown in the following program.

```
// mstat. CPP
// multiple statement in body of for loop
#include <iostream.h>
#include <iomanip.h>        // setw( )
void main ( )
   {
   int n;
   for (n = 1; n <=11; n += 2)
```

```
        {
        cout << setw(3) <<n;
        int sqr = n * n;
        cout << setw( 6 ) << sqr << endl;
        }
    }
```

The output is:

1	1
3	9
5	25
7	49
9	81
11	121

Analysis

1. The column width manipulator "setw" is going to be invoked, as evident from including "iomanip.h" header file.
2. In the "for" statement the modifier expression "n+ = 2" adds 2 to "n" after each cycle.
3. There are 3 statements in the body of the for loop. Each is punctuated by the semicolon. To indicate the beginning and end of the loop, the multiple statements are enclosed with curly braces { } .
4. The manipulator setw (3) sets 3 columns width to display n right-justified. The second manipulator setw(6) sets 6 columns to display the squared value also right-justified.
5. The variable "sqr" is defined as type int at the place where it is used. It is said to be visible from this point onwards. Once control passes outside the for loop, this definition does not hold good. It is an example of an "auto variable".

One of the most interesting illustrations is determining factorial of a number using the for statement.

```
// fact CPP
// determining factorial of a number
#include <iostream .h>
void main( )
   {
   unsigned int number; // 0 - 65536
   unsigned long factorial = 1;//defn & initialization
   cout << "\n Type number: " ;
   cin >> number;
```

```
for ( int k = number ; k > 0; k-- )
    factorial *= k;
cout<<"Factorial of" <<number<< "is" <<factorial:
}
```

The output is:

Type number : 13 < ret >
Factorial of 13 is 1932053504

Analysis

1. "number" is defined unsigned integer to hold a range of 0 to 65536.
2. "factorial" is defined as unsigned long thereby giving it a range – 2147483648 to 2147483647. Incidentally 12 is the maximum integer whose factorial can be contained in this variable. For number = 13, factorial would actually exceed and likely to give wrong result, as shown above.
3. "factorial" is set to 1 at start. This is quite obvious, as setting it to zero would end up with factorial becoming zero.
4. Look at the 3 expressions of the for statement. The first one sets k to the number whose factorial is to be determined. Its type is declared closest to the point of use.
5. The test expression k > 0, ensures that the last term of k is 1 for computation of factorial.
6. After each computation of the factorial expression, k is decremented by 1 and the loop is repeated. The loop is exited when k becomes zero. This is post decrement, ie. k is decremented after executing the body of for.
7. Note the compact form of writing the factorial expression. It can be expanded as

   factorial = factorial * k;

3.3. THE WHILE STATEMENT

The syntax of the "while " statement is

while (expression)

  statement (s);

If multiple statements are involved, they maybe enclosed within curly braces.

```
while ( expression)
   {
   statement1;
   statement2;
   ...
   }
```

"while" loop is used when we do not know the number of times the body of statement is to be executed. If the expression evaluates to true, the body is executed; if false control passes out of the while loop. Thus the body will be executed as long as the test expression is true. On the contrary there is the likelihood of the body not being executed at all if the expression is false at the very start itself.

C++ does not have an operator for exponentiation. So shall we use the while statement to do exponentiation, say, if x raised to the power of y? This is done by repeated multiplication of x by itself y times.

```
// exponent.Cpp
// shows how to do exponentiation
#include <iostream.h>
void main( )
   {
   int x, y , z, result = 1:
   cout << "Enter x: " ; cin >> x;
   cout << "Enter y: " ; cin >> y; z = y ;
   while (y > 0)
       {
       result = result * x;
       y - - ;
       }
   cout << x << " raised to power of "<< z
   << " is " << result << endl.;
   }
```

The output is

Enter x : 5
Enter y : 4 < ret >
5 raised to power of 4 is 625

Analysis

1. x, y are defined as type int. result is also of type int and initialized to 1.
2. The test expression in while statement ensures that the final value for y should be 1 only. The loop is exited when y becomes zero.
3. Let us say we enter 5 for x and 4 for y. Therefore result is computed as 5 * 5* 5* 5, for each execution of the body of while loop. After each execution y is decremented till y becomes zero.
4. y is post decremented here. It can also be predecremented. In this particular instance it does not make any difference. We'll see one more illustration of the generation of Fibonacci series as it is a favourite program of readers. Here again we use the while statement.

```
#include <iomanip.h>
// Fibonacci.cpp
// using while statement to generate the series
#include<iostream.h>
void main( )
    {
    int n = 0; int m = 1 ;
    cout << "Fibonacci series upto 100 " << endl;
    while ( n<= 100)
        {
        cout << setw( 4) << m<< endl;
    int s = n + m;
        n = m;
        m = s;
        }
    }
```

The output is:

```
Fibonacci series upto 100
1
1
2
3
5
8
13
21
34
55
89
144
```

This program doesn't need any explanation as the reader can easily understand its operation.

3.4 THE DO STATEMENT

The "do" statement is in fact a "do..while"combination. There is a difference between "while" and "do .. while". In "while", the body of the loop may or may not be executed depending upon the status of the test expression. Whereas in "do.. while" the body is executed atleast once before the test itself is done. The syntax is:

```
do
{
body of the do.. while loop;
}
while ( test expression);
```

Let's straight away see how this is used in a program.

```
// do.while , CPP
// how to use do.. while loop
# include<iostream.h>
# include<math.h>
void main ( )
    {
    double n, s ; // needed for sqrt fn
        do
        {
        cout << " \n Enter number: " ; cin >> n:
        s = sqrt (n) ; //s, n both double
        cout << "Square root of "<< n<<" is " <<s
        << endl;
        cout << ' \n';
        }
        while (n != 0.0 );
    }
```

The output is:

```
Enter number : 587.36                      <ret>
Square root of 587.36 is 24.235511
Enter number : 8973.65                     <ret>
Square root of 8973.65 is 94.729351
Enter number : 0.0                         <ret>
Square root of 0 is 0
```

Analysis

1. "math.h" header file is included in preprocessor directive, as we plan to use the "sqrt ( )" function.
2. This function must be furnished an argument of type double, and also return a value of type double. Hence n, s are defined as double.

3. See that the body of the "do" loop is enclosed within curly braces and the while statement figures just outside this loop. Proper indentation identifies the start and end of this loop.
4. Note that each statement in the body is terminated by semicolon.
5. So also the "while" statement is terminated by a semicolon. This is a statutory requirement.
6. The loop is exited when 0.0 is typed and entered against the prompt "Enter number: ". This is incidentally called a "marker" in some programs. Here 0.0 is the marker to end the do-loop.

3.5 THE IF STATEMENT

The "if" decision statement has same syntax as in any other language. The syntax is:

```
if (test expression)
    Statement(S) ; //executed when test is true
```

If the body has multiple statements they should be enclosed within curly braces. The following program shows the use of "if"

```
// ifdemo.CPP
// illustrates use of if statement
#include <iostream.h>
void main ( )
    {
    int x, y, z;
    float r;
    cout << "Enter x, y, z as int: \n";
    cin >> x; cin >>y; cin >>z;
    if ( x - y > 2)
        {
        r = float(x) + float(y) + float(z);
        float ave = r/3.0;
        cout << "\n Average of "<< x<<", "<<y<<"
        and "<<  z<<" is " <<
        ave<< endl;
        }
        cout << "Thank you."
    }
```

The output is:

```
Enter x,y,z as int:
17                                      < ret >
14                                      < ret >
21                                      < ret >
Average of 17, 14 and 21 is 17.333333
Thank you.
```

Analysis

1. There is only one prompt message asking you to enter value for x,y,z as integers.
2. However 3 separate "cin" objects are needed to assign these values to x,y,z, after typing, each value is entered by pressing the < ret > key.
3. The test expression of "if" statement determines if $x - y > 2$. If the test is true, then the statement within curly braces are executed and a valid result is output as we saw in the first run.
4. Note that $x - y$ need not be parenthesized as "–" sign has a higher precedence over the > operator.
5. As x,y,z are integers, we coerce them to become float type by using the cast operators.
6. "ave" is declared to be type float at the point of its use. This is an example of purely local variable (also called auto).
7. If the test expression of "if" statement is false, the control bypasses the statements within curly braces and executes the object cout which displays the "Thank you" message. Study the following input during a second run of the above program:

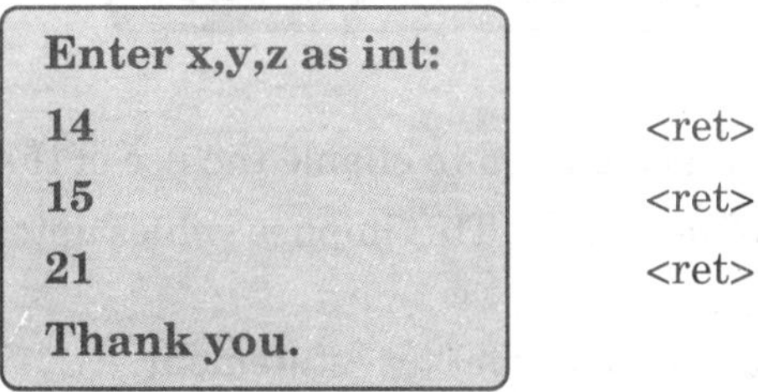

```
Enter x,y,z as int:
14                      <ret>
15                      <ret>
21                      <ret>
Thank you.
```

8. Note that the "Thank you." Message is displayed for either true or false status of the test, since it lies outside the "if" loop.

   The following program shows nesting of "if" within a "for" loop.

```
// prime.CPP
// testing for prime numbers
#include <iostream.h>
#include <process.h> // exit( ) function
```

```
void main( )
  {
  int numb, index;
  cout << " Type in the number to test: ";
  cin >> numb;
  for (index = 2; index < numb/2; index++)
      if (numb % index ==0)
      {
      cout « numb << " is not prime since
      divisible by "<<
      index << endl;
      exit(0) ; // exits program
      }
      cout << numb << " is prime.\n";
  }
```

The output for the first run is:

```
Type in the number to test: 29          < ret >
29 is prime.
```

The output for the second run is:

```
Type in the number to test: 12345       < ret >
12345 is not prime since divisible by 3
```

Analysis

1. The header file " process.h" is included to enable the use of the function exit( ).
2. "numb" and "index" are defined as int. This implies values upto 32767 only can be tested for prime.
3. The "if" statement is subordinate to the "for" statement.
4. If the test expression in for loop, index < numb /2, is true, then the "if" statement is executed.
5. If the test expression in "if" statement is true, the statements within the curly braces are executed.
6. The exit(0) causes control to pass to operating system level abandoning the program.
7. If the test expression of "if" statement is false, then "index" is incremented by 1, and the test in "for" is repeated.
8. Thus control passes between "for" and "if" statements until either the "for" test is false or the "if" test is true.

9. "for" test yielding false implies numb is prime.
10. "if" test yielding true implies numb is not prime.

Aside

The argument 0 in exit ( ) indicates successful termination. This returns control to the OS level. Any other number could be used to indicate an error condition.

3.6 THE IF.. ELSE STATEMENT

The "if .. else" statement causes a block of statements to be executed when its test expression yields true value. Otherwise the control passes out of the block to the next statement following it.

In "if.. else" construction there is a block of statements for true option and another block for false option. But only one of these block of statements will be executed in any case.

```
If (test expression)
   {
   statement(s); // true option
   }
else
   {
   statement ( s ) ; // false option
   }
// ifelse.cpp
// illustrating if.. else statement
#include <iostream.h>
void main ( )
   {
   int mark;
   cout << "\n Enter mark: " ; cin >> mark;
   if (mark >= 50)
       cout <<"Student has passed." << endl;
                                       //true
   else
       cout <<"Student has failed." <<endl;
   }
```

The output is :

```
Enter mark: 60                    < ret >
Student has passed.
For a second execution.
Enter mark: 45                    < ret >
Student has failed.
```

Aside

There is no new point to explain. Here each option is shown to have only one statement. Whereas in actual situation there may be multiple statements. In such case the block of statements concept maybe adopted.

The next program illustrates a, "while", "if.. else" nesting and also introduces the getche ( ) function, which gets a character from the keyboard and echoes it on the screen.

```
// nested.cpp
#include <iostream.h>
#include <conio.h>
void main( )
   {
   int character = 0;
   int blank = 1;
   char stream = 'x' ;            // any alphabet
   cout << "Enter any string: " ;
   while (stream != '\r')         //till carriage return
       {
       stream = getche( );        //get char from kybd
                                  //& echo
       if (stream ==' ' )
          blank++;                // true option
       else
       character++;               // false option
       }
   character-- ;
   cout << "\nNo. of letters = "<<character<<endl;
   cout <<"No. of words = "<< blank << endl;
   }
```

The output is:

```
Enter any string:
Industrial Electronics Corporation
No. of letters = 32
No. of words = 3
```

Analysis

1. Header file "conio.h" enables use of getche ( ). This function accepts one character through the keyboard and echoes it on the screen. The "e" in getche stands for echo.
2. "stream" is of type "char" and initialized to character "x".
3. The test expression in "while" determines variable "stream" does not currently hold "\r" the character for carriage return.
4. If test is true, control passes onto the block of statements following while.
5. getche ( ) function accepts one character through keyboard and assigns it to variable "stream" .
6. The "if" test determines whether contents of "stream" is blank. If true, variable "blank" is incremented and the while loop is repeated.
7. Otherwise the false option following else is executed, and variable "character" is incremented.
8. The "while" loop is exited when we type ENTER key (' \ r').
9. Just outside the while loop, variable "character" is decremented by 1 (character – –) so as to reduce the count caused by – – entering '\r' while inside the "while" loop.
10. The string "Industrial Electronics Corporation" maybe entered as one string and finally ended by typing ENTER key. Since this is done within the while loop, processing is done for each character to determine if it is a non white space or a blank and accordingly one of the variables "blank" or "character" is updated.

Aside

The getche( ) function accepts a character through the keyboard and displays it on the screen. Another function getch ( ), without the "e" simply accepts a character and does not display it. We shall have occasion to use it soon.

Nested "if .. else" structure is illustrated in the following program, which is self - explanatory.

```
// nested. CPP
#include <iostream. h>
void main( )
    {
    int city;
    cout <<"\n Enter your choice of city (1 to 4):";
```

```
    cin >> city ;
    if ( city == 1)
        cout << "Welcome to Madurai\n";
    else
        if ( city == 2)
            cout << "Welcome to Madras \n";
        else
            if ( city == 3)
                cout << " Welcome to Bombay\n";
            else
                if (city == 4)
                    cout << "Welcome to Calcutta \n";
}
```

The output is

Enter your choice of city (1 to 4) : 3 < ret >
Welcome to Bombay

Analysis

1. This illustrates a multi level "if .. else" nesting.
2. If the number entered for choice of city lies between 1 and 4, only one comparison will prove true and appropriate message is displayed.
3. We have entered 3 as our choice. Therefore the test expression in first two "if" will be false. The third test expression yields a true value.

The above program seems to be quite complex. But there are some applications, such as assessing the grade attained by a student, to decide his classification which can adopt this sort of construction despite its complexity.

The above program can also be rewritten using the "elseif" statement, which appears to be somewhat easier to understand. The program is listed without elaboration for the reader to figure out what it does.

```
//elseif.cpp
#include <iostream.h>
void main( )
   {
   int city;
   cout <<" Enter choice of city (1 to 4):";
           cin >> city;
```

```
    if (city == 1)
        cout <<"welcome to Madurai\n";
    elseif ( city = = 2)
        cout << " Welcome to Madras \n";
    elseif ( city = = 3)
        cout << "Welcome to Bombay\n";
    elseif (city = = 4)
        cout << " Welcome to Calcutta\n";
    }
```

The previous one and this program work identically and have similar logic. Don't you feel the second one is more elegant and neat in appearance and easy to write?

3.7 THE SWITCH – CASE STATEMENT

The switch statement can replace nested if .. else or elseif statements. And it can do a little more than that. Selection can be made of a particular case, and thereafter it can be made to proceed sequentially with the rest of the statements following it.

However if "break" is inserted, only the particular case statement is executed and control exits the entire switch block.

Unlike if .. else or elseif, there is no true or false decision, but merely a selection of the case statement depending on the index value associated with switch. Study the following program.

```
  // switch1.cpp
  // switch case structure shown
  #include <iostream.h>
  void main ( )
     {
     int city;
     cout << " Enter a number 1 - 4 to select city\n" ;
     cin >> city;
     switch ( city)
         {
         case 1 : cout <<" You are in Madurai \n";
                 break;
         case 2 : cout <<" You are in Madras \n";
             break;
```

```
        case 3 : cout <<" You are in Bombay \n";
            break;
        case 4 : cout <<" You are in Calcutta\n";
                break;
        }
    }
```

Analysis

1. Variable "city" is used as the index to select a case. It is obvious that "city" should be within 1 and 4 only.
2. Depending on what value is assigned to "city" control branches to that case statement and executes the object cout.
3. As "break" is inserted after this statement, control passes out of the "switch" block.

   The output is:

Enter a number 1 – 4 to select city	
3	< ret >
You are in Bombay	

Aside

The index that goes with switch need not be only integers, or in ascending order only. They can also be special characters or alphabets as shown below.

Then the next question arises, what if the index does not conform to any one of the valid case constants? This will cause control to bypass the entire switch block. Alternatively we can insert a default statement to which control will pass under this extraordinary condition. The following program shows all these.

```
// Special.cpp
// using special characters and default statement
#include<iostrem.h>
#include<process.h)
#include<conio.h>
void main( )
   {
   char pos = ' b ';  // initial value
   while ( pos != '\r')
       {
       cout << " \n Enter your grade (A, B, C, D):";
       pos = getche ( );
```

```
        switch (pos)
            {
            case 'A' : cout <<" Yourgrade:Excellent\n";
                          break;
            case 'B' : cout << "Your grade: Verygood
                          \n"; break;
            case 'C' : cout << "Your grade:Good \n";
                          break;
            Case 'D' : cout << Yor grade:Pass \n ";
                          break;
            default : cout<< "Sorry, you failed\ n";
            }
        exit ( 0 );
    }
```

Analysis

1. In addition to illustrating "default" statement, getche ( ) and exit (0) are also incorporated.
2. "pos" is char variable, initialized to constant 'b' merely to set it to some value other than '\r'.
3. The while loop is executed so long as "pos" is not '\r' (Enter Key).
4. Next the grade of the student is assigned to "pos" through getche( ) function. The grade is typed through the keyboard. It also gets echoed on the screen. Then depending on the case constant entered (A,B,C,D) one of the case statements is executed.
5. Suppose we enter any other character than A,B,C or D, the default statement is executed.
6. exit(0) causes program control to go back to Operating system level and abandon this program.

Aside

What will happen if exit(0) is removed? The while loop continues to execute till the '\r' (Enter key) is pressed.

3.8 THE CONTINUE STATEMENT

"continue" is just the opposite of break. It helps to go back to the start of the loop, whereas "break" causes control to go outside the loop. Study this program.

```
#include <math.h>
// continu. cpp
// illustrating use of continue statement
#include <iostream.h>
```

```
#include <conio.h>
void main( )
   {
   float a, b, c, disc, rl, r2; char ch;
       do
       {
       cout <<" \nEnter a,b,c values: \n";
       cin >> a; cin >> b; cin >> c;
       disc = b * b - 4 * a * c;
       if ( disc < 0)
           {
           cout <<"Roots imaginary. Try again! \n" ;
           continue // loops back to start of do
           }
           cout << " rl = " << ( -b + sqrt (disc))/
               ( 2*a) << endl;
           cout << " r2 = " << ( -b - sqrt (disc))/
               ( 2*a) << endl:
           cout << "\n Try another ( y/n) : " ;
           ch = getche( ) ;
           }
           while ( ch ! = 'n' ) ;
       }
```

The output is:

```
Enter a,b,c values:
2.5                          < ret >
4.6                          < ret >
- 16.3                       < ret >
rl = 1.794111
r2= - 3.634111
Try another (y/n) : n        < ret >
```

Analysis

1. The values for a,b,c are typed one at a time and entered so as to assign each to the respective variables.
2. The "if" tests whether "disc" is negative. When true, the body of the if statement is executed, where "continue" is encountered. Control reverts back to start of "do" loop to repeat the entries.

3. The "continue" statement causes control to go back to start of do loop and the output responses would be:

   Enter a,b,c values:

   2.5 <ret>

   4.6 <ret>

   2.116 <ret>

   Roots imaginary. Try again!

4. Thus there is no way of getting out of the do .. while except by entering correct values for a,b,c so that "disc" is +ve, and the do loop is executed at least once.
5. Towards the end of the do loop we have the option to quit by typing 'n' and entering.

Aside

The unconditional branching statement "goto" has not been discussed so far. Its syntax is

```
goto hell;
:    :
hell: statement (s);
```

The "goto" is considered an urchin, which tends to tarnish the fair name of structured programming concept. Therefore one should avoid its use at all cost.

3.9 THE TERNARY OPERATOR

The ternary operator is used to evaluate an expression and depending upon its true or false status, it is assigned a value. Its syntax is:

Conditional expression? expression1 : expression2;

For example:

value = (x > 5) ? 6 : 1;

If the expression (x > 5) is true, " value" is assigned 6. Otherwise "value" is assigned 1. You may wonder would not an if.. else statement do the same task. Yes, you are correct. However more complex decisions are possible. For example, study this. Here we assume x is already defined earlier.

amount = (x ! = 60) ? ((6 * x + 120) : (7.5 * x + 200);

Study this program.

```
// condop.cpp
// ternary operator illustrated
#include <iostream.h>
void main( )
   {
```

```
int indx = 30;
while ( indx > 0 )
    {
    char prin = ( indx % 2) ?'' : '*';
    cout << prin;
    indx - - ;
    }
}
```

The output is a series of asterisks (*) alternated by blank spaces.

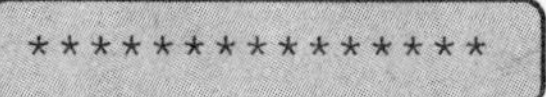

3.10 LOGICAL OPERATORS

C++ supports three logical operators AND, OR and NOT.

The symbols are

AND && OR // NOT !

The following program uses the AND and OR operators in determining if a given year is leap year or not.

```
// leapyear. CPP
// use AND , OR logical operators
#include <iostream. h>
void main ( )
   { int year;
   cout << " \nEnter year : " ; cin >> year ;
   if ( year % 4 == 0 && year % 100 ! = 0
       year % 400 == 0)
           cout << year << " is leap year";
   else
       cout << year <<" is not a leap year" ;
   }
```

The output for first run is:

Enter year : 1984 < ret >
1984 is a leap year
The output for second run is :
Enter year : 1990 < ret >
1990 is not a leap year

Analysis

1. The test expression of "if" contains both relational and logical operators.
2. The relational operators = = and ! have higher precedence than the logical operators. Therefore there is no need to use parentheses to assert further precedence

Aside

This now brings us to a review of the overall picture of different types of operators. The table holds good for other languages too. It is put in order of precedence.

Type of operator	*Operator*	*Symbol*	
Unary	=	equal to	
	!	not	
	++	increment	
	– –	decrement	
	–	negation	
Arithmetic	*	multiplication	
	/	division	
	%	modulus	
	+	addition	
	–	subtraction	
Relational	<	less than	
	>	greater than	
	<=	less than equal to	
	>=	greater than equal to	
	= =	equal to	
	! =	not equal to	
Logical	&&	and	
	||	or	
Ternary	?		
Assignment	=	+=	–=
	*=	/=	%=

Operators at higher precedence are evaluated before those at lower precedence. Operators on same level have equal precedence. Parentheses maybe used to override precedence in an expression.

The ! (NOT) operator can be used to verify the logical opposite condition of an expression.

```
if (! expression)
{
body of statement;
}
```

REVIEW QUESTIONS

3.1 What is the boolean value for true status?

3.2 What is the boolean value for false status?

3.3 How many relational operators are in C++?

3.4 What does the first expression in for statement do?

3.5 Is the body of for loop executed before or after executing the test expression in "for" statement?

3.6 Suppose the modifying expression in "for" is preincremented (+ + K) , will it be done before or after the body is executed?

3.7 Write the compact form for the index n in the "for" statement so as to be incremented by 3 after each looping.

3.8 Rewrite the following so that k + + replace k - - in the following statement : for (int k = number; k > 0 ; – – k)

3.9 What control statement do you recommend when you are not certain of the number of loopings?

3.10 Will it make any difference if y is pre-incremented here: while (y > 0) (r = r * x ; – – y)}

3.11 What header file should be included to use the manipulator setw ( )?

3.12 In which of the control statements will body of the loop be executed at least once; while or do.. while?

3.13 What type of argument be furnished to the built in math function sqrt ( )?

3.14 Where should the semicolon be used in a do .. while loop: after the curly brace or at the end of the while statement?

3.15 What does cout < <'\n' do?

3.16 Will the compiler execute the statements within do.. while loop: if indentation is improper?

3.17 Suppose a logical variable "exp" is initialized to false, write using "exp" in an "if" statement to execute the statements following it.

3.18 In using cast operators in C + + which syntax is preferred: float (x) or (float)x

3.19 Which of the operators + or > = has higher precedence when used in an expression?

3.20 Can modulus operator % be used with float type variables and constants?

3.21 What argument is associated with exit( ) if processing ends up in error?

3.22 Which of the two functions getche ( ) or getch ( ) echoes the character typed on the screen?

3.23 Is there much difference between nested if .. else and elseif statement?

3.24 Which do you feel seems easier to use for multilevel nesting?

3.25 What statement should be used with switch. case so that it works exactly like nested if .. else or elseif ?

3.26 Does switch statement involve true or false decision?

3.27 Which header file should be included to use the function exit ( ) ?

3.28 How can you still cause a statement to execute if none of the case constants match with the switch parameter?

3.29 Do you think "continue" could be replaced by a "goto" with a statement label where the label is associated with the first statement in a loop?

3.30 Does use of "continue" violate concept of structured programming?

3.31 Do you think C + + would support complex nesting of conditional operator such as: s = (x ! = 60)? ((x < 50) ? (6 * x + 100): 6.7 * x + 170) : 400;

3.32 What punctuation mark is used after a label of a "goto" statement when it indicates the executable statement (s)?

Answers

3.1 1
3.2 0
3.3 6
3.4 initialization
3.5 after
3.6 after
3.7 n + = 3
3.8 for (int k = 1; k < number; k ++)
3.9 while
3.10 No
3.11 iomanip.h
3.12 do..while
3.13 double
3.14 end of while
3.15 Introduces a new line
3.16 yes
3.17 if (!exp) { statement }
3.18 float (x)
3.19 +
3.20 No
3.21 Any number except 0
3.22 getche ( )
3.23 No
3.24 elseif
3.25 break
3.26 No
3.27 process . h
3.28 default
3.29 Yes, perhaps
3.30 No
3.31 Yes
3.32 colon (:)

Chapter 4

Structures and Enumerated Data Types

Chapter 4

Structures and Enumerated Data Types

OBJECTIVE

This chapter is about structures and enumerated data types. The latter helps us to set up our own data types. A structure is a collection of simple variables called members of a structure. Study of structure is a prelude to understanding objects and classes as they have similar syntax. A structure is compared to records in other languages, but it will turn out to be more akin to the class which is a collection of data and functions.

Keywords

struct enum class

4.1 A STRUCTURE

A structure constitutes specifying, defining and accessing data. In specifying, the keyword "struct" is used along with a structure name or tag. Specifier does not define or set apart space in memory, but merely does the work of specification. The variables of a structure are called structure specifiers. This is like saying objects are members of a class.

Definitions which are made in the main ( ) set up space in memory. Therefore we can consider definition of a structure as specification for a new data type. The following program explains the concept of structure.

```
// structur.cpp
// demo on use of structure
#include <iostream.h>
struct goods              // structure specification
   {
   int description;       // structure member
   int quantity;
```

```
    float price;
    };
void main ( )
    {
    goods list;         //defines structure variable
    list.description = 23; // accessing
    list quantity = 12;
    list.price = 1234.50
    cout << " \nDescription of 1D:"
            <<list.description
    cout << " , Quantity: " << list.quantity;
    cout << ", Price Rs. "<< list.price ;
    }
```

The output is:

Description of ID: 23, Quantity: 12, Price Rs. 1234. 499999

Analysis

1. The keyword "struct" is used to specify a structure. The structure name or tag is "goods".
2. The structure has 3 members called description, quantity and price, where first two are of type int and the third is of type float. Total space set up in memory for these variables is:

   2 + 2 + 4 = 8 bytes.
3. The elements or members of the structure are put within curly braces and terminated by a semicolon.
4. In the main ( ) the statement "goods list" defines a structure variable. The variable name is "list" and is formed like any other C++ variable name.
5. Each element of the structure is accessed by the dot or period operator (.). Each element is assigned a variable of its type.
6. The object cout displays the contents of these elements in one line as seen in the output.

Aside

In the previous program structure variable "list" was defined in the main ( ) function. Whereas it could be defined at the specifier itself and then used with the period operator as in the main ( ).

```
struct goods        // structure specification
    {
    int description;
```

```
    int quantity;
    float price;
    } list;
                    // structure variable defined
```

The rest of the program is same with the definition removed; as it is included in the specification.

4.2 INITIALIZING A STRUCTURE

The program that follows shows how to assign initial values to members of a structure, and how to assign one structure variable to another.

```
//structul.CPP
// initialization and structure variable assignment
#include <iostream.h>
struct goods
   {
   int desc;
   int quan;
   float price;
   };
void main ( )
   {
   goods list1 = {123, 12, 1234.5};
   goods list2;            // only definition
   cout << "\n Description ID: "< list1.desc;
   cout << ", Quantity : "<< list1.quan;
   cout <<" , Price Rs. "<<list1.price;
   list2 = list1;      //assignment of var to var
   cout << "\n Description ID: "<<list2.desc;
   cout <<" ,Quantity : " <<list2. quan;
   cout <<" , Price Rs. " <<list2. price;
   }
```

The output is:

```
Description ID : 123, Quantity : 12, Price Rs. 1234. 499999
Description ID : 123, Quantity : 12, Price Rs. 1234. 499999
```

Analysis

1. Two structure variables list1, list2 are defined. list1 is initialized with desc = 123, quan = 12, price = 1234.5
2. list2 is only defined. Now the structure can be accessed by using either of the variables.
3. The first 3 objects cout display the values associated with the elements of the structure accessed by list1.
4. In list2 = list1 statement each value of the member of one variable is assigned to the corresponding member of the other variable.
5. The last 3 objects cout display the values associated with the elements of the structure accessed through list2.

Aside

What is meant by defining 2 or more variables for one structure? Here list1, list2 are two variables of structure "goods". Within main, the keyword struct maybe omitted in C++, whereas it must be used in C. Let us examine the space in memory assigned to these variables.

```
struct goods                                goods
    {
    int desc;            list1     ┌─   2 bytes int desc
    int quan;                      |    2 bytes int quan
    float price;                   |_   4 bytes float price
    };
void main ( )            list2     ┌─   2 bytes int desc
    {                              |    2 bytes int quan
    goods list1;                   |_   4 bytes float price
    good list2;
    ..........
```

Thus the dot operator enables accessing each of the elements of the structure along with its relevent variable name (eg)

list1.desc   list1.quan   list1.price

list2.desc   list2.quan   list2.price

When we make an assignment such as list2 = list1, then the computer does a set of complex tasks to assign as follows:

list2.desc = list1.desc = 123

list2. quan = list1.quan = 12

list2.price = list1.price = 1234.50

We could have given different values to items of list2 by cin object. So now you know that we can create any number of variables for one structure and each one gets a replica of the structure elements. The space in memory is apportioned according to the number of variables we create.

4.3 COMPUTATION USING STRUCTURE VARIABLES

The following program shows structure variables in computations. Now that you know the significance of structure variable and how to access an element of the structure, the program should be easy to understand.

```
//strman.cpp
//how to use struct variable in computation
#include<iostream.h>
struct money
   {
   int rupees;
   float paise;
   };
void main( )
   struct money m1, m3;    // keyword struct optional
   struct money m2 = {1232, 78.6};
   cout < < "\n Enter rupees:"; cin > > m1.rupees;
   cout < < "Enter paise:"; cin > > m1.paise;
   m3.paise = m1.paise + m2.paise;
   m3.rupees = 0;
   if ( m3.paise > = 100.0)
       {
       m3.paise – = 100.0;
       m3.rupees++;
       }
m3.rupees + = m1.rupees + m2.rupees;
cout<<"Rs."<<m1.rupees<<"Ps."<<m1.paise<< "+";
cout<<"Rs."<<m2.rupees<<"Ps."<<m2.paise<<"=";
cout<<"Rs."<<m3.rupees<<"Ps."<<m3.paise<<endl;
}
```

The output is:

Enter rupees: 345 <ret>

Enter paise: 56.7 <ret>

Rs. 345 Ps. 56.7 + Rs.1232 Ps. 78.6 = Rs.1578 Ps.35.3

Analysis:

1. The structure specification by name "money" has 2 members: rupees and paise. rupees is int and paise is float.

2. In main( ) m1, m3 are structure variables. The keyword struct maybe omitted in C++.
3. m2 is defined as structure variable and also initialized as: m2. rupees = 1232, m2.paise = 78.6
4. Then using objects cout and cin, message appears prompting to assign m1.rupees and m1.paise.
5, The expression adds paise of m1, m2 and stores it m3. paise.
6. m3. rupees is initially assigned 0.
7. The if loop converts m3.paise into rupees and adds it to m3.rupees. The left over paise is held in m3.paise itself.
8. Next the compact assignment operator + = is used to add m1.rupees. m2.rupees with m3.rupees and store it in m3.rupees. The expression can be expanded as:

   m3. rupees = m3. rupees + m1.rupees + m2.rupees; Recall that + operator has higher procedence over the = or + = assignment operators.
9. The last 3 objects cout display the strings and values as seen in the output.

Aside

Now some pondering here. Suppose we define int m1, m2, m3; we can use them in an expression such as m3 = m1 + m2. This is possible with definition using built - in types. Whereas when they are user defined variables associated with a structure, writing m3 = m1 + m2 is not valid. m1, m2, m3 are structure variables encompassing the whole structure. Therefore any manipulation by them should involve the elements or members of the structure such as:

m3.paise = m1.paise + m2.paise;

4.4 STRUCTURE WITHIN STRUCTURES

This is called nesting of structures. One structure is built into another or is subordinate to the other. Of course two dot operators must be employed to access any member of the principal structure. The following program illustrates these ideas.

```
// nestst. CPP
// structure within structure
#include <iostream.h>
struct student
{
    int regno;
    float fees;
};
struct college
{
student identity;
student payment;
};
```

```
void main ( )
  {
  college details;          // definition of variable
  details.identity.regno = 1234;       //double
                                      //dot operator
  details.identity.fees = 2500.00;
  details.payment.regno = 2345;
  details.payment.fees = 3214.66;
  cout << " \n Student: " << details.
  identity.regno « endl;
  cout<< " Fees = Rs. "<< details.identity.fees
     << endl;
  cout<< " \n Student: " details.payment.regno
     << endl;
  cout<< " Fees = Rs. "<< details.identity.fees
     << endl;
  }
```

The output is:

Student : 1234
Fees Rs. 2500
Student : 2345
Fees Rs. 3214.66

Analysis

1. The principal or inner structure is named "student" and has two elements of type int and float.
2. The subordinate or outer structure is labelled "college" and has two elements called "identity" and "payment" . They appear not to belong to any data type of C++. They are simple variables of the principal structure, to enable access to the principal structure members.
3. In the main ( ) we define a structure variable called "details" which is associated with the subordinate structure name "college".
4. Therefore to access an element of the principal structure the variable name, the subordinate variable and the member variable should be involved. That is why we use 2 dot operators as:

   details. identity.regno

   details. payment . fees
5. The explanation for output need not be elaborated as it is trivial to the reader by now.

Aside

Now what have we landed ourselves into? Don't worry, an examination of the space in memory would straighten out our confusion.

```
struct                          details:
   {            identity        2 bytes            int regno
   int regno;                   4 bytes            float fees
   float fees;
   };           payment         2 bytes       into regno
struct college                  4 bytes       float fees
   {
   student identity;
   student payment;
   };
```

Therefore recognize that the entire memory area containing the structure is called "details" . "identity" and "payment" are labels on subsection of the memory having repeatable structure elements of student. Thus when we access a memory cell using 2 dot operators it has unique place in memory.

What is the depth of nesting possible with structures?

There is no such limit. But you should be able to keep track of it and don't lose your path.

4.5 ENUMERATED DATA TYPES

Enumerated data types enable one to define ones own data type, like structures. But such type do not figure prominently in C++, like structures. However if used judiciously can add clarity and simplify programming.

```
// enumer.cpp
// enumerated data type
#include <iostream.h>
enum tamil_months { thai, masi, panguni, chitrai,
   vaikasi, aani, aavani } ;
void main( )
   {
   tamil_months m1, m2;
   m1 =masi;   // integer 1
   m2 = aavani;     // integer 6
   int subt = m2 - m1 ;     // 6 - 1 = 5
   cout << " Difference = " << subt << endl;
```

```
    if ( m1 < m2)
        cout << m1 << " figures before " <<m2<<endl;
}
```

The output is:

Difference = 5
1 figures before 6

Analysis:

1. The enumerated data type has keyword "enum".
2. "tamil_months" is a variable name.
3. The curly braces holds the set of names permitted by the type. Note commas used as punctuation between names and a semicolon after the closing brace. These values are called members.
4. The set of values has integer values associated as follows:
   {thai, masi, panguni, chitrai, vaikasi, aani, aavani}.
   0 1 2 3 4 5 6
5. In the main ( ) function two variables m1, m2 of "enum" type are defined. These variables can be assigned any of the set of values in the enum specifier.
6. So when we assign m1 = masi, actually the integer 1 is assigned. m2 has 6 assigned to it because of its relative position.
7. Now you would understand the meaning of the expression: int subt = m2 – m1; which is performed with the integers, rather than the names. Here it is 6 – 1 = 5.
8. In the "if" expression, integers are tested. So you have a fair idea of how enum type data and variable is handled.

Aside

It is hoped you understand why relational and arithmetic operations are possible on enumerated data types. Internally the set of names are treated as integers starting from 0 onwards. However it is possible to start from 1 instead of 0.

enum tamil_months (thai = 1, masi, ...;.}.

One unfortunate fact is input/output statements do not recognize enum types as evident from the output. For example:

```
cout << m1 <<" figures before "<< m2 <<endl;
```

The output we got is

1 figures before 6

Don't you think it would have been perfect if it had been "thai figures before aavani".

REVIEW QUESTIONS

4.1 What 3 tasks are associated with a structure?

4.2 Is space set up in memory on specifying a structure?

4.3 When actually is space set up for a structure?

4.4 In C++ is it necessary to use the keyword "struct" during definition?

4.5 Suppose structure has 2 integer type and 2 float type variables as members and 2 structure variables are used to access it, how much of memory space are allocated in all?

4.6 Is it always necessary to define the structure variable within the main ( ) function?

4.7 Where else can it be defined?

4.8 Explain why is the following initialization in error.

struct goods void main ( )

```
{
int desc;          goods 11 = { 123, 12, 12.50 };
float type; goods 12;
int quan;          ......................
}
```

4.9 Is there any limit to nesting of structures?

4.10 Is enum data type specified outside or inside main ( )?

4.11 What is the default integer associated with the first name in the set of names listed in the enumerated data specifier?

4.12 Can it be modified to start with 1?

4.13 Within main ( ) is it necessary to use the keyword enum during variables definition?

4.14 Do input/output objects of C++ rgcognize enum data types?

4.15 Why do you think relational and arithmetic operations are possible on enumerated data types?

Answers

4.1 Specifying, defining, accessing 4.2 No

4.3 definition 4.4 No

4.5 24 bytes 4.6 No

4.7 Structure specifier between closing brace and semicolon

4.8 Data mismatch: float assigned integer constant

4. 9 No 4.10 Outside

4.11 0 4.12 Yes

4.13 No 4.14 No

4.15 Internal storage is treated as integer.

Chapter 5

Functions

Chapter 5

Functions

OBJECTIVE

Functions are of 2 types: pre-defined and user-defined. Predefined functions are coded in machine language and defined in the CS.LIB file. The user must merely declare it by including the header files and furnish relevant arguments to execute it. It will return the result to the point from where it was called. User-defined functions are written by the programmer and form part of the source file. It is compiled along with the other functions and can be invoked as usual.

KEYWORDS

return inline auto static

5.1 FUNCTIONS

Functions aid the conceptual organization of a program. It conforms to structured programming and object oriented programming concepts. It helps to reduce the program size.

How to determine the best candidate for a function? Any sequence of instructions appearing several times in a program can be evoked into a function.

Functions are subjected to 3 processes called declaration (or prototypes), calls and definition. By declaration we mean the presence of the function in the file is made known to the program. This should figure before the first function call is made.

Calling or invoking a function locates the function in memory, furnishing it with arguments and causing it to execute. The arguments or parameters maybe of different data types depending on the type of function.

Defining the function means developing the code and assigning it a name, conforming to the rules governing naming of a variable. The function maybe placed even before the main ( ) program, however, its presence should be declared before using it.

However built-in library functions need not be declared, as relevant header files in which they figure are included as preprocessor directives.

In passing-by-value constants or variables maybe passed. These must match the data types of the arguments, which automatically get initialized to the values passed. Entire structure may also be passed, provided it is properly declared.

A function normally returns a value. If it does not do so, it is prefixed with the keyword "void".

When a function returns a result it must be defined using proper data type. The keyword return is used when variable names are different in the main ( ) program and the function.

We shall be discussing about passing by reference, overloaded functions, inline functions, default arguments, storage classification and returning by reference in this chapter.

5.2 A SIMPLE FUNCTION

Let's first get an idea of how to declare, call and define a function by a simple example.

```
// function.cpp
// simple function to draw line
#include <iostream.h>
void border( );          // function declaration
void main ( )
   {
   border( );                //function call
   cout << "Thiagarajar Coll of Engg. "<< endl;
   cout << "Thiruparankundram " << endl;
   cout << "Madurai - 625015 " << endl;
   border( );
   }
// border( ) function
void border( )          // function definition
   {
   for ( int ind = 0; ind < 35; ind ++)
   cout << " - ";
   cout << '\n';
   }
```

The output is:

Thiagarajar Coll of Engg.
Thirupparankundram
Madurai – 625015

Analysis:

1. The presence of border( ) function is made known to the program by its declaration. The keyword "void" implies the function does not return any value, but merely carries out a task, like drawing the dotted line.
2. The declaration is done outside main( ) . It could as well be included as first statement within main. It does not make much difference.
3. The function does not need any argument or parameter, and therefore no value is passed on to it.
4. The function border( ) draws the dotted lines when ever it is invoked, as seen from the output.

Aside

We have said earlier that the function definition maybe placed before the main( ) function.

```
// function .CPP
// placing function definition before main( )
#include < iostream.h>
// border( ) defined
void border( )
    {
        . . .
    }
void main( )
    {
    border ( ) ;
    . . . .
    border( ) ;
    }
```

Don't you feel something is amiss with this coding? Where is the declaration ? There is no need for a separate declaration as the function itself has been defined before the main ( ) function, where it is invoked. In this section we shall tell the function which parameter or argument to use.

5.3 PASSING OF PARAMETERS

```
// paramete.cpp
// passing parameters to functions
#include <iostream.h>
void passing ( int, char) ; // declaration
void main ( )
   {
   passing (34, '*');                    //first call
   cout << "Computer courses offered by: " << endl;
   passing (34, '-');                    //second call
   cout << "Thiagarajar college of engineering "
   <<endl;
   cout << "Thiruparankundram " << endl;
   cout << "Madurai - 625015 " << endl;
   passing '( 34, '^');                  //third call
   {
// passing function
void passing ( int in, char chr)
   {
   for ( int ind = 0; ind < in; ind ++)
       cout << chr;
   cout << '\n';
   }
```

The output is:

```
**********************************
Computer courses offered by:
----------------------------------
Thiagarajar college of engineering
Tirupparankundram
Madurai 625015
^^^^^^^^^^^^^^^^^^^^^^^^^^^^^^^^^^
```

Analysis

1. During declaration we specify the type of data to be passed. Here we have an int and char type data.
2. During the function call the actual values of the parameters are specified. The function is called 3 times. Each time the int value is 34 but the char value is different such as * – or ^.

3. Now see the passing( ) function definition. It has 2 dummy arguments which specify the data type and name of the variables: "in" is of type int and "chr" is of type char.
4. When main ( ) calls passing( ), it passes two parameters, viz. 34 and *. The passing( ) function receives them and assigns 34 to "in" and * to "chr".
5. The function is executed which results in the character* displayed 34 times in a row.
6. Thus during subsequent calls the integer 34 is same but character constants are – and ^ respectively.

Aside

In the above function calls, the parameter values were stated directly. we can exercise the freedom to specify variables, which are predefined, as seen in this example.

```
// parameter.CPP
// passing arguments as variables.
#include <iostream.h>
void passing ( int, char);
void main ( )
    {
    char ch; int in;
    . . . . . .
    cin >> ch; cin >> in;
    . . .
    passing ( in, ch) ;
    }
// passing
void passing ( int in, char ch)
    {
    . . . .
    }
```

5.4 PASSING STRUCTURE VARIABLES AS ARGUMENT

We saw how to pass values or predefined variables as arguments to function. Here we shall pass structure variable as argument to a function. This is great, as the function receives the structure as a parameter and is able to acces and operate on the individual elements of the structure. The following program illustrates the idea.

```
// struct.cpp
// passing structure variable as argument
#include <iostream.h>
```

```
struct currency
   {
   int rupees;
   float paise;
   };
void passing ( currency ) ; // fn declaration
   void main ( )
   {
   currency rs, ps; // structure variables defined
   cout << " \nType rupees: "; cin >> rs. rupees;
   cout << " \Type in paise  "; cin >> rs. paise;
   cout << " \nType rupees : "; cin >> ps. rupees;
   cout << " \Type in paise  "; cin >> ps. paise;
   passing (rs);
   passing (ps);
   }
// passing ( ) definition
// display the structure constants
void passing (currency cur)
   {
   cout << " \nRs. " << cur.rupees <<"Ps. "<< cur.paise;
   }
```

The output is:

Type rupees: 1234	< ret >
Type in paise: 67.5	< ret >
Type rupees: 345	< ret >
Type in paise: 75.4	< ret >
Rs. 1234 Ps. 67.5	
Rs. 345 Ps. 75. 400002	

Analysis

1. The structure with tag "currency" is defined. It has two members: "rupees" of type int and "paise" of type float.
2. Following the structure definition is the declaration of a function passing( ) with the structure tag or name "cur" as argument.
3. In the main( ) function, "rs" and "ps" are structure variables. They can be used with dot operator to access any element of the structure.
4. The objects cout and cin respectively display a prompt and accept any element of the structure.

5. The function passing ( ) is invoked twice using the structure variables "rs" and "ps".
6. The function is defined to receive the structure variables "rs", "ps" and associate it with parameter "cur". Therefore "cur" can access the elements of the structure using, the dot operator, just like rs, ps were able to do it in main ( ).

Aside

Structure parameter "cur" is different from the arguments "rs", "ps". It is possible to modify "cur" without affecting "rs", "ps", whereas in the above program no such modification is attempted.

5.5 FUNCTION RETURNS A VALUE

So long we concentrated on passing of values, variables and structures to a function. Now let us see what the function returns in turn.

```
// return.CPP
// function returns a value
#include <iostream.h>
float func(float);
void main( )
    {
    float rupees, dollars;
    cout<< "\nHow much rupees?:";
    cin >> rupees;
    dollars = func ( rupees); // function invoked
    cout <<"\nRs. "<<rupees<< "="<<" $ "<<dollars;
    }
//  func( )
//  converts rupees to dollars
    float func  ( float rs) // func ( ) defined
    {
    float doll = rs / 31.65;
    return doll;
    }
```

The output is

How much rupees? : 12345.65	< ret >
Rs. 12345.67 = $390.067930	

Analysis

1. The function "func" is of type float and will accept an argument of type float. Since this function must return a value, the keyword "void" is replaced by float, indicating the type of value returned by it.
2. The function "func" is invoked using float type rupees.
3. In the function definition of "func" the type float is used. Its argument "rs" is also type float. The value passed as argument by rupees is receieved by "rs" in "func".
4. In func ( ) the conversion is done and stored in "doll" which is defined as float.
5. "return doll" writes the contents of "doll" into "dollars" of the main ( ). The keyword "return" is used as the two variable names "doll" and "dollars" are different and local to each function.
6. The output of $ is shown to have 6 decimal places as this is the default mode of display.

Aside

The above program can be coded with less number of variables. For example "dollars" and "rs" could be eliminated.

```
// returnl. CPP
// function, returns a value
#include <iostream.h>
float func( float);
void main( )
    {
    float rupees;
    cout << "\nHow much rupees?:";cin >> rupees;
    cout << "\nRs. "<<rupees<<" = "<<func (rupees);
    }
// func ( 0 )
float funct ( float func)
    {
    return rupees / 31.65;
    }
```

This program gives identical output as above. The function invocation is done as part of object cout rather than separately. The passing and receiving parameters are called by one name, viz. rupees. In func( ) , the conversion is done in return statement itself. Look there is no need to enclose the computation within parentheses. However if you have a doubt you can pretty well use parentheses.

5.6 RETURNING A STRUCTURE VARIABLE

Here we are going to analyse how structure variables maybe passed as arguments to a function. In turn the function returns a structure variable as result.

```
// strvar.CPP
// returning structure variable
#include <iostream.h>
struct currency              // structure defined.
   {
   int rupees;
   float paise;
   };
currency func(currency, currency);
void display(currency);
void main ( )
   {
   currency r1, r2, r3;          //structure variables
   cout << "\nHow much rupees :"; cin >> r1.rupees;
   cout << "How much paise :"; cin >> r1.paise;
   cout << "\nHow much rupees :"; cin >> r2.rupees;
   cout << " How much paise :"; cin >> r2.paise;
   r3 = func ( r1, r2 );
   display (r1) ; cout << " +";
   display (r2) ; cout << " =";
   display (r3) ; cout << " \n";}
// func ( )
// adds structures currency, returns total
currency func ( currency rr1, currency rr2)
   {
   currency rr3 ;  // structure var defined
   rr3.paise = rr1.paise + rr2.paise;
   rr3.rupees = 0;
   if (rr3.paise >=100.0)
       {
       rr3.paise - = 100.0;
       rr3.rupees++;
       }
```

```
        rr3.rupees += rr1.rupees + rr2.rupees;
        return rr3;
    }
// display ( )
// displays structure of type currency
void display ( currency rr)
    {
    cout <<"Rs" << rr.rupees <<" Ps." << rr.paise;
    }
```

The output is:

```
How much rupees: 123                          < ret >
How much paise: 67.5                          < ret >
How much rupees: 345                          < ret >
How much paise: 85.4                          <ret>
Rs. 123 Ps. 67.5 + Rs. 345 Ps. 85. 400000
= Rs. 469 Ps. 52. 899994
```

Analysis

1. The structure "currency" has 2 elements: "rupees" of type int and "paise" of type float.
2. The first declaration declares a function "func" of type "currency". Its 2 arguments refer to the 2 members of the structure, viz. rupees and paise. In passing structure to a function we need only to use the structure name, and not the member names.
3. The next declaration makes known the presence of a function display, where again we pass the structure name only.
4. In main ( ) we define 3 structure variables r1, r2, r3 of type "currency" .
5. The next 4 statements use objects cout, cin to display messages and accept inputs and store them in relevant structure elements.
6. The expression r3 = func(r1, r2) used only structure variables. r3 is determined by invoking func ( ). The arguments passed are structure variables r1, r2.
7. The function func( ) receives these variables through rr1, rr2 which are also of type "currency". This means rr1, rr2 are now treated like 2 structure variables just like r1, r2 and can access the members of the structure "currency" using dot operator.
8. In the func definition another structure variable rr3 of type "currency" is defined to hold the total amount.
9. The expression rr3. paise = rr1. paise + rr2. paise adds up the paise components of the structure and assigns it to rr3. paise.
10. rr3. rupees = 0 initializes the rupees component.

11. The "if" statement extracts whole rupees from the rr3.paise and adds it to rupees.
12. The next expression now adds the rupees element by the compact method . The expression can be expanded for easier understanding as:

    rr3.rupees = rr3. rupees + rr1.rupees + rr2.rupees
13. The statement "return rr3" returns the entire structure variable to the main ( ) where structure variable r3 receives and stores it. Note that when a structure variable is returned, its constituent elements rupees and paise are returned. On inspection you'll find:

    r3.paise = rr3.paise

    r3.rupees = rr3.rupees
14. The dispaly function is called thrice, with a different structure variable like r1, r2, r3 each time. The structure variable passed from main ( ) is received by structure variable rr of type "currency" to cause appropriate display.

5.7 PASSING ADDRESS (PASSING BY REFERENCE)

The following program illustrate passing by value as well as passing by reference.

```
// passaddr.cpp
// illustrate passing of addresses
#include <iostream. h >
void main ( )
    {
    void convert (float, int&, float&);
                                        // declaration
    float amount; int wholers; float wholeps;
    do
    {
    cout<< " \n How much amount?"; cin >> amount;
    convert (amount, wholers, wholeps); // invocation
    cout<< " Whole rupees is:"<< wholers<<",
        wholepaise is :"
        << wholeps;
    }
    while (amount ! = 0);
    }
// convert ( )
// pulls out rupees, paise from amount
```

```
void convert (float a; int& wr, float& wp)
  {
  wr = long (a) ; // convert to long int, no decimal
  wp = int ( (a - wr) *100 + 0.5 ); //pulls paise
  }
```

The output is:

How much amount ? 1234.567 <ret>
Whole rupees is: 1234 whole paise is : 57

Analysis

1. The function declaration for "convert" has 3 arguments: float, int& and float&. The first float implies a simple variable. The other two imply addresses of type int and float. In function declaration only the types are specified without the variable names.
2. In the "do" loop the function "convert" is invoked with 3 arguments: amount, wholers, wholeps, which are respectively of type float, int and float, "amount" is a simple variable while wholers and wholeps are reference arguments.
3. The reference arguments wholers, wholeps passed from main are received by wr and wp in the convert function. This implies wholers and wr refer to the same memory location with different names. Similarly wholeps and wp refer to another one location by two different names.
4. The simple float type variable "amount" passed from main ( ) is received by float type "a".
5. In the convert function wr is assigned the truncated integer value of "a". The decimal or paise portion is chipped off.
6. To evaluate wp whole rupees is subtracted from "a" yielding fractional paise. This is converted to whole number by multiplying by 100 and rounding off by adding 0.5. Then the int conversion is done to get wp.

Aside

In passing by reference the ampersand (&) symbol is used to imply reference of a variable. Actually when we pass reference argument, it maybe taken as the address being passed, so that having different names for one location, all such names refer to the single address only.

5.8 CONCEPT OF OVER LOADED FUNCTIONS

A function is branded as overloaded when it has a common name, but is capable of performing different tasks depending on the type of data furnished. Such functions can use several arguments. The data types associated with them distinguish them from one another. However for each type, there must be a separate definition, which means, their coding is different. The advantage of employing over loaded function seems to be to reduce number of function names. If this description is still vague read through the program and you'll get an idea.

```
// funcover.CPP
// overloaded function illustrated
#include<iostream.h>
void func ( );                          // func defn, no arg
void func (char);                       // func defn with arg
void func (int, char);        // func defn with 2 args
void main( )
   {
   func ( );
   func ( 'x' );
   func ( 30 , 'u' );
   }
// first func ( )
void func ( )
   {
   for ( int k = 1 ; k < 35 ; k++)
       cout<< ' $ ' ;
   cout << endl;
   }
// second func ( )
void func (char chr)
   {
   for (int k = 1; k <35; k++)
       cout << chr;
   cout << end;
   }
// third func ( )
void func ( int n, char chr)
   {
   for (int k = 1; k<n; k++)
   cout << chr;
   cout << endl;
   }
```

The output is:

```
$$$$$$$$$$$$$$$$$$$$$$$$$$$$$$
xxxxxxxxxxxxxxxxxxxxxxxxxxxxxx
uuuuuuuuuuuuuuuuuuuuuuuuuuuuuu
```

Analysis

1. There are 3 declarations of function "func" : the first with no argument, the second with char type argument and the third with an int and a char type argument.
2. In the main ( ) these functions are called separately. The first has no argument. The second has 'x' as char argument. The third has 30, 'u' as int and char arguments conforming to the 3 declarations.
3. The 3 functions find separate definitions to match with the declarations.
4. In first function for func ( ) the int and char constants are built into it.
5. In the second definition for func ( ), the char constant was furnished, the int constant is built in the function itself.
6. In the third definition for func ( ), both int and char constants are furnished. These are received by "n" and "chr" of the function used.

In the next example we will slightly stretch the example of overloaded function, involving a structure and structure variables. You have already seen how to pass a structure variable to a function. This is exactly what we will do here.

```
// complex.cpp
// overloaded function, structure, struct variables
#include <iostream.h>
struct currency
    {
    int rupees; float paise;
    };
void display (currency);
void display (float);
void main ( )
    {
    currency r1; float r2; // struct variables
    cout << "\n How much rupees?"; cin >> r1.rupees;
    cout << "How much paise ( 2 digits): "; cin>> r1.paise;
```

```
    cout << "\nWhat is the total amt in paise?" ;
        cin>>r2;
    cout << "\nr2 = ";
    display ( r1) ;              // display ( ) called
    cout << "\nr2 = ";
    display (  r2); // display ( ) called
    }
// display ( ) function definition
void display (currency rr)
    {
    cout << "Rs." << rr.rupees << "Ps."
    << rr.paise;
    }
// display ( ) another function defined
void display (float rr)
    {
    int rupees = rr/100;
    float paise = rr - rupees *100;
    cout << "Rs. "<< rupees <<" Ps. " << paise;
    }
```

The output is;

How much rupees ? 123	< ret >
How many paise (2 digits): 45	< ret >
What is the total amt in paise? 12345	< ret >
r1 = Rs. 123 Ps. 45	
r2 = Rs. 123 Ps. 45	

Analysis

1. A structure called "currency" is defined with members; rupees of type int and paise of type float.
2. The display function is declared with structure name currency as an argument.
3. The display ( ) function is again declared with float type as an argument.
4. In main ( ) two structure variables are defined: r1 of type currency and r2 of type float.
5. The display ( ) function is called twice in main ( ), once with structure variable r1 and a second time with float variable r2.

6. There are two separate definitions for display ( ). The first definition uses structure variable "rr" as argument. The second definition uses float variable "rr" as argument.
7. The same function name display is used in both definitions. However they receive different types of data from main ( ) , and therefore their coding is different.

5.9 INLINE FUNCTIONS

Before describing "inline" functions see what happens with ordinary functions. When a function is called, control has to pass to the function and after executing it, control passes back to the calling program. This may appear to save memory, but time of execution is long. Therefore one way of reducing this time is to use inline functions.

Now what is this inline function? An inline function is a short code written and placed before the main ( ), and compiled as an inline code. Whenever this function is invoked in a program, the lines of code are inserted at the point of calling. This works only for a few lines of code. For longer ones it is better to write ordinary functions.

As inline function is defined before main ( ), there is no need for a declaration. This maybe construed as the define macros of C language, with better type checking.

```
// inline fn.CPP
#include <iostream.h>
inline float dolrs ( float dollars)          // inlinefn
                                           //defined
   {
   return 31.65 * dollars;
   }
void main ( )
   {
   float doll; // variable defined
   cout << "s \nHow much US$ : " ; cin >> doll;
   cout << " US$ : " << doll << " = "<<" Ind Rs. "
       << dolrs (doll) << '\n' ;
   }
```

The output is:

```
How much US$: 123.65                      < ret >
US$: 123.650000 = Ind Rs. 3913.522461
```

Analysis

1. The keyword "inline" is used while defining the function, which is of type float. The argument is of float "dollars".

2. The function "dolrs" consists of just one line of coding, which is a return statement, to convert "dollar" into Indian rupees.
3. In main ( ) a float type variable "doll" is defined to interact with "dollars" of the inline function "dolrs".
4. The inline function "dolrs" is invoked in the object cout. Actually the coding of this function is presumed to be inserted at this point of call. Therefore the result of evaluating the function is substituted here.

Aside

In section 5.8 on overloaded function we discussed how the function "func" was called three times; first with no arguments at all, the second with one argument only. In such cases of missing arguments, the function furnishes default arguments, provided the prototype was defined with default arguments.

In the case of both arguments missing, it uses the default values. If only one is missing, it uses the previous value along with the furnished value for the other one to execute the function.

The following program illustrates the case of function without and with arguments. The reader is encouraged to figure out its operation.

```
// noargfn. CPP
#include <iostream. h>
void chdisp (char = '-' , int = 30 );
void main ( )
    {
    chdisp ( ); // both args missing
    chdisp (' ^'); // one arg missing
    chdisp ( '#' , 20)// no missinq args
    }
// chidisp ( )
void chdisp ( char chr, int m)
    {
    for ( int k = 1; k <m; k++)
            cout << chr;
    cout << '\n';
    }
```

The output is:

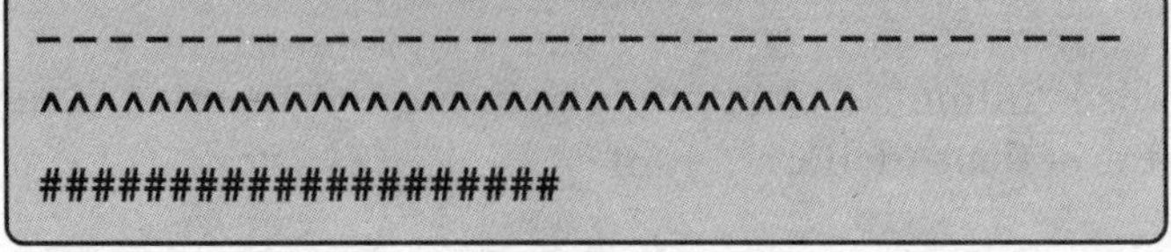

```
-----------------------------
^^^^^^^^^^^^^^^^^^^^^^^^^^^^^
###################
```

5.10 STORAGE CLASSES

There are several types of storage classes, of which we shall discuss 3 prominent ones. They are automatic (or auto), static and external (global). There is yet another class called the register class, which is best left out, as few in-built registers are available in most CPUs (Central Processing Units), for the programmer to use.

In describing these storage classes and their variables, we use two indices called visibility (or scope) and lifetime.

Visibility implies the setting up of space in memory for a variable and used by the program. Lifetime implies the duration or period for which the variable remains active or defined.

An "auto" class variable is defined inside the main ( ) or function program. It is created only when called , and get removed when the function or segment is exited. Thus we can say its visibility and lifetime coincide and limited to the function execution. Generally the keyword auto maybe dropped as it is implied. Auto variable is not initialized , and will normally contain garbage.

Despite the limited visibility and lifetime of auto storage class, it helps to organize and modularize programs. There is little chance of accidental altering of its contents. It is very useful in structured and object-oriented programming. Auto variables are also known as local variables, as they are accessible only to the function where it is defined.

External or global variables are defined outside the main or function program. These variables are set up in memory immediately on definition and remain active for the entire period of the program file. Its visibility (scope) and lifetime is that of the source file. If they are not initialized they assume zero values. External or global variables can be accessed by all functions in the file.

The third class is static variables. Static variables are defined inside main ( ) or function programs, with keyword static prefixed to it. They are sometimes called static auto variables as they have visibility of a local (or auto) and the lifetime of external (or global) variable. Static variables are initialized once at the first call only.

In MS-DOS machines auto variables are stored in the stack segment, while external and static variables are stored in the data segment.

We have all along been using auto class variables so far in our programs. Therefore the following program illustrates external or global storage class variables.

```
// external.cpp
#include <iostream.h>
#include <conio.h>              //getch() function
char chr;  // global variable
void fetchchr( );           // function declaration
void placechr( );
```

```
void main( )
    {
    chr = 'x';              // arbitrary initialization
    while( chr != '\r' )
        {
        fetchchr ( );
        placechr ( );
        }
    }
void fetchchr( )                    // fetchchr func defined
    {
    chr = getch( ) ;
    }
void placechr( )            // placechr defined
    {
    cout << chr;
    }
```

The output is:

A good demonstration on global class.

Analysis

1. One global or external variable is defined: "chr" of type char. Since it is not initialized it will assume NULL.
2. Two functions fetchchr( ) and placechr ( ) are declared.
3. Inside main( ) chr is arbitrarily initialized to 'x'.
4. The while loop calls the two functions to get a char through keyboard and display it on the VDU screen, until carriage return key is pressed.
5. In the fetchchr ( ) function definition, predefined function getch ( ) is used to get the character entered through keyboard and stored in global variable chr.
6. The placechr ( ) function leaves one line blank and displays the characters in the next line, as seen in the output. The carriage return key is assumed to be pressed after the period following "class".
7. This program should be run with Alt-R key only to get the output displayed.

5.11 STATIC STORAGE CLASS

The static storage class has been discussed earlier. Here a program is illustrated showing its use.

```
// stattype.cpp
#include <iostream.h>
float total (float);                          //fn total defined
void main( )
   {
   float info = 1.0;                         //float var info defined,
                                             // initialized
      do
      {
      cout << "\nType in a float value: " ; cin >> info;
          tot = total(info);
      cout << " Current total value = "<< tot <<
      endl;
      }
      while (info != 0) ;
   }
// total ( )
float total( float c)
   {
   static float sum = 0.0 ;                  // static type defined,
                                             // initialized
   sum += c;
   return sum;
   }
```

The output is:

```
Type in float value: 357.34              < ret >
Current total value = 357.3339996
Type in float value: 654.32              < ret >
Current total value = 1011.660034
Type in float value: = 0                 < ret >
Current total float value: = 0
```

Analysis

1. Inside main( ) "info" is initialized to 1.0 to avoid garbage value.
2. Within the do-loop we give it the first correct value.
3. The function total( ) is called with "info" as an argument. After the function execution, the result is returned and stored in "tot"

4. In the function total( ), "sum" is a static float type variable. We have seen its scope or visibility is limited to the function call, but its lifetime is for the entire range of the program source file.
5. The static variable "sum" is initialized only once at definition. Thereafter values are added to it until the function call is terminated by entering 0 for info in main( ).
6. The output shows you the result of calling the function total( ) twice.

5.12 RETURN A VALUE BY REFERENCE

Just as we can pass a value by reference, a function can return a value by reference. This is a unique feature of C ++. Normally a function is invoked only on the right hand side of the equal sign. But here we'll use it on the left side and the value returned is put on the right side. This is a weird looking application, but seems to have its own utility in overloaded operators, which we shall study later on.

```
// refval.CPP
#include <iostream.h>
float v;    // global
float& func( );                    // return by ref func declared
void main( )
    {
    func ( ) = 1234.0    // func invoked
    cout << "\nReference value is returned: "<<endl;
    cout <<"\nv = " << v<<"\n";
    }
float& func( )
    {
    return v;
    }
```

Analysis

1. See the definition of the function func ( ) which returns a value by reference. The address operator & is used after the data type float. The reference variable "v" is defined global and type float .
2. The function is executed and the value is returned through reference variable "v" to the main ( ).

   The output is:

Reference value is returned:

V = 1234.000000

REVIEW QUESTIONS

5.1 What is the prototype of a function?

5.2 Does memory get allocated during declaration or definition of a function?

5.3 Can a function be placed before main ( ) program?

5.4 If a function is placed before main ( ), which of the 3 processes of declaration, definition or call is not required ?

5.5 How is the function described if it does not return any value?

5.6 Can keyword "return" be omitted when variable names in main ( ) and called function are the same?

5.7 Which of the two statements is a function call: the first or the second?

```
void border ( );
border ( ) ;
```

5.8 What is wrong with this coding?

```
void passing ( int, char);
void main ( )
{
passing ( ' *', 34);
. . .
}
```

5.9 Can predefined variables be used in function calls as arguments?

5.10 When passing a structure as argument to a function which is furnished as argument: structure name or structure variable?

5.11 In function declaration where a structure is passed as argument , should it be structure name or variable.

5.12 Can a function which receives structure variable as argument, in turn return a structure variable for result?

5.13 What type of passing is implied by the last two arguments in this declaration? void convert (float, int &, float &);

5.14 Can an overloaded function have a common definition for different data type arguments?

5.15 Suppose rr = 12345, what value is stored in rupees by executing the following statement? int rupees = rr/100;

5.16 Should inline function be defined before or after the main ( ) program?

5.17 Suppose you have 5 lines of coding, would you treat it as inline function or normal function?

5.18 What storage class does 'x' belong to in this segment: void main ( ) { int x; .... }

5.19 What storage class does x belong to? int x; void main ( ) { .... }

5.20 What storage class does a variable with limited visibility in a function but unlimited lifetime belong to?

5.21 Should static variable be defined inside or outside a function?

5.22 Where do you think returning a value by reference be useful?

Answers

5.1 declaration

5.2 definition

5.3 yes

5.4 declaration

5.5 void
5.6 yes
5.7 second
5.8 wrong data constants
5.9 yes
5.10 structure variable
5.11 structure name
5.12 yes
5.13 passing by reference
5.14 yes
5.15 123
5.16 before
5.17 normal function
5.18 auto
5.19 external or global
5.20 static
5.21 inside
5.22 overloaded operator

Chapter 6

Objects and Classes

Chapter 6

Objects and Classes

OBJECTIVE

Structures help to group data elements; functions help to organize program that perform a task. Here we discuss class and objects. Objects of class are similar to variables to structures. Class contain data items and member functions. The principal objective of object oriented programming is putting data and functions into one class and data hiding. This chapter further discusses constructors to initialize objects on creation and destructors to remove the space setup up in memory by the constructor. Over loaded constructors, memory allocation and static class data are also explained.

KEYWORDS

private public class

6.1 CLASS AND OBJECT

A class is specified just like a structure with a name. The body of the class is enclosed with curly braces and terminated with semicolon. By using the keyword "private" in a class, we can hide data, which can be accessed by functions defined within the class. In contrast "public" data or functions, which are also specified within the class, are accessible by any function even from outside the class. Generally data is private and functions are public. The reverse may also be true.

Member functions need to be defined within the class specification, just as inline functions were done. Function definitions within a class are automatically considered to be inline, therefore there is no need to associate keyword inline with these function definitions.

Space in memory is set up only when objects are defined in the main ( ) program, and not during the class specification. Member functions are accessible only through the objects of that class using the class member access operator, which is the dot operator.

The following program illustrates class and objects.

```
// object.CPP
// Class and object illustrated
#include <iostream.h>
class sample            // class called sample
   {
   private:
        int informat;
   public:
        void memfunc( int x)      // member func
                    {informat = x;}
        void display( )       // member func
            {cout << informat;}
   };              //note closing brace & semicolon
void main( )
   {
   sample d1, d2; // 2 objects of class sample
   d1.memfunc (3547):
   d2.memfunc (8843);
   cout << "\nHome phone is:";
   d1.display ( );
   cout << "\nOffice phone is:";
   d2.display ( );
   }
```

The output is:

Home phone is: 3547
Office phone is: 8843

Analysis

1. The class is specified by keyword "class". It's name is "sample".
2. The body of the "class" is enclosed within braces. The closing brace is punctuated by a semicolon.
3. It has a private class data called "informat" of type int.
4. There are 2 public class functions called memfunc( ) and display ( ). Each function is defined as public class.
5. The memfunc ( ) has an int type argument x, which is assigned to the private class data informat.

6. The display ( ) has no argument, It's body causes the value stored in "informat" to be displayed. Both memfunc ( ) and display( ) are treated as inline functions.
7. Remember that a mere class specification is equivalent to a declaration, and no memory is set up at this stage. Memory is set up only on creating objects of this class in the main( ) function.
8. Within main ( ) the first job we do is to define objects d1, d2 of class "sample". Now memory is apportioned to the class .
9. d1.memfunc (3547) is a way to invoke the memfunc ( ). The class member access operator or dot operator is used between the class object and member function. This function assigns the value 3547 to private class data called informat. The data is now identified as d1. informat and assigned 3547.
10. Similarly d2.memfunc (8843) assigns d2.informat with 8843.
11. Then the function invocation d1.display ( ) causes to display the value stored in d1.informat.
12. The function invocation d2.display ( ) causes to display the value stored in d2.informat. Thus we have the output as shown above.

Aside

Does it seem confusing? Recall that we have talked of class, public functions, private data and objects to class. Let us now try to consolidate our idea what all these mean.

We created two objects to class sample called d1 and d2. These can be considered as the keys to access the memory locations of private data and public functions. Therefore these have to be associated with the private data and public member functions to access their memory locations by using the dot or period operator.

Objects	*d1*		*d2*
function		memfunc ( )	
data:	d1.informat (3547)		d2. informat (8843)
Objects:	d1		d2
function:		display ( )	
data;	d1.display ( )		d2.display ( )

6.2 CLASS WITH MULTIPLE DATA OBJECTS

The following program has 3 private data and 2 public functions. First go through the program then you'll appreciate the niceties built into this program.

```
// multidat.cpp
// student record as object
# include <iostream .h>
```

```
class student
  {
  private:
     int reg_no; char grade; float fees;
  public:
     void assign ( int x, char y, float z )
     {reg_no = x; grade = y; fees = z ;}
     void display ( )
     {
     cout <<"\nReg number : "<<reg_no;
     cout <<" Grade obtained: "<< grade;
     cout <<", Fees Rs . "<< fees;
     }
  };
void main( )
  {
  student s1; // defining object of student
   s1.assign (3547, 'p' , 370.60);
   s1.display ( );
  }
```

The output is:

Reg number: 3547, grade obtained: P, Fees Rs. 370. 600006.

Analysis

1. The "student" class has 3 private data items:

   reg_no of type int,

   grade of type char,

   fees of type float.

   This is only a specification. Memory allocation will be done only on creating object of this class called "student". This is done within the main ( ) function. The total number of bytes for object s1 is 2 + 1 + 4 = 7.

s1.reg_no	←	2 bytes
s1.grade	←	1 bytes
s1.fees	←	4 bytes.

2. There are 2 public functions: assign( ) and display ( ). "assign" has 3 dummy arguments, matching the data types specified in private class. These are used for assigning values to the data items.

3. display ( ) is an argumentless function, which causes display of the contents of the memory location, which it accesses with the aid of the relevant object.
4. In the main ( ) program a single object s1 of class student is defined.
5. The object s1 is associated with each of the public functions to access the data items. During the first call s1.assign ( ), the real arguments furnished are assigned to the relevant data items as shown:

   s1.reg_no - 3547

   s1. grade - 'P'

   s1. fees - 370.60
6. The second function s1.display ( ) accesses these elements and displays values stored in them on the monitor.

Aside

What is significant about the public functions is that they handle all 3 data items collectively.

6.3 MULTIPLE DATA MULTIPLE OBJECTS EXAMPLE

The following program and its output are given merely to show how memory is apportioned when several data items and several objects are defined. The example is confined to 2 data items and 2 objects for sake of simplicity. The idea could be extended for any number of data or objects.

```
#include <iostream.h>
// complex. CPP
// objects using Indian currency
class currency
  {
  private:
      float paise; int rupees;
  public:
      void getf( )
         {
         cout <<" \nRupees in integer: "; cin >>
                 rupees;
         cout << "Paise as real: "; cin >> paise;
         }
         void setf ( int rs, float ps )
            {rupees = rs; paise = ps;}
         void outf ( )
```

```
            {cout <<"Rs."<< rupees <<"Ps."<< paise
                << endl;}
    };
void main ( )
    {
    currency c1, c2;          // objects created
    c1.setf(13, 7.85);
    c2.getf( );
    cout <<"\nFirst amount = "; c1.outf( );
    cout << "\nSecond amount = "; c2.outf( );
    }
```

The output is:

```
Rupees in integer: 345                    < ret >
Paise in real: 67.6                       < ret >
First amount = Rs. 13 Ps. 7.85
Second amount = Rs. 345 Ps. 67.599999
```

Analysis

1. The 3 public functions getf ( ), setf ( ) and outf ( ) perform different tasks.
2. getf ( ) receives data through keyboard and assigns to data items.
3. setf ( ) is specified with dummy arguments so that when real parameters are furnished during a call it simply assigns it to data items.
4. outf ( ) simply accesses the data items to display the values.
5. The outcome of invoking the 3 functions using objects are shown pictorially:

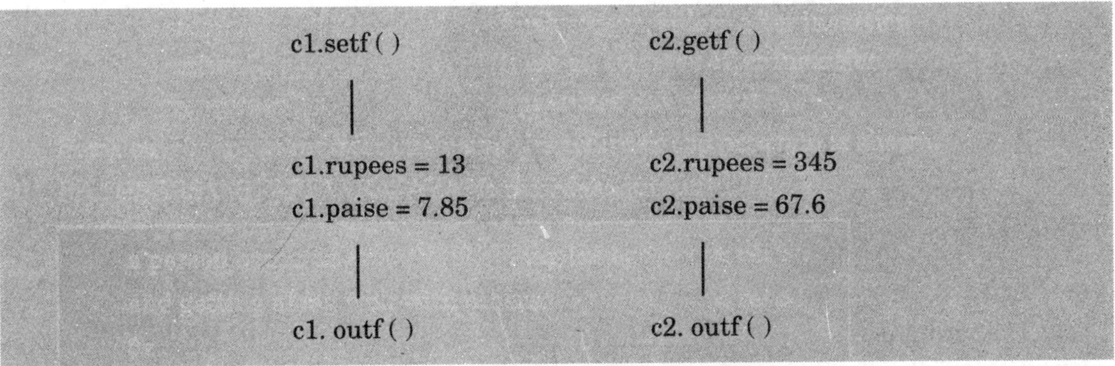

6.4 CONSTRUCTOR

A constructor enables the initialization of an object as it is created. Memory is set up and, the initial value written into it as soon as the object is defined in the main( ). The constructor is written using the class name as a function, and the initialization of the variable done within braces. For example "measure" is a class name, "meas" is a data item.

The following statement is an example of a constructor which assigns zero value to data item meas.

```
measure( ) { meas = 0; }
```

Study the following program:

```
// construc.CPP
// illustrating setting up of constructor.
#include <iostream.h>
class measure
    {
    private
        int meas;
    public:
        measure ( ) { meas = 0 ; }  // constructor, no
                                     //argument
        void raise_meas ( ) { meas++; } //underscore
        int fetchmeas ( ) { return meas;}
        };
void main ( )
{
measure ml, m2;
cout << "\nStarting m1 = "<<m1.fetchmeas ( );
cout << "\nStarting m2 = "<<m2.fetchmeas ( );
for (int k = 0; k < 5; k++)
    m1.raise_meas ( ) ;
for (int k = 0; k < 3; k++)
    m2.raise_meas ( ) ;
cout << "\nNew m1 = "<< m1.fetchmeas( );
cout << "\nNew m2 = "<< m2.fetchmeas( ):
}
```

The output is:

```
Starting m1 = 0
Starting m2 = 0
New m1 = 5
New m2 = 3
```

Analysis

1. See how the constructor is set up within the class specification as a public function.
2. "raise _ meas" increments "meas" each time it is invoked.
3. "fetchmeas ( )" returns the recent value stored in "meas" when it is called.
4. Let us now examine the memory cells assigned to object m1, m2 of class "measure" at start and at end of program.

   At start of program:

```
        m1.meas <- 0           m2.meas <- 0
```

   At end of program:

```
        m1.meas <- 5           m2.meas <- 3
    m1.raise_meas ( ) called   m2.raise_meas ( ) called
```

   5 times   3 times

Aside

A constructor helps to set up memory space and initialize it with a value specified in class specification upon defining the object. The opposite of the constructor is the destructor, which deallocates the memory space set up. A destructor has same name of the constructor and preceded by the tilde (~) sign. A destructor need not be furnished any argument.

```
class measure
  {
  private:
      int meas;
  public:
     measure( ) {meas = 0;}       //constructor
     . . . . .
  ~measure( ) { }     //destructor with no argument
```

6.5 OBJECTS AS FUNCTION ARGUMENTS

This section shall show objects being used as function argument. Constructor overloading and defining member function outside the class.

The following program incorporates all these 3 features:

```
//objectfn.cpp
#include <iostream.h>
class currency                //class specification
  {
```

```
    private:
        float paise; int rupees;
    public:
        currency ( ) { }            // constructor
         currency ( int rs, float ps )
                                //constructor 2 args
            {rupees = rs; paise = ps;}
        void fetcurr ( )
        {
        cout << "\n Type rupees in int: " ;
            cin >> rupees ;
        cout << " Paise in float: " ; cin >> paise;
        }
        void sumcurr (currency, currency);
                                    // declaration
        void display ( )
            {cout << "Rs. " << rupees << "Ps."
                << paise << endl; }
    };
void currency::sumcurr (currency c2, currency c3)
    {                                               // fn outside class
    paise = c2.paise + c3.paise;
    rupees = 0;
    if (paise > = 100.0)
        {
        paise -= 100.0;
        rupees++;
        }
    rupees += c2.rupees + c3.rupees;
        }
void main ( )
        {
        currency m1, m3;            // objects defined
        currency m2 (14, 56.98);    // objs defined,
        m1.fetcurr( );              // initialized
        m3.sumcurr(m1, m2 );        // objs as arguments
                                    // to add
        cout <<"\nFirst amt = ";    m1.display( );
        cout <<"\nSecond amt = ";   m2.display( );
        cout <<"\nTotal amt = ";    m3.display( );
        }
```

The output is:

```
Type rupees in int: 123              <rt>
Paise in float: 76.85                <rt>
First amt = Rs. 123 Ps. 76.849998
Second amt = Rs. 14 Ps. 56.98
Total amt = Rs. 138 Ps. 830002
```

Analysis:

1. There are two constructors: One without argument and the other with 2 arguments. These two constructor definitions are needed as you shall see shortly.
2. The definition currency ( ) { }, that is, the constructor without argument is called an implicit constructor. It must be defined so that later on in the main( ) we shall be able to create the two objects m1, m2. Thus the implicit constructor helps to define objects without being initialized.
3. The second definition

   currency (int rs, float ps)

   { rupees = rs; paise = ps; }

   is a constructor with 2 arguments. This is the usual way of defining a constructor. Here this constructor helps us to initialize values to the arguments by simple function invocation.

   ```
   currency m2  (14,   56.98)
                  |      |
        rupees= rs       |
                    paise = ps
   ```

4. The two public functions declared are fetcurr( ) and display ( ). They have assigned specific task as seen from the inline coding.
5. Now look at the declaration without a body:

```
void sumcurr (currency, currency);
```

   This declaration is required within class so that function can be defined outside the class structure.

6. So now we see a new feature in class and objects; defining a function of a class outside the class specification.

```
void currency : : sumcurr (currency c2, currency c3)
```

The following terms are to be noted:

```
currency <- class name
: : <- scope resolution operator
sumcurr <- member function name
currency c2 <- first object as dummy argument
currency c3 <- second object as dummy argument
```

Read through the heading carefully. The keyword void implies the function does not return any value. The class name follows void. The scope resolution operator (: :) is put between class name and function name. The function sumcurr( ) has two dummy arguments, which are objects of class currency.

7. The body of this function simply pulls out whole rupees from total paise and adds it to rupees. Then the total rupees is evaluated.
8. In main( ) two objects m1, m2 of class "currency" are defined. This is possible due to the definition of constructor without any argument within class.
9. The second is a definition cum initialization. This object is created and initialized due to the definition of the second constructor which has two arguments.
10. The invocation of m1.fetcurr( ) enables values to be entered for the class variables rupees, paise through the keyboard.
11. The invocation of m3.sumcurr (m1, m2) is again a special feature of class and objects to be re-emphasised. The function is invoked with the third object m3, and is furnished two arguments m1, m2 which are objects of class currency. The values associated with m1, m2 are added by the function to determine total amount.
12. The display of output is shown with appropriate responses.

Aside

The following pictorial representation strives to summarise the program activity.

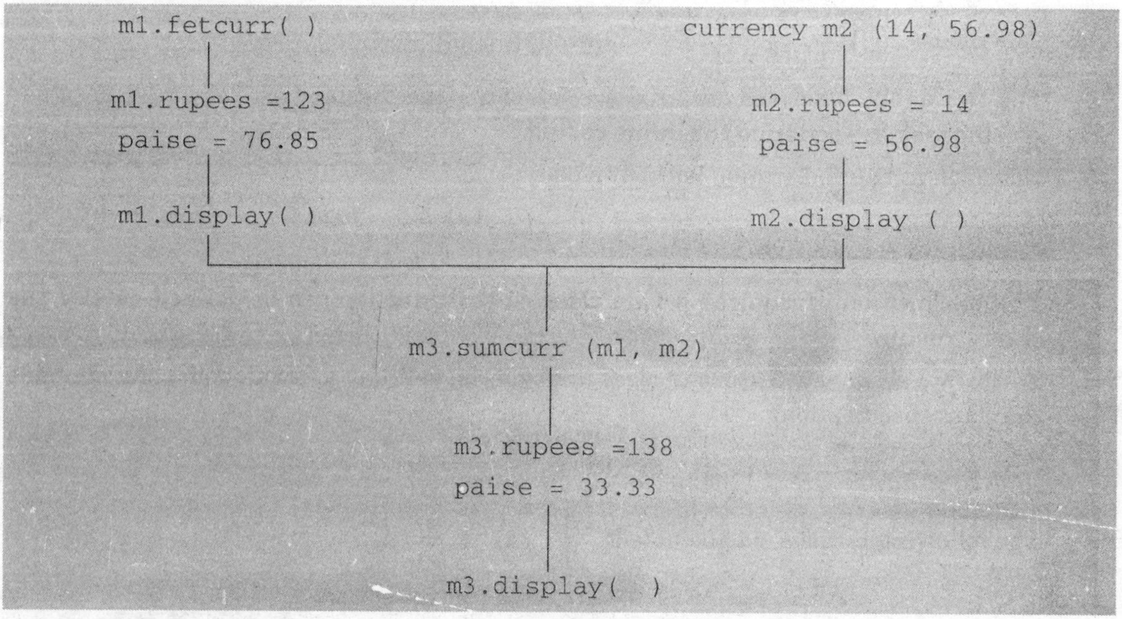

```
m1.fetcurr( )                          currency m2 (14, 56.98)
    |                                           |
m1.rupees =123                           m2.rupees = 14
paise = 76.85                            paise = 56.98
    |                                           |
m1.display( )                            m2.display ( )
    |                                           |
    ---------------------------------------------
                        |
              m3.sumcurr (m1, m2)
                        |
                 m3.rupees =138
                 paise = 33.33
                        |
                  m3.display(  )
```

6.6 FUNCTION RETURNING AN OBJECT

Here we are about to examine a function which returns an object for an answer. The previous program is modified slightly to do this. Therefore the changes in coding alone are indicated and explained, the rest of the coding remains unaltered.

```
//object.CPP
// function returns an object to calling function
#include <iostream.h>
class currency
   {
   private:
       float paise; int rupees;
   public:
       currency( ) { rupees = 0.0; paise = 0.0;}
   . . . .
   };
   currency currency: :sumcurr (currency c2)
   {                                   //1 arg constructor
   currency rest;                      // object defined
   rest.paise = paise + c2.paise;
   if  (rest.paise > = 100.0)
       {
       rest.paise - = 100.0;
       rest.rupees++;
       }
   rest.rupees += rupees + c2.rupees;
   return rest;    // returns object rest
   }
void main ( )
   {
   currency c1, c3;
   m3 = m1.sumcurr ( m2 );
                                 //note function invoked
   . . . . . . .
   }
```

Analysis

1. The output and responses of this program is identical to the previous one.

2. Wherever modifications are done, some comment has been included, so that it is easy to recognise the changes.
3. The point to be highlighted is calling of the function for adding two amounts in the main( ). It is done as follows:

```
m3 = m1.sumcurr (m2);
```

4. Now examine the function definition for sumcurr( ) outside the class

```
currency  currency      : :        sumcurr     (currency c2)
   |          |          |            |              |
 return     class      scope       member          object
  type      name     resolution     func          argument
                      operator      name          (dummy)
```

5. In the function invocation of sumcurr( ), object m1 is used to invoke it with object m2 as dummy argument. The result returned after executing the sumcurr ( ) function is assigned to object m3. Therefore one should be able to recognize the relationship that exists between

```
m3 = m1.sumcurr ( m2 ) and the sumcurr ( ) definition.
```

6. Since sumcurr( ) is defined to return class currency, it has a return statement, which returns the object "rest" to the calling function.

6.7 STATIC CLASS DATA

A static class data has limited visibility and lifetime of an ordinary static variable. Refer to Section 5.11 for a note on static storage class.

All along we bragged that each object has separate data type. But now we are confronted with a data item in a class of static type. This then must have a special significance. Yes it does have. It will be the only one of its type for the whole class, which all objects of the class can share and use. The following program shows its use.

```
// statict.cpp
// data of static class illustrated
#include <iostream.h>
class book
   {
   private:
        static int number; // static class data
   public:
```

```
        book( ) {number += 3;}  //constructor
        int fetch( ) { return number; }
    };
int book: :number = 0;
void main ( )
    {
    book b1, b2, b3:     // 3 objects defined
    cout << "\nNo of I books: "<<b1.fetch( );
    cout << "\nNo of II books: <<b2.fetch( );
    cout << "\nNo of III books: "<<b3.fetch( );
    }
```

The output is:

No of I books: 9
No of II books: 9
No of III books: 9

Analysis

1. A static data type is declared with keyword "static", its type and name. It must normally be initialized. Some compilers may assume zero value if simply defined without initialization. Static variable must be initialized before main ( ) using scope resolution operator (::) to avoid linker error.
2. The public function book( ) is actually a constructor which gets incremented by 3 for each object definition in main( ).
3. The fetch( ) function merely returns the result stored in static data type "number".
4. In main( ) 3 objects b1, b2, b3, are defined which belong to class "book".
5. As each object is defined, the constructor causes the static type variable to increment by 3, so that for defining 3 objects, the value stored in "number" is 9 in each case, as seen from the output.
6. "number" being static data type, is shared and accessed by all objects. Hence the same result holds good for all objects.

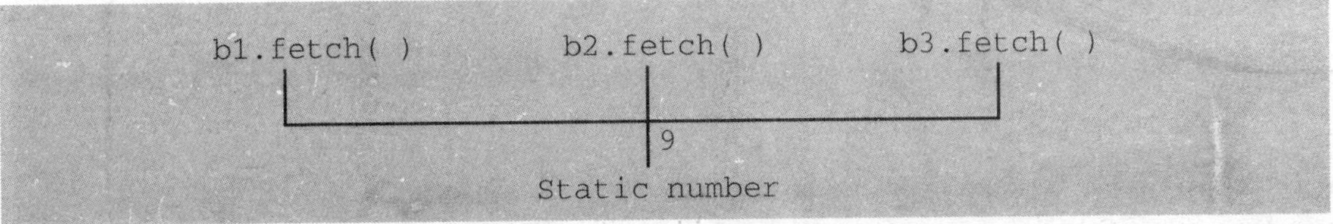

Aside

Suppose the keyword static is removed, and "number" is defined as an ordinary int type variable, then the memory allocation would be:

```
b1.number          b2.number          b3.number
    3                  3                  3
```

Since each definition of the object could increment its separate data only. In very large program static data maybe used to keep count of how objects were defined.

REVIEW QUESTIONS

6.1 What do you call a specification when it has data items and member functions.

6.2 What would you consider the principal objective of OOPs?

6.3 What keyword in class specification helps to hide data?

6.4 Can a class have public data and private functions?

6.5 What type do you call member functions when defined within a class: ordinary or inline?

6.6 When is memory space set up in class specification?

6.7 What is the dot operator called when it is used with class functions?

6.8 What is the number of bytes of memory for the following specification and definition?

```
    class student
    {
    private:
        int reg-no; char mark; float fees;
    public
        . . . . .
    }:
void main ( )
    {
    Student s1, s2;
    . . .
    }
```

6.9 Find out what is wrong with this segment?

```
class currency
    {
    private:
        . . . .
    public:
        void setf ( int rs, float ps ){ }
void main ( )
    {
    currency c1, c2;
    c1.setf (7.85, 13);
    . . . .
    }
```

6.10 What do you call the C+ + feature which enables you to initialize an object on creation?

6.11 What name does the constructor assume?

6.12 What does the destructor do?

6.13 What symbol is used before a destructor?

6.14 By what name should destructor be defined?

6.15 Can objects be furnished as function arguments?

6.16 What is double colon (: :) known as?

6.17 Can a class function be defined outside the class?

6.18 To enable a function definition outside the class definition what should be done within the class?

6.19 Suppose m1, m2 m3 are 3 objects. Write an expression so that object m1 invokes a function sumcurr ( ) using object m3 as argument, and the result returns to object m2.

6.20 What class does a variable with limited visibility and lifetime of a program belong?

Answers

6.1 Class

6.2 data hiding

6.3 private

6.4 Yes

6.5 inline

6.6 when objects defined

6.7 class member access operator

6.8 14 bytes

6.9 float and int type interchanged

6.10 constructor

6.11 class name

6.12 deallocate memory

6.13 tilde (~)

6.14 class name or constructor name

6. I5 Yes

6.16 scope resolution operator

6.17 Yes

6.18 function declaration

6.19 m2 = m1.sumcurr (m3);

6.20 static

Chapter 7

Numeric and String Arrays

Chapter 7

Numeric and String Arrays

OBJECTIVE

Structures and objects can hold different data types in one declaration. But arrays can hold only one data type such as int, char, float. Each element of an array is accessed by an index. Arrays maybe data members in classes and arrays can hold objects. Strings are character arrays terminated with a null character. Some string handling functions are used. Classes of string objects are illustrated to make string copying easier.

KEYWORD, FUNCTIONS, OPERATORS AND HEADER FILES

strcpy( ) strlen( ) string.h stdlib.h
time.h

7.1 INTRODUCTION TO ARRAYS

An array is defined by specifying its type, name and size. The size maybe directly given as an integer or an expression that evaluates into an integer. Array elements are accessed by the array index. The first element starts from 0. Actually there is no need to specify the size or dimension of the array during definition. When an array name is used as argument during a function call, it is assumed that memory address of the first element is passed. Now examine the following program.

```
// simple.CPP
// illustration of a simple array
#include <iostream.h>
void main( )
   {
   int numb [5] ; // array definition
```

```
cout <<"\nEnter 5 Numbers : \n";
for (int k = 0 ; k <5; k++)
    {cin >> numb [k] ;}
float sum = 0 . 0 ;
for (int j = 0; j < 5; j++)
    {sum += numb[j];}
float average = sum/5;
cout <<"\nAverage value = "<< average<< endl;
}
```

The output is:

```
Enter 5 numbers :
23          < ret >
45          < ret >
54          < ret >
65          < ret >
2           < ret >
Average value = 37.79999
```

Analysis

1. The array definition

   `int numb [5] ;`

   specifies the type as int, name of array is "numb" and size of the array is 5. The size may be omitted in the declaration.
2. In the first for-loop 5 values are entered for the array, each time pressing the RET key. The values are stored in

   `numb [0], numb [1] , . . . numb [4]`
3. The second for-loop adds the values in this array called "numb" and stores the total in float variable "sum" .
4. The "average" which is of type float is evaluated and the result is displayed.

Aside

The array of type int has 5 elements. Each element occupies 2 bytes of memory. In all, the entire array needs 10 bytes of memory space.

7.2 INITIALIZING ARRAYS

The next program shows how arrays can be initialized and how a particular element maybe accessed.

```
// initial.cpp
// initializing and accessing an array element
#include <iostream.h>
const int SIZE = 5;
void main( )
   {
   int k;
   float amount [SIZE] = { 23.45 , 43.55 , 33.67, 67.89 , 46.54);
   cout <<"\nWhich amount? ";
   cin>> k;
   cout << k <<" -th amount is: "<< amount [k];
   }
```

The output is:

```
Which amount?                    < ret >
4-th amount is : 46.540001
```

Analysis

1. The dimension of the array is defined by the following:

`const int SIZE statement. It is 5.`

2. The float type array "amount" is initialized with five elements so that

```
amount [0] = 23.45  amount [1] = 43.55
amount [2] = 33.67  amount [3] = 67.89
amount [4] = 46.54
```

3. In the cout statement, the array is accessed with the index k entered through the keyboard.

7.3 TWO-DIMENSIONAL ARRAY

The program shows how to handle a 2-dimensional array

```
// twodarr.CPP
#include <iostream.h>
#include <iomanip.h>
const int clas = 3;
const int sess = 2;
void main( )
   {
   int c, s;
```

```
float fees [clas] [sess];
                            //2-d array defined
for (c = 0; c < clas; c++)
    for (s = 0; s<sess; s++)
        {
        cout << "\nType fees for class: "<< c+1;
        cout << " , Session: "<< s+1 << endl;
        cin>> fees[c] [s] ;
        }
cout <<"\n\n Session";
cout <<" First Second";
for (c = 0; c<clas; c++)
    {
    cout <<"\nClass "<< c+1;
    for (s = 0; s<sess; s ++)
        cout << setprecision (2) << setw (10) <<
            setiosflags(ios: : showpoint)
            << setiosflags(ios: :fixed)
            << fees [c] [s];
    }
}
```

The output is:

Type fees for class: 1, Session:1	
1234.56	< ret >
Type fees for class: 1, Session:2	
234.76	< ret >
Type fees for class: 2, Session:1	
456.85	< ret >
Type fees for class: 2, Session:2	
675.42	< ret >
Type fees for class: 3, Session:1	
854.47	< ret >
Type fees for class: 3, Session:2	
746.77	< ret >

	Session	
	First	Second
Class 1	1234.56	234.76
Class 2	456.85	675.42
Class 3	854.47	746.77

Analysis

1. The const int type statements set the row and column. The array is a 3 x 2 one.
2. The array is float type, named fees. It has 3 rows and 2 columns.
3. The nested "for" statements assign values to the array rowwise. For every value of c of the outer for-statement, the inner for-statement executes twice in this program. c + 1, s + 1 enable the values to begin with 1 instead of 0.
4. Now study the last cout statement where several manipulation functions are used. This is possible by invoking the iomanip.h file.
5. setprecision(2) causes float type constants to be displayed to 2 decimal places.
6. setw(10) allows 10 columns for each output and right justified.
7. setiosflags (ios: : showpoint) is a flag invocation function, which avoids display in the exponential form.
8. setiosflags (ios: : fixed) is another direction to use a fixed decimal format.
9. These manipulators maybe placed in any random fashion. There is no rule that one should precede the other.
10. The output is shown above.

Aside

2-Dimension array was illustrated. Theoretically an array can be of any size such as even 7-dimension, depending upon the user.

7.4 INITIALIZING A 2-D ARRAY

In the previous program we entered the values of the 2-D array through the keyboard. In the ensuing program, the values are built into the program itself in a procedure known as initialising the array.

Except for this new feature, the program is similar to the earlier one. Therefore no further explanation is given.

```
// arrayarg.cpp
#include <iostream.h>
#include <iomanip.h>
void getshow( float (3][2] );
void main( )
   {
   float fees [3] [2]
```

```
        = {
            { 234.00,   456.00 },
            { 123.65,   543.89 },
            { 321.76,   675.78 }
        };
getshow(fees);            //function invocation
}
//getshow( )
void getshow ( float cfees [3] [2] )
    {
    int c, s;
    cout << endl; cout << endl;
    cout << " Fees Structure\n";
    cout << " Session\n";
    cout << " 1 2" ;
    for ( c = 0; c <3; c++)
    {
    cout << "\nCourse "<< c+1 ;
    for (s = 0; s < 2; s++)
        cout << setiosflags (ios::showpoint)
        <<  setiosflags(ios::fixed)
        <<  setw(10)
        << setprecision (2)
        << cfees [c] [s] ;
    }
}
```

Analysis

1. The output of this program is similar to the previous one.
2. The presence of function getshow( ) is declared by

   ```
   void getshow( float [3] [2] ) ;
   ```

   The "void" implies it does not return any value. Name of the function is getshow( ). It is furnished an argument, which is an array of type float of 3 rows and 2 columns.
3. Within main ( ) the float type array called "fees" of size 3 x 2, is initialized. Each row is enclosed by curly braces and separated by a comma. So also each element item is punctuated by a comma. The whole array is put within curly braces and terminated by a semicolon.
4. The getshow( ) function is invoked with the array name "fees" furnished as an argument.

5. In the getshow( ) the receiving parameter is "cfees" which is of dimension 3 x 2.
6. Thereafter the nested for-loop output the array values in a set format, as decided by the manipulators.

Aside

In a 2-D array the row size need not be specified in the declaration. The following declaration would work equally well in the above program.

```
void getshow( float [ ] [2] );
```

However while accessing a particular element, both indexes must be furnished.

7.5 STRUCTURE VARIABLES AS ARRAY ELEMENTS

Arrays can also contain structure, as this program shows:

```
// arrstr.cpp
// array of structures
#include <iostream.h>
#include <iomanip.h>
const int NUM = 2;
struct comp
   {int idno; int ptno; float price; } ;
void main( )
   {
   int k;
   comp spt [NUM] ;          //structure variable is
                             //an array
   for ( k = 0; k< NUM ; k++)
       {
       cout << '\n' ; cout <<"What is ID No?" ;
       cin >> spt[k].idno;
       cout << "Type in PT No"; cin >> spt[k].ptno;
       cout<<" Type in price : "; cin>> spt[k].price;
       }
   for ( k = 0 ; k< NUM; k++ )
       {
       cout <<'\nID of prod: "<<spt[k].ptno;
       cout <<"Type : "<<spt[k].ptno;
       cout <<"price "<< setprecision (2)
       << setiosflags(ios::fixed)
       << setiosflags (ios::showpoint)
```

```
        << spt[k].price
        }
    }
```

The output is:

```
What is ID No? 7                          < ret >
Type in PT No? 2                          < ret >
Type in price: 1234.57                    < ret >
What is ID No? 4                          < ret >
Type is PT No? 3                          < ret >
Type in price: 345.67                     < ret >
ID of prod: 7 Type: 2 Price: 1234.57
ID of prod: 4 Type: 3 Price: 345.67
```

Analysis

1. The structure by name "comp" has two int type and one float type variable.
2. The array of structure is defined within main( ) as comp spt [NUM] ;
3. Thereafter each element of the structure is accessed by using the structure variable with dot operator and the element name.

```
spt[0].idno <- 2 bytes
spt[0].ptno <- 2 bytes
spt[0].price <- 4 bytes

spt[1].idno <- 2 bytes
spt[1].ptno <- 2 bytes
spt[1].price <- 4 bytes
```

4. The program output and responses are shown above.

7.6 STACK CLASS

A stack is a space set apart in memory to store and retrieve addresses when control passes from one function to another. Generally a stack is implemented as last-in-first-out (LIFO) basis in the RAM . The following program illustrates arrays as data items in classes and shows data structure called the stack.

```
// stack.CPP
// Using stack as a class
#include <iostream.h>
```

```
const int LAR = 20;
class haystalk
   {
   private:
       int hs[LAR] ; int summ;
   public:
       haystalk( ) { summ = 0; }          //no arg
                                          //constructor
   void thrust(int ch)
       {hs [++summ] = ch; }               //PUSH operation
   int eject ( )
       {return hs[summ- - ];}             //POP operation
   } ;
void main ( )
   {
   haystalk hl;
   hl.thrust (23);
   hl.thrust (27);
   hl.thrust (58);
   cout << "First out: "<<hl.eject( ) << endl:
   cout << "Second out: "<<hl.eject( ) << endl:
   cout << "Third out: "<<hl.eject ( ) << endl;
   }
```

The output is:

First out: 58
Second out: 27
Third out: 23

Aside

Before going into the analysis of the above program, the action of the stack maybe understood from these diagrams.

```
(PUSH)   Empty Stack   hl.thrust (23)   hl.thrust(27)   hl. thrust (58)
hs [0]                       23               27               58
hs [1]                                        23               27
hs [2]                                                         23

(POP)    Full stack    hl.eject ( )     hl.eject ( )     hl.eject ( )
             58         27 ⟶ 58         23 ⟶ 27          23 --->
             27         23
             23
```

During the "thrust" operation data at top is pushed down to contain the incoming one. Thus each time a thrust( ) is done the existing data gets pushed down. As we "eject" the topmost data, the ones below come up to occupy the empty space at top. In computer parlance it is known an PUSH and POP operations.

Analysis

1. The usual class specification with private data and public functions is implemented.
2. But note the private class data is of int type array and not the simple data type. This array hs[ ] will be used to point to the stack top, that is, the highest memory address occupied currently.
3. The constructor merely initializes the index "summ" to 0.
4. The function thrust (int ch) pushes a value on the top of the stack. The index "summ" is pre-incremented so that it points to the next available memory location.

```
                thrust( )                     eject( )
        0          58          0                 27
        1          27          1                 23
        2          23        hs [2]      --->hs [summ --]
   hs [3] ->
              hs [++summ]
```

5. The eject( ) function pops out the topmost value from the stack. The index "summ" is post-decremented so that it points below the next occupied memory space.

7.7 ARRAY OF OBJECTS

The next program shows the creation and use of an array of objects.

```
// arrayobj. CPP
// array of objects illustrated
#include <iostream.h>
#include <stdio.h>
const int LAR = 40;
class currency
  {
  private:
        int rupees; float paise;
public:
        void fetch ( )
        {
        cout << \nRupees in int: "; cin >> rupees;
```

```
        cout <<" Paise in float :"; cin >> paise;
        }
    void display ( )
    {cout <<"Rs." << rupees<<"Ps." << paise;}
    };
void main ( )
{
    currency cr [LAR];       // array of objects
    int k = 0; char chr; cout = '\n';
    do
    {
    cout <<"Amount: "<< k+1;
    cr [k++].fetch ( ) ;
    cout <<"Another?(y/n) : ";cin = getchar( );
    }
    while (chr != 'n');
    for (int m = 0; m<k; m++)
        {
        cout <<"\nAmount : " <<m + 1<<" is ";
        cr [m].display( );
        }
}
```

The output is:

Amount: 1
Rupees in int: 345 < ret >
Paise in float: 67.85 < ret >
Another? (y/n): y < ret >

Amount: 2
Rupees in int: 456 < ret >
Paise in float: 56.98 < ret >
Another? (y/n): n < ret >

Amount: 1 is Rs. 345 Ps. 67.85
Amount: 2 is Rs. 456 Ps. 56.98

Analysis:

1. By now the class specification would be quite familiar to the reader. There is no need for an elaborate explanation for the program.

2. The new feature in this program is the array of objects defined in the main( ).

```
currency cr[LAR] ;
```

This array can contain upto 40 elements of data type "currency" Maybe the following diagram shall convey the meaning of creating an array of objects.

	Array of objects	Simple objects
int rupees	cr [0]	co
float paise	cr [0]	co
int rupees	cr [1]	c1
float paise	cr [1]	c1
. . . .	. . .	. .
int rupees	cr [39]	c39
float paise	cr [39]	c39

The difference between simple class objects and an array of objects is in the name only. Whereas in simple objects several names may have to be used such as c1, c2, .. c39. Note that in array of objects the same name is used with the index alone changing.

3. The do.. while loop prompts to enter an amount and invokes the fetch( ) function using the array object such as

```
cr[k++].fetch( );
```

The k is post-incremented; the starting value for k is 0 and after executing the fetch( ) function k is incremented.

4. The do.. while loop cycles till 'n' is entered for the query another? (y/n) :

5. The for-loop causes an output by invoking the display( ) function using the array object.

```
cr[m].display( );
```

6. The size of m is limited by the last k value evaluated when control exits the do.. while loop.

Aside

Now the question of array overflow is disquieting. Though we set a bound of 40, the array will continue to accept data even beyond this prescribed maximum. This may lead to unpredictable results or even lead to system crash. Therefore bound (limits of upper and lower values) checking is the responsibility of the programmer. Though such a likelihood is remote, a check maybe included at the start of the do. while loop itself as a precaution.

```
if (k >= 40 )
   {
   cout <<"\nArray bound exceeded";
   break;
   }
```

7.8 STRING HANDLING AS CHARACTER ARRAYS

Strings are treated as an array of characters terminated by the null character ('\0'). Let's examine a simple program to enter in a series of characters through the keyboard, store it in a variable and display it.

```
// Simpstr.cpp
// String variable illustrated
#include <iostream.h>
const int LAR = 40;
void main( )
   {
   char chr[LAR];  // defining character array
   cout <<"\nType in series of characters:";
   cin >> chr;
   cout <<"The string is: "<<chr;
   }
```

The output is:

Type in series of characters; Tirupparankundram <ret>
The string is: Tirupparankundram

Analysis

1. The string is treated as an array of characters terminated by null character '\0'.
2. Each character is stored in one byte of memory in successive locations. When the <RET> key is pressed the null character is automatically stored, and the series of characters is assigned to the char array "chr[ ]".

```
      0 1  2  3  4  5  6  7  8  9  10  11  12  13  14  15  16  17
chr[]T  i  r  u  p  p a  r  a  n  k   u   n  d    r   a  m  '\0'
```

3. The last object cout displays the contents of this array upto the null character.

Aside

It is fortunate that the above char array has only 17 characters, which was well within the provision of 40 characters. What if more than 40 characters were entered? In such a case there is likely to be an overflow of the buffer leading to a chaos! The following program uses the manipulator setw( ) to avoid buffer overflow. It will accept one character less than the maximum to accommodate the null character.

```
// bufover.cpp
// avoiding buffer ovefflow by setw manipulator
#include <iostream.h>
```

```
#include <iomanip.h>
const int LAR = 20;
void main( )
   {
   char chr [LAR] ;
   cout <<"\nType in series of characters: ";
   cin >> setw(LAR) >> chr; //setw( ) manipulator
   cout << "The string is: "<< chr;
   }
```

7.9 HANDLING SENTENCES

A sentence is also treated as an array of characters with blanks embedded between words. The following program handles this sort of array.

```
//sentenc.CPP
// sentences with blanks embedded between words
#include <iostream.h>
const int LAR = 100;
void main ( )
   {
   char chr [LAR];
   cout <<"\nType a sentence: ";
   cin.get (chr, LAR);
   cout <<"Your sentence is: "<< chr;
   }
```

The output is:

Type a sentence: Heartiest Pongal Greetings. < ret >
Your sentence is: Heartiest Pongal Greetings.

Analysis

1. The new feature in this program is the cin.get( ) function. get() is a member function of the "cin" class. Actually it should be expressed as cin: : get( ). However the above shown use is also valid. Either the period operator or the scope resolution operator maybe used.
2. There are 2 arguments for cin: : get ( ). The first is the character array name" chr" , which holds the starting address of the array. The second argument LAR holds the size of the array.

   This automatically avoids buffer overflow.

Aside

The cin: : get( ) function can take one more argument to indicate the end of multiple line inputs. The following program shows how this works.

```
// paragrap.cpp
// reading a paragraph
#include <iostream.h>
const int LAR = 140 ;
void main ( )
   {
   char chr [LAR] ;
   cout <<"\nType in a paragraph: ";
   cout << "\nEnd each line by pressing <RET> key: ";
   cout << "\nEnd each para with # symbol : \n";
   cin.get (chr, LAR , '#') ;  // terminator #
   cout <<"Your paragraph is: \n"<< chr;
   }
```

The output is:

```
Type in a paragraph:
End each line by pressing <RET> key:
End each para with # symbol:
Everyman needs a wife, because                 <ret>
sooner or later something goes wrong           < ret >
that you just can't blame on the               <ret>
government. #                                  <ret>
Your paragraph is:
Everyman needs a wife, because
sooner or later something goes wrong
that you just can't blame
on the government.
```

Analysis

1. Examine the cin: : get( ) function which now has 3 arguments.
   The first holds the starting address of the array "chr" , the second tells the size to avoid overflow. Third is the character '#' which when entered would terminate the paragraph.
2. The paragraph is from the popular monthly Reader's Digest(1993).

7.10 ELEGANT WAY TO COPY A STRING

This section will introduce an elegant string function to duplicate contents of one string variable into another string variable.

```
// duplicat.CPP
// copying a string to another variable.
#include <iostream.h>
#include <string.h>          // strcpy( )  func
const int LAR = 80;
void main ( )
   {
   static char chr [ ] = "Thiagarajar coll of engg\n"
       "Madurai - 625015";
   char chr1 [LAR];
   strcpy (chr1, chr);
   cout <<"\n";
   cout << chr1;
   }
```

The output is:

Thiagarajar coll of engg
Madurai - 625015

Analysis

1. The char array chr[ ] is of static type, which has limited visibility and lifetime of the program. But here a predefined function strcpy( ) of type "string" is invoked , so that the char array can be accessed even from outside the main( ) program.
2. The strcpy( ) copies character by character from "chr" and writes it into "chr1".

Aside

What is shown above is the best way to copy one string into another string.

In another method the length of the string can be determined using the strlen( ) function. Then a loop can be devised to copy this string into another string array and then insert the null character at the end. Of course this is a very crude method.

7.11 ARRAYS OF STRINGS

An array of string is similar to an array of arrays. The program handles array of strings using the latter concept.

```
// arraystr. CPP
//array of strings
#include <iostream.h>
const int CITY = 5;
const int TOT = 12;
void main ( )
    {
    char city [CITY] [TOT] = (" madurai", "madras",
        "tirunelveli", "salem","coimbatore" };
    for (int m =0; m<CITY; m++)
        cout << city [m] << endl;
    }
```

The output is:

```
madurai
madras
tirunelveli
salem
coimbatore
```

Analysis

1. The char array city [5] [12] has five row, with 12 columns in a row. The string names have been so selected that maximum is 11 characters and the last can be null character.
2. The array will be organised as shown

		0	1	2	3	4	5	6	7	8	9	10	11
	0	m	a	d	u	r	a	i	'\0'				
	1	m	a	d	r	a	s	'\0'					
city [ ] [ ]	2	t	i	r	u	n	e	1	v	e	1	i	'\0'
	3	c	o	i	m	b	a	t	o	r	e	'\0'	

3. While accessing it for reading only the first index, viz row number is specified. In 2 dimensional arrays the column index need not be specified.

7.12 STRINGS AS MEMBERS OF CLASS

The program illustrates strings as members of a class.

```
//strclass.cpp
#include <iostream.h>
```

```
#include <string.h>
class stud
    {
    private:
        char name [25]; int reg_no; floatfees;
    public:
        void fetch ( char n[], int i, float c)
            {
            strcpy (name, n);
            reg_no = i;
            fees = c;
            }
        void display( )
            {
            cout <<"\nName = "<<name;
            cout <<", Reg No = "<<reg_no;
            cout <<", Fees = Rs. "<<fees;
            }
        } ;
void main( )
    {
    stud s1, s2;
    s1.fetch ( "R. Jayaram", 1234, 876.00);
    g2.fetch( "J. Vivek", 2345 , 675.00);
    cout <<"\Details of I student:" ;s1.display( );
    cout << "\n Details of II student : "; s2.display( );
    }
```

The output is:

Details of I student:
Name = R. Jayaram, Reg No = 1234, Fees = 876.00
Details of II student:
Name = J. Vivek, Reg No = 2345, Fees = Rs. 675.00

Analysis

1. The only new feature in this program is the use of the strcpy( ) function in the public function fetch( ).

2. In declaring the private class data, "name" is of type char of size 25. In fetch( ) , n is also declared to be char type and no size is mentioned. It will automatically assume the size of each string stored in name[ ] array during the strcpy( ) process.
3. In main( ) two objects s1, s2 are defined of class "stud".
4. These objects are used with member function fetch( ) to assign constants.
5. The member function display( ) is invoked by the objects to display these values.

7.13 USER DEFINED STRING TYPE

How nice it would be to simply assign one string to another char array just as we do in Basic language. This is exactly what is achieved by the following program. It enables defining our own string type, so that assignment statements maybe employed for handling strings.

```
// userdef.CPP
// user defined string as class
#include <iostream.h>
#include <string.h>
const int s = 35;
class sentence
   {
   private:
       char chr [s];
   public:
       sentence( ); { chr[0] = '\0' ; }    // no arg
                                           // constructor
       sentence( char st [ ] ) //1 arg constructor
           {strcpy ( chr, st) ; }
   void show ( ) { cout <<chr; }
   void join ( sentence sr)
       {
       if (strlen ( chr) + strlen (sr.chr) < s)
           strcat ( chr,  sr.chr);
       else
           cout <<"\n Wow! Sentence too unwieldy. ";}
       };
   void main ( )
       {
```

```
sentence sa("Happy Deepavali!");
                                //1 arg constructor
sentence sr="Wishing you a happy birthday. ";
     // alternate call to 1 arg constructor
sentence sc; // call no arg constructor
cout <<"\n Wishing you a"; sa.show( );
cout <<"\nCongratulations! "; sr.show( );
sc = sa;
cout <<"\n Greetings on "; sc.show( );
sc.join(sr); cout <<"\nWow!";
sc.show( );
}
```

The output is:

Wishing you a Happy Deepavali!
Congratulations! Wishing you a happy birthday.
Greetings on Happy Deepavali !
Wow! Sentence too unweildy.

Analysis

1. The sentence class has one data item which is of type char. It is an array called chr[35].
2. The constructor with no argument sets the first element of this array to null character. The object to call this constructor is defined by following definition.

   `sentence sc;`

3. The constructor with 1 argument copies the string in char array st [ ] to the object's data "chr". It is called by following statement:

   `sentence sr = "Wishing you a happy birthday."`

4. The member function show( ) simply displays the contents in the object data array "chr".
5. The member function join(sentence sr) concatenates two strings. One is in the object "sr" and another is in the object by which this function is invoked. Suppose the following invoking is done:

   `sc.join(sr);`

   Then the immediate contents of object "sc" and "sr" are concatenated, subject to string length being less than 35 characters, including the null character. If the resulting string length exceeds 35 characters, then the error message "Wow! Sentence too unwieldy" is displayed.

7.14 RANDOM NUMBER GENERATOR

The random number generator has many useful roles in games such as dice, cards. Here a brief discussion is included regarding two important functions relating to random number generation.

They are randomize( ) and random( ). Both are built-in functions of Turbo C++. Both these functions use the system time as the seed, therefore there is a need to include two header files in the preprocessor directive.

stdlib.h and time.h

In a typical program they are included as shown:

```
randomize(  ): // seed random number generator
int game(  )
{
int k = random(12);
. .
}
#include <time.h>
#include <stdlib.h>
#include <iostream.h>
int game (  )
   (randomize ( ); int k = random (12);
   cout <<"\n Random number is:" << k;
   return ( 0 );
   }
void main ( )
   {
game ( );
   }
```

The Output is :

Random number is: 6	**//First Run**
Random number is: 8	**//Second Run**
Random number is: 9	**// Third Run**

"k" will now have a value between 0 to 11. Those who are familiar with random number generation in Basic would recall that it generates a decimal number. Whereas in C ++ the number generated is an integer within the seed value prescribed.

REVIEW QUESTIONS

7.1 Can an array contain different data types like structure?

7.2 Is there a separate data type called "string" in C++?

7.3 How is a string treated in C and C++?

7.4 What 3 specifications characterize an array?

7.5 What is the index of the first element of an array?

7.6 Should size or dimension be specified during array declaration?

7.7 When an array name is used as an argument in a function call, what is passed: the value or its address?

7.8 How many bytes of space in memory is required to store this array? float fees[8];

7.9 An array is declared as

```
float amt [5] =(23.45, 43.55, 55.32, 67.89, 46.5;)
```

what value is displayed when the following statement is executed:

```
cout << amt [2] ;
```

7.10 Which manipulator enables setting number of digits to be fixed after the decimal point?

7.11 What does the setiosflags (ios: : showpoint) do?

7.12 What flag manipulator enables a float type number to be displayed with a decimal point?

7.13 Which header file should be included to use the flags and precision manipulators?

7.14 Point out the errors if any in this declaration:

```
float fees [ 3] [2] = { { 234.0, 456.0}
{ 123. 0 , 543.0}
{ 323. 0 , 675.0  }
}
```

7.15 Is this declaration correct?

```
void getshow (float [3] [2]) ;
```

7.16 Examine the following structure struct comp

```
 struct comp
{int i; int p;float p;)
void main ( )
{
comp spt[2];
. . . .
}
```

Compute the total number of bytes required to store the array of structures.

7.17 What is the basis of stack organisation in C ++?

7.18 Is array of objects and array of structures similar?

7.19 Does C++ have a built-in mechanism to check array overflow?

7.20 By what character should an array of characters be terminated to call it a string?

7.21 Which manipulator helps to avoid buffer overflow while handling string inputs?

7.22 What is special about the get( ) function which is a member function of cin class [cin: : get ( )] ?

7.23 Write the member function of cin class so that the end of a multi-line sentence is indicated by an asterisk. Array name is chr, size of array is MAX.

7.24 The following declaration is made with main( ) . Mention any errors in it.

```
static char str[ ] = " Rolling stone gathers no"
                                   "moss".
```

7.25 An array of strings is considered as a 2-d array. While accessing it, which index maybe omitted: row or column?

7.26 Can a built-in function be used in a public member function of a class?

7.27 Examine the following specifications.

```
class student
{
private :
    char name [25]:
public:
    student( )  ( name = '\0';)
. . . .
} ;
void main( )
{
student s1("Congratulations");
student s2 ;
. . .
}
```

which object definition calls the constructor without any argument?

7.28 To use the built-in library function randomize( ) and random( ) , which header files must be included?

7.29 What is the range of numbers generated by the following:

```
randomize( ):
random(45):
```

Answers

7.1	no	7.2	no
7.3	array of chars	7.4	type, name, size
7.5	0	7.6	no
7.7	address	7.8	32 bytes
7.9	55.32	7.10	setprecision()
7.11	avoids exponential form of display	7.12	setiosflags (ios: : fixed)
7.13	iomanip.h	7.14	commas missing

7.15 yes

7.16 16 bytes

7.17 LIFO

7.18 yes

7.19 no

7.20 null'\0' character

7.21 setw()

7.22 recognizes embeded blanks

7.23 cin.get(chr, MAX, '*');

7.24 \n missing

7.25 column index

7.26 yes

7.27 student s2

7.28 stdlib.h time.h

7.29 0 to 44

Chapter 8

Operator Flexibility

Chapter 8

Operator Flexibility

OBJECTIVE

This chapter discusses about how to give additional meanings to operators like + * < = + = when dealing with objects of user-defined class. This is also known as operator overloading, as these operators perform more than their conventional role. Data type conversion is also discussed. Finally some pitfalls in employing over loaded operators is mentioned.

KEYWORD

operator

8.1 OVER LOADED UNARY OPERATOR

We shall see how the increment operators + + and – – can be used on objects of user-defined class. Generally they work well with basic data types such as int. Now we shall assign it with special provisions, so that they can perform the same operations on objects of user-defined classes. Study the following program for a model.

```
//operover.cpp
// illustrates - operator overloading
#include <iostream.h>
class operation
   {
   private:
       unsigned int C;
   public:
       operation( ) { c = 4;}
       int fetch ( ) { return c;)
```

```
        void operator --( ) { c--;}
    };
  void main( )
        {
        operation o1, o2;
        cout <<"\nInitial o1= "<<o1.fetch( ) ;
        cout <<"\nInitial o2 = "<<o2.fetch( );
        o1--; o1--;
        o2--; o2--; o2--; o2--;
        cout <<"\nFinal o1 = "<<o1.fetch( );
        cout <<"\nFinal o2 = "<<o2. fetch( );
          }
```

The output is:

Initial o1 = 4
Initial o2 = 4
Final o1 = 2
Final o2 = 0

Analysis

1. In the "operation" class declaration, the public function operation( ) { c = 4; }

   is a constructor without argument. It initializes the private data c with 4. A constructor without argument helps to initialize a class data with any initial value.

2. The next public function

   ```
   int fetch( ) {return c;)
   ```

   simply returns the current value available in "c".

3. The next function

   ```
   void operator--( )  {c--;}
   ```

   assigns the unary operator – – the added flexibility to use it with particular object of a class. Here it decrements the "c" data in the object of which it is a member function. Note the word "operator" is a C++ keyword.

4. Inside main( ) two objects o1, o2, are defined, which are used with the dot operator and the fetch( ) function to display the initial values stored in "c".

5. Now we are able to use the overloaded operator – – with objects o1, o2, so that they decrement "c".

6. Then again we use the objects o1, o2, with the dot operator and fetch( ) function to display the current values stored in data c.

Aside

Examine the following member function:

```
void operator - - ( ) { c - - ; }
```

It is designed to perform decrement of the class objects o1, o2 only as stand alone operands. They cannot return any value due to the use of the classifier "void" . Therefore it is not possible to write such expressions as follows within the main( ):

```
o2 = o1 - -;
```

8.2 CLASS MEMBER FUNCTION TO RETURN A VALUE

We shall overcome the above shortcoming by enabling the member function to return a value. This will enable us to write the above expression as

```
o2 = o1 - - ; or o2 = o1++;
```

The following program illustrates this point.

```
// operovrl . CPP
#include <iostream.h>
class operation
   {
   private:
       unsigned int c;
   public:
       operation ( ) { c = 4; }
       int fetch( ) ( return c; }
       operation operator ++ ( )
       {
       c++;
       operation ord; // temporary object
       ord.c = c;
       return ord;
       }
   };
void main ( )
   {
   operation o1, o2;
   cout <<"\nInitial o1 = "<< o1.fetch( );
   cout <<"\nInitial o2 = "<< o2.fetch( );
   o1++; o1++;
```

```
o2 = o1++; o2 = o1++; o2 = o1++; 02 = o1++
cout <<"\nFinal o1 = "<< o1.fetch( );
cout <<"\nFinal o2 = "<<o2.fetch ( ) ;
}
```

The output is:

```
Initial o1 = 4
Initial o2 = 4
Final o1 = 10
Final o2 = 10
```

Analysis

1. Now examine the member function

   ```
   operation operator ++ ( )
                           { }
   ```

   Here a temporary object of type operation called "ord" is declared to return a value for the + + operator. This will leave the content of data type "c" intact, and use its copy in "ord.c" to be returned.

2. Otherwise this program is similar to the previous one. Here the increment operator + + is shown in its overloaded role. o1 + + causes increment by 1. It figures twice therefore o1 will have 6.

3. In the expression o2 = o1 ++; it is incremented and then assigned to object o2. The pre-increment value of o1 was 6. Now due to the present expression, o1 is incremented and copied into o2. Repeating this 4 times makes o2 = o1 ++ to become 10, as obvious from the output.

Aside

Now that was quite a task to create a temporary object and use it to return a value. In a more elegant method we can eliminate the temporary object and return the value directly. The member function is recoded as follows to do this:

```
operation operator ++( )
    {c++; return operation(c);}
```

In the earlier and this instance, the overloaded operator can be used as follows also:

```
cout << o2++.fetch( );
```

The meaning should be quite clear. The object is made to display itself using the fetch( ) member function.

Alert

When + + or – – is used in its overloaded role, there is no difference between pre and post-operations. In turbo C++ or Borland C++ it is always assumed to be preincrement, *i.e.*

```
++o1 or o1++ have identical effect.
operator ++( ); prefix(++o1);
operator ++(int ); postfix (o1++);
```

8.3 FLEXIBLE BINARY OPERATION

The next program shows how the + or - binary operators can be given the flexibility to operate on objects of class data using member functions. Study the following program.

```
//operplus.cpp
// overloaded '+' operator add 2 amount
#include <iostream.h> '
class currency
  {
  private:
       float paise; int rupees;
                                    //constructor without arg
  public:
       currency( ) {rupees=0; paise=0.0;)
                                    //2arg constrtr
       currency (int rs, float ps)
           {rupees = rs; paise=ps;)
       void fetch ( )
           {
           cout <<"\nType in rupees (int) :; cin
               >>rupees;
           cout <<"\nType in paise (float):"; cin
               >>paise;
           }
       void display ( )
           { cout <<"Rs . " << rupees <<" Ps.
               "<<paise<<"\n"; }
           currency operator + (currency);
                                            // declarator
           };
currency currency::operator + (currency d2)
  {
```

```
        int r = rupees + d2.rupees;
        float p = paise + d2.paise;
        if (p >= 100.0)
            {
            p -= 100.0;
            r++;
            }
        return currency ( r, p);
        }
    void main( )
        {
        currency c1, c3, c4;
        c1.fetch( ) ;
        currency c2 (104, 67.89);
        c3 = c1 + c2;
        c4 = c3 + c3;
        cout <<"\nAmount1 = "; c1.display ( );
        cout <<"\nAmount2 = "; c2.display ( );
        cout <<"\nAmount3 = "; c3.display( );
        cout <<"\nAmount4 = "; c4.display( );
```

The output is:

Type in rupees (int): 123 <ret>
Type in paise (float): 67.85 <ret>
Amount1 = Rs. 123 Ps. 67.849998
Amount2 = Rs. 104 Ps. 67.889999
Amount3 = Rs. 228 Ps. 35.739999
Amount4 = Rs. 456 Ps. 71.479981

Analysis

1. By now one should be quite familiar with constructors with and without arguments. So no more elaboration is done about them.
2. Look at the last declarator among member functions:

```
currency operator + ( currency);
```

The definition immediately follows the class declaration outside class structure before the main( ) function.
3. The definition uses the scope resolution operator (: :) to assign the + sign its overloaded role within the body of the definition. We are able to use the + sign on data objects such as rupees and paise which belong to data type "currency", and assign it to "r" and "p".

4. The "if" loop pulls out whole rupees and adds it to "r" . "p" now contains the remaining paise. The function is able to return the objects "r" and "p" , when invoked in the main( ) in such expressions like c3 = c1 + c2; c4 = c3 + c3;

   The returned values are stored in objects c3 and c4.
5. Within main( ) 3 objects c1, c3 and c4 are defined which can then access the member functions for adding, assigning and displaying the values.
6. Object c2 invokes the constructor with 2 arguments to assign initial values to itself.

8.4 JOINING STRINGS (CONCATENATION)

Here the use of the + sign as an overloaded operator to concatenate two string variables using simple expression like

```
x3 = x1 + x2;
```

is shown. x1, x2 and x3 are string objects. The following program shows the use.

```
//strjoin.cpp
//using + as overloaded operator to join 2 strings
#include <iostream.h>
#include <string.h>
const int S = 100;
class senten
   {
   private:
        char chr [S] ;
   public:
        senten( ) { strcpy ( chr, " ") ; }
                                        // constructor
        senten ( char x[ ] ) { strcpy (chr , x );}
                                        // constructor
   senten show ( ) { cout <<chr ; }
   senten operator + (senten.xx)
        {
        if (strlen (chr) + strlen (xx.chr) <S )
            {
            senten just;//temporary object
            strcpy (just.chr, chr);
            strcat ( just.chr, xx.chr);
            return just;
```

```
            }
            else
            cout <<"\nSentence overflowed";
        }
    };
void main( )
    {
    senten x1 = "\nHappy Deepavali ! ";
    senten x2 = " Enjoy your reading.";
    senten x3;
    x1.show( ); x2.show( );
    x3 = x1 + x2;
    x3.show( );
    }
```

The output is:

Happy Deepavali! Enjoy your reading.
Happy Deepavali! Enjoy your reading.

Analysis

1. There are 2 constructors as member function in public class. First one has no argument and initializes "chr" to null. The second constructor with one argument, copies the array x[ ] into chr [ ].
2. The member function

   ```
   senten operator + ( sente.xx)
                         { }
   ```

   overloads the + symbol so that it can be used to concatenate (join) two strings.
3. The if-loop in this member function tests if the length of the two strings to be joined is less than the maximum size 100.
4. With the body of the if-loop a temporary object called "just" is set up, so that it can be used in different manipulations without affecting the contents of the original object "chr" . It also serves to return the copied string wherever the overloaded + operator is invoked. The strcat( ) function joins the two strings.
5. If the length exceeds the maximum size of 100. Then the false option following "else" clause is executed, to give a message "Sentence overflowed".
6. In the main( ), the two objects x1 and x2 are initialized with string constants "Happy Deepavali !" and "Enjoy your reading." with the aid of the constructor with one argument.
7. A third object x3 is created and used in an expression

```
x3 = x1 + x2;
```

where the overloaded operator + is used to join two objects and return the result to object x3.

8. In the output, note that 2 blanks spaces between the first and second strings. This is due to the 2 spaces entered in the string stored in object x2.

8.5 OVERLOADED RELATIONAL OPERATOR

In this section the relational operator " > " shall be overloaded, just as the + operator was overloaded in the previous section. The value returned shall depend on a relational test and it shall be "true" or "false".

```
// relover.CPP
// relational operator > overloaded
#include <iostream.h>
enum relation {false, true};
class currency
   {
   private:
       float paise int rupees;
   public:
       currency( ) {rupees=0; paise=0.0;}
                              //no arg constr
   currency (int rs, float ps) //2 arg constructor
       {rupees = rs; paise = ps;}
void fetch ( )
   {
   cout <<"\nType rupees (int): "; cin >>rupees;
   cout <<"\nType paise ( float) : "; cin >> paise;
   }
void display( )
   {cout << "Rs. "<< rupees<<"Ps. "<< paise; }
   relation operator > (currency) ; // declaration
   } ;
relation currency: :operator > (currency c2)
                                         // definition
   {
   float cu1 = rupees + paise /100;
   float cu2 = c2.rupees + c2.paise/100;
```

```
        return (cu1 > cu2)? true : false;
        };
    void main( )
        {
        currency c1; c1.fetch( );
        currency c2( 8, 5.6) ;
        cout <<"\nAmount1 = "; c1.display ( );
        cout <<"\nAmount2 = " = ; c2.display( );
    if ( c1 > c2)
        cout <"\nAmount1 is greater than Amount2.";
    else
        cout <<"\nAmount1 is less than Amount2.";
        }
```

The output is:

Type rupees(int): 7 <ret>
Type paise (float) : 54.65 <ret>
Amount1 = Rs. 7 Ps. 54.650002
Amount2 = Rs. 8 Ps. 5.6
Amount1 is less than Amount 2.

Analysis

1. The class "currency" structure is quite strightforward with its private data and public member function. Therefore no further explanation is offered.
2. Examine the last declaration of a member function where the relational operator " < " is assigned its overloaded role.
3. The definition of this function uses the scope resolution operator (: :) in data type "currency" . We use two objects cu1 and cu2 to hold the two amounts in decimal form. That is, paise is divided by 100 and converted into rupees and added. This function has a dummy parameter c2 furnished during its definition. The real parameter is used during its invocation.
4. The return statement is a conditional one.

   ```
   return (cu1 > cu2) ? true:false;
   ```

   If the expression (cu1 > cu2) is true, a boolean value "true" is returned. If it is false, a boolean value "false" is returned.
5. Now in the main( ) the if-statement.

   ```
   if (c1 >c2)
   ```

receives a "false" value returned by the member function, for the particular values associated with the objects c1, c2 namely,

```
c1 = 7.5465 c2 = 8.56
```

8.6 STRINGS COMPARED USING OVERLOADED OPERATORS

The same idea of applying overloaded operator > can be extended to comparing strings. However for a change the not equal to (! =) operator is tried here.

```
// notequal.CPP
// overload not equal to operator an strings
#include <iostream.h>
#include <string.h>
const int S = 100;
enum relation { false , true);
class sentenc
   {
   private:
       char chr[S];
   public:
       sentenc( ) { strcpy ( chr, " " ) ; }
       sentenc (char c[S]), {strcpy (chr, c);}
       void screen( ) { cout << chr; }
       void fetch ( ) {cin.get (chr, s); }
       relation operator != ( sentenc xx)
           {return (strmp ( chr, xx.chr) ! = 0)
       ? true:false; }
   } ;
void main( )
   {
   sentenc c1 = "madurai"; // 1 arg constructor
   sentenc c2 = "madras";
   sentenc c3;
   cout <<"\nEnter 'madurai' or 'madras' : ":
   c3.fetch( );
   if (c3 != c1)
       cout << "You belong to Madras, :";
   else
       cout << "You belong to: "; c3.screen( );}
   }
```

The output is:

Enter 'madurai' or 'madras' : madras < ret >
You belong to madras.

Aside

This program works exactly like the last one. Only thing is strings are used in the comparison instead of floating point numbers. Therefore the reader may analyse it and strive to understand it.

It is needless to mention that operators like + = – = < < = * = / = can all be overloaded and used in any expression within a program.

8.7 DATA CONVERSION

There are 2 types of data called "basic" type and "user defined" type. Normally there are implicit predefined functions available to convert from one basic type to another basic type such as float to int, double to float, etc. Or one can use case operators to coerce (force) one basic data type to be of another type. In this case it is termed an explicit conversion.

In this section the focus is on the conversion from "basic" to "user-defined" data type and vice versa. Study the following program which employs such conversions.

```
// dataconv.cpp
// conversion of US$ into Indian rupees
#include <iostream.h>
const float DTR = 31.75 ;
class currency
{
private :
    float paise; int rupees;
public:
    currency( ) { rupees =0; paise= 0.0;}
    currency ( float doll)
    {
    float fr = DTR * doll;
    rupees = int(fr);
    paise = 100* {fr- rupees);
    }
carrency ( int rs, float ps)
    {rupees = rs; paise = ps; }
void display ( )
```

```
        {cout <<"Rs. "<< rupees<<" Ps. "<<paise; }
    operator float ( )
        {
        float frr = paise/100;
        frr += float (rupees);
        return frr/ DTR;
        }
    } ;
void main ( )
    {
    currency c1 = 12.78;
    cout <<"\nEquiv "; c1.display ( );
    currency c2 (12345, 56.78) ;
    float dolrs = float( c2);
    cout << '\n' ;
    c2.display( ) ;
    cout <<"is US$ = "<< dolrs ;
    }
```

The output is:

Equiv Rs. 404 Ps. 48.699951
Rs. 12345 Ps. 56.77999 is US$ 390.065338

Analysis

1. Now analyse the member function which converts "$" into rupees and paise. It is a constructor with one argument. It converts a basic data type to user-defined type.

```
        currency (float doll)
        {
        float fr=DTR * doll:
        rupees =int (fr);
        paise =100 *(fr-rupees);
        }
```

It is invoked within main( ) by the first definition

```
        currency c1 = 12.78;
```

c1 is an object of class "currency" and initialized with value 12.78. The member function accepts this as an argument and converts it into rupees and paise.

2. The next member function to be noted is the one which converts rupees to dollars.

```
operator float( )
{
float frr = paise /100;
frr += float ( rupees);
return frr/DTR;
}
```

It is invoked with main ( ) by the statement

```
float dolrs = float (c2);
```

Notice the left and right sides of this expression. "dolrs" is a basic variable of type float. Whereas c2 is an object of type currency. Thus data conversion from basic type to user-defined type has been achieved.

3. The body of this function converts paise into fractional rupees and assigns it to "frr". Then the rupees of type int is converted into float by cast operator and added with "frr" and the sum is assigned to "frr" itself.
4. The return statement transfer $ value to the main and stores it in "dolrs".
5. Besides the special features mentioned, the above program is otherwise quite simple.

8.8 STRING CONVERSION: STRING TO OBJECT AND REVERSE

```
// strstrob.CPP
// string to class and reverse conversion
#include <iostream.h>
#include <string.h>
const int S = 100;
class sentenc
{
private:
    char sen[S];
public:
    sentenc( ) { sen[0] = '\0'; }
    sentenc (char c[ ]) { strcpy ( sen , c);}
    void screen( ) { cout << sen; }
    operator char* ( ) {return sen;}
    } ;
void main( )
{
sentenc c1;
```

```
char ssen[ ]= "\nWelcome to Madurai !";
c1 = ssen; c1.screen( ); // class to str
sentenc c2 =" Madurai Meenakshi Our Divine Lady.";
c2.screen( );// str class to string
}
```

The output is:

Welcome to Madurai! Madurai Meenakshi Our Divine Lady.

Analysis

1. This program has 2 important member functions which enable string to class conversion and class to string conversion. Examine the string to class conversion first. The function which does this is:

   ```
   sentenc (char c[ ]) {strcpy ( sen, c);}
   ```

   This is a constructor with one argument, which copies the string in the main( ) as follows:

   ```
   sentenc c2 ="Madurai Meenakshi Our Divine Lady."
   ```

2. The other function which converts a class to ordinary string is

   ```
   operator char*( ) { return sen;}
   ```

   The statement that invokes in main( ) is

   ```
   cout <<c2;
   ```

   c2 is an object of type "sentenc". The overloaded operator < < converts it into normal string and displays it on the screen. c2 is initialized with string "Madurai Meenakshi Our Divine Lady."

8.9 DIVERSE POINTS ON CONVERSIONS

1. It is possible to convert between basic type and user-defined types and the reverse as we have seen in the above example.
2. Conversion between two user-defined types is also possible by defining a 1-argument constructor or by means of a conversion function.
3. When to use a 1-argument constructor or a conversion function? One argument constructor is used with a library of class: object of such class is source argument and destination is of user-defined type. On the other hand if library class object is destination, user-defined conversion function is the source.
4. The following operators cannot be overloaded:

   (.) dot operator

   (: :) scope resolution operator

   (?:) conditional operator

   (.*) point to member operator

REVIEW QUESTIONS

8.1 Is "operator" a keyword or a function?

8.2 What is achieved by the following declaration in class structure:

```
void operator ++ ( ) { C++; }
```

8.3 Suppose we declare a class structure, and then define objects within the main( ), what type do these objects belong to?

8.4 When you declare a member function within class structure as void operator – – ( ) { c – – ;)

```
will the following expression be valid
02 = 01 - -;
```

8.5 What strategy would you suggest so that the unary operator + + or – – can be overloaded to be used in an expression such as in (8.4)?

8.6 Do you think that it is possible to return an object directly without using an intermediate temporary object?

8.7 Suppose a unary operator like + + is overloaded, does it make any difference if it is used as pre or post increment with an object?

8.8 Is it possible to define member functions so that the distinction between pre and post operation is evident?

8.9 Assume c1, c2, and c3 are objects of a class, which handle data elements like rupees and paise. If we write an expression using the overloaded operator + such as c3 =c1 +c2; what does it imply?

8.10 Is it possible to overload the + operator so that it can be used in string expressions such as x3 = x1 + x2 ; to perform concatenation?

8.11 Can relational operators such as < > < = > = ! = also be overloaded?

8.12 A overloaded relational operator > is used in a member function as: return(s1 > s2) ? false : true; What value is returned for s = 1, s2 = 3?

8.13 A overloaded relational operator != is used in string handling as:

```
return (strcmp (s, x.c) != 0? true: false;)
Assume s and X.c
contain different
strings, what value
is returned
```

8.14 Can a basic data type be converted into user-defined type?

8.15 Is it possible to convert a user-defined data into a basic data?

8.16 Can one object class be converted into another object class?

8.17 Suppose a library of class uses a source argument, and the destination is user-defined, what should you use for the conversion?

8.18 If the source argument is used with a user-defined function and the destination is a library of class, what should be used for the conversion?

Answers

8.1 Keyword

8.2 ++ overloaded

8.3 class type

8.4 No

8.5 set up temporary object and assign it with class object and return the value in temporary object.

8.6 Yes

8.7 No

8.8 Yes

8.9 rupees in c3 <– rupees in c1 + rupees in c2
paise in c3 <– paise in c1 +paise in c2

8.10 Yes

8.11 Yes

8.12 true

8.13 true

8.14 Yes

8.15 Yes

8.16 Yes

8.17 1-argument constructor

8.18 conversion function

Chapter 9

Inheritance: Derived Class

Chapter 9

Inheritance: Derived Class

INTRODUCTION

Inheritance is the process to set up derived classes from base class. It inherits all the characteristics of the base class and can add refinements and improvements, while the attributes of the base class remain intact. A great advantage of inheritance is reusability, which ensures ease of distributing class libraries. It improves a program reliability. The problem of accessibility is discussed. A member function in base class can be accessed by objects of a derived class. Member functions of derived class can access members of base class if public or protected, but not if it is private. Objects of base class cannot access anything of the derived class. As an extension of inheritance, class hierarchies, multiple inheritance and levels of inheritance are discussed. Finally inheritance as a kind of relationship called containership is also discussed.

KEYWORD

protected

9.1 AN EXAMPLE OF INHERITANCE

The program in this section makes a brief introduction to the idea of inheritance or derived class. In the base class the + + operator is overloaded. In the derived class the – – unary operator is also overloaded, so that both can be used in the main program. Note that the base class is intact. Now study the following program and analyse it.

```
// inherit.cpp
// inheritance and derived class illustrated
# include<iostream.h>
class meas                              // base class
{
protected:
```

```
            unsigned int measure;
        public:
            meas ( ) {measure = 0;}       //constructor
                                          // no arg
            meas (int m) { measure = m; }
            intfetch ( ) { { return measure;}
            meas operator ++ ( )
                {
                measure++;
                return meas ( measure);
                }
            };
    class measdr: public meas          // derived class,
                                       // inheritance
            {
            public:
                measdr ( ) :meas ( ) { }
                        //no arg constructor
                measdr ( int m) : meas( m) { }
                meas operator - - ( )
                {
                measure - - ;
                return meas (measure);
                }
        };
  void main ( )
    {
    measdr m1 = 6; // using constr with 1 arg
    cout <<"\n Initial m1 = "<<m1.fetch ( );
    ++m1; ++m1; ++m1; ++m1; ++m1;
    cout << "\nAfter increment m1 = "<<m1.fetch ( );
    -- m1; -- m1; -- m1; -- m1;
    cout <"\nAfter decrement m1 = "<<m1.fetch ( );
    cout <<"\n\n"<< endl;
    }
```

The output is:

```
Initial m1 = 6
After increment m1 = 11
After decrement m1 = 7
```

Analysis

1. By now the reader should be able to recognize the various constructs in the base class.
2. The notable feature in the base class called "meas" is a new specifier called "protected". It replaces private specifier of earlier declarations. A private member cannot be accessed by objects of a derived class even if it is derived from the base class. However a member of the protected class can be accessed by member functions of the derived class. Morever it affords data hiding like private specifier. A public member is accessible by all and any functions from anywhere.
3. The public member functions of the base class constitute an argumentless constructor, a 1-argument constructor, a function which returns an integer and a function which enable overloading the + + unary operator.
4. Now examine the declaration of the derived class called "measdr". It is a derivative of the base class, and see how it is declared:

   ```
   class measdr: public meas
   ```

   A single colon followed by specifier "public", and the base class name. Now we have set up a dependent class whose objects will be able to use all member functions in public specifier and members of the protected specifier in the base class.
5. The derived class of inheritance as it is called, overloads the – – unary operator, so that it can be used with objects of this derived class to cause decrement. Since it returns the value it can be used in expressions also.
6. Within main( ) an object of derived class "measdr" is defined and initialized with the value 6. This makes use of the 1-argument constructor of derived class. The definition is

   ```
   measdr m1 = 6;
   ```

   If it was simply declared as

   ```
   measdr m1;
   ```

   then m1 would be automatically initialized with zero using the no-argument constructor of base class.
7. Now m1 an object of the inheritance or derived class, is used within the body of main( ) in conjunction with member functions and member elements of base class. See how both + + and – – operators are used liberally with this object.
8. The output is as shown. Now go through the main( ) program and see how overloaded operators + +, – – have been combined.

Aside

1. Is it possible to define an object of base class and avail the – – overloaded operator ? No! This is not possible, as the base class is not aware of the presence of the derived class. An object of the base class can access only its own member functions and member elements.
2. If a constructor is declared within derived class, then the object automatically invokes this, rather than the one declared in base class.
3. In the derived class a 1-argument constructor is included:

```
measdr ( int m ) { }
```

which is invoked in the main( ) to initialize object m1 to 6. Examine the syntax of this definition. The derived class name "measdr" has an argument "m" of type int. This is followed by single colon and name of base class "meas" with the argument. The empty set of curly braces automatically includes the constructor in base class.

9.2 OVERLOADING FUNCTION

In this section overloading member functions of base and derived classes are explained. Member functions in both have same names. It is important to remember that declarations must be made in both base and derived classes, an object of the derived class automatically invokes only the member functions of the derived class and not that of the base class. The following program shows setting up of a stack and ensuring that it does not overflow or attempt to "pop" up more than the stored values.

```
// overidfn.CPP
// base and derived class function overloaded.
# include <iostream.h>
# include <process.h>
const int L = 120;
class arrange
   {
   protected:
       int arr [L]; int up;
   public:
       arrange ( ) { up = 0; }
       void put (int symb) { arr [up++] = symb; }
       void get ( ) { - - up; }
   };
class array1 : public arrange  // derived class,
                               // inheritance
   {
```

```
public:
     void put (int symb)
          { if (up < L)
               arrange : : put (symb);
          else
               cout <<"\nDon't overload me! \n\n";
          }
     void get ( )
          { if ( up > 0 )
               arrange: : get ( );
               cout <<arr [up] <<endl;
     else
          cout <<"\nHa Ha! You - - are trying to
     get too many. \n\n";} };
void main ( )
     {
     array1 a1;            // a1 initialized to zero
     a1.put (32);
     a1.put (54)
     a1.put (78)
     a1.get ( );                //pops 78
     a1.get ( );                //pops 54
     a1.get ( );                //pops 32
     a1.get ( );                // sends message Ha Ha!
     }
```

The output is:

78
54
32
Ha Ha! You are trying to get too many.

Analysis

1. Base class is quite familiar to the reader, therefore no explanation is given.
2. Analyse the structure of the derived class. The names of member functions put( ) and get( ) are the same in the base and the derived classes.

3. The put( ) function tests if the stack size is not exceeded. If true, then it puts value into it by using the put( ) of the derived class. It is declared as:

   ```
   arrange: :put (symb);
   ```

   The scope resolution operator (: :) enables the derived member function to use the put( ) function declared in base class.

   If the condition test is false, the else clause gives an error message "Don't overload me!" and exits.

4. A similar structure is used for the get( ) function. It is assigned the capability of the get( ) of base class by declaring it as

   ```
   arrange: :get ( );
   ```

   For false status the error message "Ha Ha! You are trying to get too many" is displayed.

5. The put( ) and get( ) of derived class overrides those of the base class. Thus in the main( ) object "a1" of derived class "array1", invokes put( ) and get( ) declared in the derived class, which of course, acquire the capabilities on the corresponding base class member functions, with some additional feature of their own.

6. In the main( ) the three values 32, 54 and 78 are pushed down into the stack and then popped out in the last-in-first-out order.

7. If an attempt is made to pop out more than the stored values, there is an error message.

9.3 INHERITANCE FOR PROGRAM DESIGN

This section introduces the concept of inheritance. A base class is declared. Then some derived classes are defined with some additional data pertaining to the individual.

```
// derivedr.cpp
// inheritance with added features
#include <iostream.h>
const int CHAR = 25;
class teachers                          // base class
   {
   private:
       char empn[CHAR]; int numb;
   public:
       void read ( )
       {
       cout <<"\nType name of individual :";
   cin>>empn;
       cout <<"Type his number: "; cin >>numb; }
   void write ( )
```

```
        {
        cout <<"\nName of individual:" <<empn;
        cout <<"Emp No." << numb;
        }
    };
  class principal : public teachers
    {
    private:
        char desig [CHAR] ; float ded;
    public :
        void read ( )
            {
            teachers: :read ( );
            cout <<"\nType desig:"; cin >> desig;
        cout "\nType deduction: "; cin>>ded;
            }
        void write ( )
            {
            teachers: :write ( );
            cout <<"\n Designation:" >>desig;
            cout "\nDeduction:">>ded;
        }
    };
 class expert : public teachers
    {
    private:
        int papers;
    public:
        void read ( )
            {
            teachers: :read ( );
            cout"\nHow many papers?";
            cin>>papers;
            }
            void write ( )
            {
            teachers: : write ( );
            cout "  \nNo of papers: "<< papers;
```

```
            }
    };
class luscar : public teachers
    { };
void main ( )
    {
    principal p1, P2;
    expert e1.;
    luscar 11;
    cout <<endl;
    p1.read ( );
    cout <<"\nType in detail of VP: ";
    p2.read ( );
    cout << "\nType in detail of expert: ";
    e1.read ( );
    cout <<"\Type in detail of luscar: ";
    11. read ( );
    cout <<"\nPrincipal : "; p1.write ( );
    cout <<"\n Vice Principal : ";p2.write ( ) ;
    cout <<"\nExpert : "; e1.write ( );
    cout <<"\nLuscar: : "; 11.write ( );
    }
```

The output is:

Type name of individual: R. Jayaram	<ret>
Type his number: 1234	<ret>
Type desig: Principal	<ret>
Type deduction: 1234.44	<ret>
Type in detail of VP:	<ret>
Type name of individual: V. Ramprakash	<ret>
Type his number: 1235	<ret>
Type desig: Vice principal	<ret>
Type deduction: 333.56	<ret>
Type in detail of expert:	<ret>
Type name of individual: J. Vivek	<ret>
Type his number: 1236	<ret>
How many papers: 6	<ret>

```
Type in detail of luscar:                          <ret>
Type name of individual: J.Veeriah                 <ret>
Type his number: 1237                              <ret>
Name of individual: R. Jayaram
Emp No: 1234
Designation: Principal
LIC Deduction: 1234.439941
Name of individual: V. Ramprakash
Emp No. 1235
Designation: Vice principal
LIC deduction: 333.559998
Name of individual: J. Vivek
No of papers: 6
Name of individual: J. Veeriah
Emp No: 1237
```

Analysis

1. The base class "teachers" has 2 member functions: read( ) and write( ).
2. The first derived class "principal" declares its own private data called "desig[CHAR]" of type char and "ded" of type float. It also uses the scope resolution operator to access the read( ) and write( ) of the base class.

```
teachers: :read ( );
teachers: :write ( );
```

   In the derived class additional data regarding designation and deduction is solicited through read( ). This is in addition to data acquired by read( ) of base class. Thus an object of "principal" will be using read( ) of base and derived classes.
3. The second output is displayed by write( ) of both the base class and the derived class.
4. The second derived class "expert" also has its own private member called "paper" which is of type int. Here also the scope resolution operator enables access to the read( ) and write( ) of the base class due to the following declarations.

```
teachers: :read ( );
teachers: :write( );
```

   The object of this class accesses the member functions of both base and derived classes.
5. The third derived class "luscar" simply accesses the base class and does not have any read( ) or write( ), unlike the earlier two classes.

6. In main( ) "principal" has 2 objects p1, p2; "expert" has one object e1; and "luscar": has one object 11. These member functions are invoked thus:

```
p1.read ( ); p2.read ( ); e1.read ( ) l1.read ( ) ;
p1.write ( ); p2.write ( ); e1.write ( ); l1.write ( );
```

These member functions are executed in the order in which they are invoked.

Alert

While entering a string against any prompt such as (say)

```
Type desig;
```

there should be no intermediate blank in it. That is why "Vice-Principal" is entered with a hyphen or underscore. Names like R. Jayaram, V. Ramprakash, J. Vivek and J. Veeriah are all entered continuously without intermediate blank. Do you wonder what happens if a blank is introduced such as?

```
Vice principal
```

Control exits the loop and returns to the DOS mode.

Aside

So far we have been generously declaring derived classes using keyword public with the base class name. For example:

```
class principal: public teachers
class expert: public teachers
class luscar : public teachers
```

The objects of such derived classes had free access to member functions of base class.

Now what will happen if keyword"private" is used with base class name. Say for example

```
class principal: private teachers
class expert : private teachers
class luscar : private teachers
```

In this case none of the objects of "principal" "expert"or "luscar" will have access to member functions of base class teachers. The following table summarises accessibility of various specifiers. Each has accessibility from their own class.

Specifier	*Public*	*Protected*	*Private*
From derived class	Yes	Yes	no
Objects outside class	Yes	no	no

If no access specifier is stated while declaring a class, the default private is assumed. For example:

```
class A: X // private assumed
{ }
structure A : X // public assumed
{ }
```

whereas for a structure declaration, public is assumed by default. One may wonder what is the need for the complicated access specifiers? Sometimes one may want member functions of a base class to be accessed only by its own objects and deny access to objects of a derived class. In such cases the derived class mayabe made private.

9.4 DERIVED CLASS OF DERIVED CLASS (MULTIPLE INHERITANCE)

In this section a class is derived from a derived class. This is called levels of inheritance, or multiple inheritance, for example:

```
class X { };
class Y : public X { };
class z : public Y { };
```

What level of inheritance is possible in C++?

There appears to be no limit. However the programmer should keep track of what is being done at each level. The following program uses the idea for a one-level inheritance.

```
// levelin.CPP
// multi level inheritance
#include <iostream.h>
const int L = 120;
class hired
{
private:
   char n [L]; int num;
public:
   void fetch ( )
      {
      cout <<"\nName :"; cin >> n;
      cout << "No : "; cin>> num;
      }
   void show ( )
      {
      cout <<"\nName: "<<n;
```

```
        cout <<"\nNumber: "<<num;
        }
};
class lect : public hired      // derived class
   { };
class nonteach : public lect   // derived derived
                               // class
   {
private:
   float targ;
public:
   void fetch ( )
   {
   lect: : fetch ( );
   cout <<"\nTarget? ";cin>>targ;
   }
void show( )
   {
   lect: :show( );
   cout<< "\nTarget:"<<targ;
   }
};
void main ( )
   {
   lect l1; nontech n1;
   cout <<"\nLecturer: "; l1.fetch ( );
   cout <<"\nNon teaching: "; n1.fetch ( );
   cout <<"\nLecturer' details : "; 11.show ( ) ;
   cout <<"\nNon teaching details:'; n1.show ( );
}
```

The output is:

Lecturer:	
Name: R. Jayaram	<ret>
No: 1234	<ret>
Non teaching	
Name: J. Vivek	<ret>

```
No: 1235                        <ret>
Target? 456.79                  <ret>
Lecturer's details:
Name: R. Jayaram
Number: 1234
Non teaching details:
Name: : J. Vivek
Number: 1235
Target: 456.790009
```

Analysis

1. Note that the derived class "lect" is an inheritance of base class "hired" . It has an access specifier "public" , so that all member functions of base are accessible to it.
2. Next another derived class called "nonteach" is derived from the "lect" . This is known as a one level inheritance. This derived class "nonteach" also has access to base member functions and elements through "lect", which is the first derivative of "hired".
3. In the derivative of the derived class "nonteach", there is private data element called"targ", which is of type float. It has its own member functions of the same names as in base class. This means derived class"nonteach" accesses the member functions of the base class, followed by its own member functions.
4. The base class member functions fetch( ) and show( ) are included in the derived class by means of the scope resolution operator (: :).
5. Within main( ) two objects l1 of class "lect" and n1 of class "nonteach" are defined. They are used to access the member functions of base class and derived class in succession of one another.

Aside

To make this example simple only one level of inheritance has been illustrated. There have been multilevel inheritance, if needed. The above program could have a few more derived class declarations of base class such as:

```
class hired { };                    // base class
class principal: public hired       // derived class
class professor : public hired
```

This is in addition to whatever is existing

9.5 DERIVED CLASS FROM SEVERAL BASE CLASSES

So far it was seen how to derive one class from a base class, or how to derive a class from a derived class itself. In this section it is shown how to derive a class from several base classes. The following program illustrates this idea.

Before examining the program a summary of the program organisation is given.

```
class categ { };              // base class 1
class curr { };               // base class 2
class ind: public categ, public curr
              {   };          // derived using 2
                          // base classes
```

The program listing is

```
// multinh.cpp
// multiple inheritance
#include <iostream.h>
#include <string.h>
const int L = 120;
class categ {
protected:
   char meas [L] ; char stat [L]; float rate;
public :
   categ ( ) {strcpy (meas,'\0'); strcpy
   (stat,'\0'); rate = 0.0;}

   categ ( char m[ ] , char s[ ] , float r)
       {strcpy (meas, m); strcpy
       (stat, s); rate = r;}
   void fetchcateg ( )
       {
       cout <<"\nCurrency: "; cin>>meas;
       cout <<"Country: "; cin>> stat;
       cout <<"Rate: ";cin >> rate;
       cout <<"\nConversion from "<<meas<<" to
       Rs."<<' \n' ;
       }
   void dispcateg ( )
       {
       cout <<"\ncurrency: "<<meas;
       cout << "\nCountry: "<< stat;
       }
};
```

```
class curr
   {
   private:
       int rupees; int paise;
   public:
       curr ( ) {rupees = 0; paise = 0;}
                                      // no arg constr
       curr (int rs, int ps) {rupees = rs; paise = ps;)
   void fetchcurr ( )
       {
       cout <<"\nRupees: "; cin>> rupees;
       cout <<"\nPaise:"; cin>>paise;
       }
   void dispcurr ( )
       {cout << "Rs."<< rupees<<" Ps. " <<paise<<
           "converted to $ "; }
   };
   class ind: public categ, public curr
                                      // derived class
       {
       private:
           float numb; float foreign;
       public:
           ind ( ) : categ ( ) , curr ( ) // no arg constr
               {numb = 0.0 ; foreign = 0.0; }
           ind (char c [ ] , char r [ ] , float
           rat, int,rs, int ps):
               categ ( c, r, rat ), curr ( rs, ps )
           {numb = ( rs + ps/100 ) / rat; }
       void convert ( ) { cout << numb; }
   void dispind ( )
       {
       categ: :dispcateg ( );
       cout << "\nIndia: ";
       curr: :discpurr ( );
       }
   void fetchind ( )
       {
```

```
        categ: :fetchcateg ( );
        cout << meas<< ": "; cin>> foreign;
        cout << "\n" << meas<<" " << foreign<<
    "converted to Rs. "<< foreign * rate;
        }
    };
void main ( )
    {
    cout << "\n\nConversion from Rs. to $";
    ind peop ( "$" , "U.S.A",31.65, 50, 35);
    peop.dispind ( );
    peop.convert( );
    cout <<"\n\n";
    ind money ;                 // object of ind
    money.fetchind ( );
    }
```

The output is

Conversion from Rs. to $ <ret>
currency: $ <ret>
Country: U.S:A <ret>
India: Rs. 50 Ps. 35 converted to $1.579779 <ret>
Currency: Lira <ret>
Country: Italy <ret>
Rate: 2.5 <ret>
Conversition from Lira to Rs.
Lira: 150 <ret>
Lira 150 converted to Rs. 375 <ret>

Analysis

1. The first base class" categ" has protected data members and public member functions.

```
    meas [L] , stat [L] are char type
    rate is float type
```

2. There is no argument constructor which initializes "meas" and "stat" to null and "rate" to zero.
3. The 3 argument constructor assign values to "meas" , "stat" and "rate".

4. fetchcateg function prompts for "meas", "stat" and "rate" and stores the values entered through the keyboard. The cout object displays the string with value for "meas".
5. The dispcateg( ) function displays strings and values stored in the variables "meas" and "stat".
6. The second base class curr has its own private data elements rupees and paise, both of type int.
7. This has a no-argument constructor to initialize variables and 2 argument constructor to assign values to variables.
8. Member function fetchcurr( ) gets values through keyboard and assigns to rupees and paise.
9. Memer function dispcurr( ) displays the string following the object cout.
10. Now we have declared the derived class "ind". It is derived using both the above two base classes.
11. It has its private data elements "numb" and "foreign", both of type float.
12. It has a no-argument constructor to initialize the variables "numb" "foreign" with zero. The constructor is declared as

    ```
    ind ( ) : categ ( ), curr ( )
    ```

    This indicates that class "ind" depends on the 2 base classes "categ" and "curr".
13. Next is a 5 argument constructor, which is also dependent on the base classes. Its structure is

    ind(char c [ ], char r [ ], float rat, int rs, int ps);

    ```
    categ ( c , r, rat ) , curr (rs, ps)
    { numb = (rs + ps/100 ) /rat; }
    ```

    The 5 arguments can be identified as:

    ```
              char c [ ], char r [ ], float rat
              < - arguments to 3 - argument
         constructor of base class "categ"
    int rs, int ps < - arguments to 2 - argument
         constructor of base class "curr"
    ```

    These are used in the expression

    ```
    numb = (rs + ps / 100) / rat
    ```

    to convert Indian currency into a foreign currency.
14. The dispind( ) function invokes two display functions of base class as follows, using scope resolution operator.

    ```
    categ: :dispcateg ( );
    curr: :dispcurr( );
    ```

15. The fetchind( ) function invokes one display function of first base class using scope resolution operator

```
categ: :fetchcateg( );
```

16. Within main( ) examine the object "peop" being defined and also furnished with the 5 arguments, as declared in derived class "ind".

```
ind peop ("$","U.S.A", 31.65, 50, 35);
```

which can be related as

```
c [ ] <-$          r [ ] <-U.S.A        rat <-31.65
rs <- 50                ps <- 35
```

These are the parameteres of base class "curr".

17. The object "peop" invokes display function dispind( ) and uses the 5 arguments.
18. "peop" also invokes the convert ( ) function of derived class "ind".
19. Another object "money" is defined. This is used to invoke the function fetchind ( ) of derived class.
20. The output has been shown with the responses.

Aside

Note that in the derived class functions, the names used in the base class themselves are used. Suppose the base class has :

```
class ceteg { void fetch ( ) { } }; // base class
class curr { void fetch ( ) { } }; //base class
class ind :public categ, public curr // derived class
      {       };
```

Then these same functions can be used in the derived class by using the scope resolution operator as follows:

```
void main ( )
   {
   ind obj;
   obj.categ: :fetch ( );
   obj.curr: :fetch ( );
      . .
   }
```

9.6 NESTED CLASSES

When classes are declared within classes, they are known as nested classes. The following is an example of nested classes.

```
class X
   {
   Y   y;                          // y is an object of Y
   };
class Y
   {        };
```

This is called containership. The following program shows an elementary way of using containership or class within a class to convert Indian rupees to $.

```
// contain. cpp
// illustrating containership
# include<iostream.h>
# include<string.h>
const int L = 20;
class basel
{
private:
   char coun [L]; char curr [L];
public:
   basel ( ) {strcpy (coun,'\o');
   strcpy (curr,'\o');}
   basel (char co [ ], char cu [ ] )
   {strcpy (coun, co); strcpy (curr, cu);}
void fetbl ( )
   {
   cout <<"\nCountry : "; cin>>coun;
   cout<<"Currency; "; cin>>curr;
   }
void shobl ( )
   {
   cout<<"\nCountry: "<< coun;
   cout<<"\nCurrency:"<<curr;
   }
};
```

```
class base2
    {
    protected:
        float amt; float rate;
    public:
        base2 ( ) {amt = 0.0; rate = 0.0}
        base2 (float a, float r)
                { amt = a; rate = r; }
        void fetb2 ( )
            {
            cout <<"\nAmt to convert:"; cin >>amt;
            cout <<"Rate of cov:"; cin >>rate;
            }
        void shob2 ( )
            {
            cout <<"\nAmt to Convert : "<<amt;
            cout <<"Rate of conv: "; cin >> rate;
            }
        float conv ( )
            {return amt * rate};
    class cont
    {
    private:
        basel b1;
        base2 b2;
    public:
        void fetc ( )
            {
            b1.fetb1 ( );
            b2.fetb2 ( );
            }
        void shocon ( )
            {
             b1.shob1 ( );
            b2.shob2 ( );
        cout <<"\nConversion is:    "<<b2.conv ( );
                    }
            };
```

```
void main ( )
    {
    cont c;
    cout <"\n";
    c.fetc ( );
    c.shocon ( );
    }
```

The output is:

```
Country: USA                                          <ret>
Currency; $                                           <ret>
Amt to convert; 1234.56                               <ret>
Rate of conv: 31.65
Country: USA
Currency: $
Amt to convert: 1234.560059 Rate of conv: 31.65
Conversion is : 39073.824219
```

Analysis

1. The first declaration consists of a class "base1" with 2 char type variables, "coun" and "curr".
2. There are constructors of zero argument and 2 arguments, which are used in public functions fetb( ) and shob1( ) to assign constants to "coun" and "curr".
3. The second declarations consists of two float type variables, "amt" and "rate".
4. Here again two constructors, one without argument and the other with 2 arguments are declared.
5. The public functions fetb2( ) and shob2( ) use these constructors to assign values to "amt" and "curr".
6. The float conv( ) function uses variable "amt" and "rate" and returns the product when invoked by relevant object.
7. The third class declarator for "cont" has two objects declared as follows under private class.

   ```
   base1 b1;
   base2 b2;
   ```

   This is the highlight of this particular program which illustrates containership. The object "b1" can access all functions of class b1 and object b2 can access all functions of class b2.

8. The public function fetc( ) in this class simply uses the objects b1 and b2 to invoke fetb1( ) and fetb2( ) of their respective classes.
9. Similarly shocon( ) function invokes the correponding functions in their respective classes by the following means:

```
b1.shob1 ( );
b2.shob2 ( );
b2.conv ( );
```

The last one, namely, b2.conv( ) is a return type, which evaluates and returns the float type value when called by the object cout.

10. Within main( ) only one object is defined for cont,

```
cont c;
```

This invokes the functions in class cont;

```
c.fetc ( );
c.shocon ( );
```

Aside

Containership or class within class illustrates the reusability feature of C++.

REVIEW QUESTIONS

9.1 Is inheritance identical to overloading?

9.2 Where do you use inheritance: base or derived class?

9.3 Can a member function in base class be accessed by an object of its derived class?

9.4 Can an object of the derived class access member functions of a base class if declared private?

9.5 What type of declaration of a base class enables an object of a derived class to access member functions?

9.6 Does protected class afford data hiding feature?

9.7 To what value is object m1 initialized if "meas" is a derived class of another base class.

9.8 Can an object of a base class access member functions of a derived class?

9.9 If a constructor is declared in base and derived classes, which of this is accessible to an object defined in main( ).

9.10 What is wrong with this declaration?

```
meas (m) : base (m) { }
```

9.11 How do you invoke a member function putc( ) of class "arrange" in a derived class?

9.12 Can an object of a derived class of a derived class access member functions of both the base and first derived classes?

9.13 What term do you use to describe a derived class when its object is able to access member functions of another derived class and its base class?

9.14 Suppose a prompt request for a particular string data, how should it be entered?

9.15 Suppose a derived class is declared as

```
class principal : private teachers
```

can an object of "principal" access member functions of "teachers"?

9.16 In a derived class declaration suppose we leave out the type specifier, what class is assumed by default?

9.17 Suppose we declare as follows:

```
struct A : X
```

What class does X belong?

9.18 What do you understand by level of inheritance?

9.19 Is there are limit to the level of inheritance?

9.20 Is it possible to derive a class using several base classes?

9.21 Is there any limit to the number of arguments that maybe used in a constructor?

9.22 A constructor with 5 arguments is invoked as follows:

```
ind people ("$" , USA, 3.1 , 50, 35);
```

What is wrong with this definition?

9.23 Which of these constructors is correct?

```
base1 ( ) { strcpy (c, '\0') }
base1 ( ) { strcpy (c, "\0") }
```

9.24 What header file should be included to use strcpy( ) function?

Answers

9.1	No	9.2	derived class
9.3	Yes	9.4	no
9.5	public or protected	9.6	no
9.7	zero	9.8	no
9.9	derived class constructor	9.10	type of m not given
9.11	arrange: : putc(variable)	9.12	Yes
9.13	hierarchy	9.14	Without intermediate blank
9.15	no	9.16	private
9.17	public	9.18	deriving a class out of derived class
9.19	no	9.20	yes
9.21	seems none	9.22	USA within double quotes
9.23	both are correct	9.24	string.h

Chapter 10

Pointers and Arrays

Chapter 10

Pointers and Arrays

INTRODUCTION

A pointer is a variable that holds an address of a memory location. An address is an integer, but pointers are of various target types such as char, integer, float, double. This distinction is required as each data type requires different number of bytes of memory, so that when a pointer is incremented, it is done in block of bytes of memory of the particular target type. Pointers enable efficient way of accessing array elements, passing arguments, passing arrays and strings to functions, obtaining memory from system, creating data structures such as linked lists and binary trees.

KEYWORD AND OPERATORS

new delete

10.1 INTRODUCTION TO POINTER VARIABLES

By now the reader should be familiar with what is implied by contents of a memory location and the address of the memory location. The content is what is stored within a memory location. Its address is a label that identifies its location. Using this simple concept a program is presented.

```
//content.cpp
//contents and address of a memory
#include <iostream.h>
void main( )
   {
   int loc1 =37; int loc2 = 73; int loc3 = 96;
   cout <<"\nloc1 contains: "<<loc1;
   cout<<"\nloc2 contains: "<<loc2;
```

```
cout<<"\nloc3 contains: "<<loc3;
cout<<"\nAddr of loc1: "<<&loc1;
cout<<"\nAddr of loc2: "<<&loc2;
cout<<"\nAddr of loc3: "<<&loc3;
}
```

The output is:

```
loc1 contains: 37
loc2 contains: 73
loc3 contains: 96
Addr of loc1: 0x4do2fff4
Addr of loc2: 0x4do2fff2
Addr of loc3: 0x4do2fff0
```

Analysis

1. Three integer variables loc1, loc2, loc3 are defined and initialized.
2. The cout objects cause the contents and addresses of these variables to be output.
3. "&" is called the address operator. When this operator is prefixed to a variable, the address of the variable is implied.

```
&loc1 <- address of loc1
&loc2 <- address of loc2
&loc3 <- address of loc3
```

4. Simply using the variable name implies the content of the memory location.

```
loc1 <- content of loc1
loc2 <- content of loc2
loc3 <- content of loc3
```

Aside

Note that the addresses of the int type variables differ by 2 bytes and are arranged in a descending order. This is because the variables are set up in a stack. Normally "internal" variables are organized as stores in stack.

Whereas "external" variables are organized with increasing addresses, as they are stored in the RAM. However this is an internal working of the computer and the programmer need not be concerned with this matter, except out of academic interest.

The address commences with "0x" implying hexadecimal numbers. The addresses displayed are not unique and may vary during each run, particularly in multi-user computer systems. What is shown above is the addresses assigned to the internal variables during a particular run only.

The following program uses pointer variables.

```
//pointer.cpp
//creating and using pointer variables
#include<iostream.h>
void main( )
    {
    int *ptr; int locl = 37; int loc2 = 73;
    ptr = &locl;
    cout<<"\nlocl contains: "<<locl<<" in addr:"
    <<ptr;
    ptr = &loc2;
    cout<<"\nloc2  contains: "<<loc2<<" in
    addr: "<<ptr;
    }
```

The output is:

```
1ocl contains: 37 in addr: 0x4cffff4
1oc2 contains: 73 in addr: 0x4cffff2
```

Analysis

1. A pointer variable is defined by

   `int *ptr;`

   Now "ptr" is said to be a pointer to target type "int". It can hold any hexadecimal address. The above definition may also be written with asterisk associated with int, such as:

   `int*   ptr;`

   The asterisk '*' implies "pointer to".
2. Two int type variables are defined and initialized.
3. Then the address of "1oc1" is assigned to "ptr" by the following

   `ptr =&1oc1;`

   By this the address of "1oc1" is assigned to the pointer variable "ptr".
4. The object cout then outputs the contents of "1oc1" and "ptr".
5. In the next statement the address of "1oc2" is assigned to "ptr" and the object cout causes the contents of 1oc2 to be output.

Aside

So far pointer of target type int alone were considered. Pointers can be set up for other data types such as char, float or even for a user-defined class variable.

```
char* chrptr:             //one byte memory location
float*  fltptr;           //4 byte memory location
currency* currptr;        //class variable of user-
                          //defined type
```

pointers to user-defined class variable will have memory bytes depending on the data mix constituting the private data class.

It is possible to have multiple pointers defined in one lines:

```
int *loc1, *loc2,*loc3;
```

where all 3 pointers are of type int.

loc1, loc2, loc3 are pointer variables. Their contents constitute pointer constants.

10.2 MORE ABOUT POINTERS

In this section pointers are defined and then used to access locations pointed to by them. Thereafter a general purpose pointer is defined which can accept any address regardless of its target type.

```
//general.cpp
//location pointed to , void type pointer
#include<iostream.h>
void main( )
   {
   char cp = 'a' ; int ip = 27; float fp = 12.34;
   char *cpt; int *ipt; float *flpt;
   cpt =&cp; ipt = &ip; fpt =&fp;
   cout<<"\nchar "<<*cpt<<" is in loc" <<cpt ;
   cout<<"\nint"<<*ipt<<" is in loc"<<ipt;
   cout<<"\nfloat "<<*fpt<<" is in loc "<<fpt;
   }
```

The output is:

```
char a is in loc a
int 27 is in loc 0x517afff2
float 12.34 is in loc 0x517affee
```

Analysis

1. Three different types of variables are defined and initialized.
2. Three different pointers are defined.
3. These are used to retrieve the contents in their respective locations and display their addresses.

Aside

So far pointers of different target type such as char, int, float etc. were seen. The next section demonstrates that it is possible to set up a general purpose pointer, which can point to any location regarless of its target type. Such a pointer is declared with keyword "void" preceding it. The following program illustrates its creation and use.

```
//void type.cpp
//general purpose pointer using the void declarator
#include<iostream.h>
void main( )
  {
  void *ptr;
  int in = 27; char ch = 'a'; float fl = 12.34;
  ptr = &in;
  cout<<"\ninteger"<<in<<" is in loc "<<ptr;
  ptr = &ch;
  cout<<"\nchar"<<ch<<" is in loc " <<ptr;
  ptr =&fl ;
  cout<<"\nfloat "<<fl<<" is in loc "<<ptr;
  }
```

The output is:

```
integer 27 is in loc 0x5l7afff4
char a is in loc 0x5l7afff3
float 12.34 is in loc 0x517affee
```

10.3 POINTERS TO ARRAY

The versatility of pointers is established due to its ability to handle arrays. The following program illustrates an elementary idea of pointer to an array.

```
//ptrarray.cpp
//pointer to an array
#include<iostream.h>
void main ( )
  {
  float array[ ] = { 12.34, 23.45, 34.56, 45.67, 56.78} ;
  float *ptr;
```

```
    ptr = array;
    for(int k = 0; k<5; k++)
        cout<<"\narray["<<k<<"] ="<<*(ptr++);
    }
```

The output is:

array[0] = 12.34
array[1] = 23.450001
array[2] = 34.560001
array[3] = 45.669998
array[4] = 56.779999

Analysis

1. A float type array called array [ ] is defined and initialized with 5 floating point constants.
2. A pointer called "ptr" of target type float is set up.
3. It is made to point to the starting address of array [ ] by the following assignment.

   ```
   ptr = array;
   ```

   "ptr" now points to memory Location where array [0] is located.
4. Within the for loop, the pointer "ptr" is used to access the location whose address it holds to retrieve the constants stored in it.
5. Then the pointer increments to point to the next array element which is 4 bytes away, as it is of type float.

Aside

In the above program examine the for loop:

```
    for (int k=0; k<5; k++)
        cout <<"/narray ["<<k<<"] ="<<* (array++) ;
```

If array [0] is at a particular address, then array [1] is 4 bytes away from that location; array [2] is 4 bytes away from array [1] and so on. For char array the addresses would be advanced by 1 byte only. For int type array the addresses would be advanced by 2 bytes for successive elements.

10.4 PASSING BY POINTER

Arguments can be passed to a function by value, by reference or by pointer. Passing by value is quite easy. Passing by reference implies passing the address of a variable or an element of an array. This is the same as passing of pointer. The following program illustrates the idea.

```
//reference.cpp
//passing by reference
#include<iostream.h>
void main( )
    {
    void convert(float&);    //called a prototype
    float amt = 123.45;
    float dollars = amt;
    convert(amt);
    cout<<"\n amt"<<dollars<<" converted to Rs.is"
    <<amt;
    }
void convert (float& a)
{ a *= 31.65;}
```

The output is:

amt 123.449997 converted to Rs. is 3907.192383

Analysis

1. A prototype is declared for the function called "convert" with an address argument, which is pointing to a location having float type data.
   `void convert(float&):`
2. The function is invoked with argument "amt" , which is actually an address.
3. The function "convert" receives the address passed by "amt" in "a" which is also an address variable.
4. The contents of this address is multiplied by 31.65 and the result stored in "a". Remember that "a" and "amt" point to the same address, and therefore there is no need to return the result to the calling program. Hence convert( ) function is of type void.

The next program shows how to pass a pointer.

```
// ptrpas.cpp
// passing by pointer
#include <iostream.h>
void main( )
    {
    void convert (float* );    // prototype
    float amt = 123.45;
    float dollars = amt;
    convert(&amt);
```

```
    cout << "\namt $ "<< dollars <<" converted
    to Rs. is Rs. "<< amt;
    }
void convert ( float *a)
        { *a *= 31.65; }
```

The output is:

amt $123.449997 converted to Rs. is Rs. 3907.192383

Analysis

1. A prototype of type void is set up for convert( ) with a pointer of type float.

   `void convert(float*);`

2. The convert( ) function is declared to be type void with a pointer "a" of target type float. Thus "amt" passes an address which is received by pointer "a".

3. In the main( ) the function convert( ) is invoked with address variable.

   `convert(&amt);`

4. In the function

   `*a  *= 31.65;`

   implied the contents of location pointed to by pointer "a" is multiplied by 31.65 and the result is written back into the same location.

5. Since "amt" and "a" point to same memory cell there is no need for a return statement. Hence convert( ) is of type void.

Aside

So far it was seen how individual addresses were passed to a function. In the ensuing program it is shown how to pass a whole array by pointers to a function.

```
//arrayptr.cpp
//passing of array by pointer
#include <iostream.h>
const int L = 4;
void main( )
   {
   void convert(float*);         // prototype
   float indrs [L] = ( 12.34, 23.45, 34.56, 45.67};
   convert (indrs) ;             // function invoked
   for (int k = 0; k <L ; k ++)
       cout <<"\nindrs ["<<k <<" ] = $"<<indrs [k] ;
   }
```

```
void convert ( float* ptr)
        {
        for ( int m = 0; m < L ; m++)
        *ptr++ *= 31.65 ;
    }
```

The output is:

```
indrs[0] = $390.561005
indrs[1] = $742.192505
indrs[2] = $1093.824097
indrs[3] = $1445.455444
```

Analysis

1. An array of type float indrs [ ] is defined and initialized.
2. The function convert ( ) is invoked with the array name "indrs". Here it represents the first address of the array which is the address of indrs[0]. This address is passed to function convert() and received by parameter "ptr" which is a pointer of target type float.
3. The expression

   ```
   *ptr++ *= 31.65;
   ```

   is to be read as the "contents" of "location" pointed to by "ptr" is multiplied by 31.65 and assigned back into the same location.
4. The pointer variable "ptr" is post incremented, therefore it points to the next element in the array, namely indrs[1]. Thus the pointer automatically advances to the next location as the expression is evaluated each time.
5. Here again the function is of type void, as the contents in memory locations are modified. While outputting the result the contents of these locations are read and the result is displayed.

10.5 SORTING USING POINTERS

Here sorting an array containing floating point values is done by pointers. The technique used is called bubble sort. In this technique the first element value is compared with all other elements, until a value less than this is encountered. Then a swap is made. Next the second element is compared with the others and if need be a swap is made. Thus the process is continued until the array values are arranged in an ascending order. The program is given.

```
//ptrsort.cpp
//sorting float type values by pointers
#include<iostream.h>
void main( )
   {
   void bubble(float*, int); //prototype
   const int L =12;
   float val [L] = { 9.1, 6.3, 5.5, 8.7, 1.2,
       4.3, 6.5, 7.8, 11.2, 3.2, 2.4, 1.1} ;
   cout <<"\nThe original array is: \n";
   for(int k= 0; k<L; k++)
       cout <<val [k] <<"  ";
   bubble(val, L);
   cout<<"\nThe sorted array is: \n"
   for(int j= 0; j<h; j++)
       cout<<val[k]<<"  ";
   }
void bubble(float* ptr, int n)
   {
   void sort(float*, float*) ;
   int m, k;
   for (m=0 ; m<n - 1; m++)
       for (k=m +1; k<n; k++)
           sort (ptr + m, ptr + k) ;
   }
void sort(float* nl, float* n2)
   {
   if (*nl > *n2)
   {
   float temp = *nl;
   *nl = *n2;
   *n2 = temp ;
   }
}
```

The output is:

The original array is:
9.1 6.3 5.5 8.7 1.2 4.3 6.5 7.8 11.2 3.2 2.4 1.1
The sorted array is:
1.1 1.2 2.4 3.2 4.3 5.5 6.3 6.5 7.8 8.7 9.1 11.2

Analysis

1. A prototype is declared for bubble with a float type pointer and an integer.
2. The array val [ ] of type float is defined and initialized with 12 elements.
3. The elements of the original array are displayed.
4. The function bubble( ) is invoked with the first address of the array val [ ], which corresponds to val [0], and the number of elements in the array.
5. The sorted array is then displayed.
6. The function bubble( ) is furnished two arguments:

   "ptr" is a pointer of type float, which receives the first address of val [0], and int "n" receives 12, which is the number of elements in the array val [ ].
7. Within bubble( ) another prototype is declared

   ```
   void sort (float*, float*);
   ```

   The function sort( ) has two float type pointers, which can receive the addresses of 2 elements of array val [ ].
8. The function bubble( ) invokes the sort( ) function, furnishing two pointer values, to do bubble sort of the array val [ ].
9. The sort( ) function does the sorting of the float values by the technique called bubble sort, which was described at the beginning.

Aside

In bubble( ) function address arithmetic has been used.

```
ptr + m, ptr + n
```

Recall that "ptr" received the address of val [0] and thereafter it remains constant. By varying m and n, it is possible to point to different elements of the array val [ ].

For example, when m=0, n=1, sort ( ) is furnished the address of val [0], val [1]. When n becomes 2, the addresses are that of val[0] and val[2]. Then the process is repeated till n is exhausted, and restarted with the next value of m. Thus the nested for - loops are repeated for all combinations of m and n.

10.6 POINTERS IN STRING HANDLING

A string is an array of char type. While array notation itself is sufficient to point to the elements of a string, in the next program pointers are used to point to the various elements of the string.

```
//strl.cpp
#include<iostream.h>
void main( )
  {
  void show(char*);
```

```
    char s1[ ] = "Love thy neighbour as thyself.";
    char* s2 = "Do unto others as thou
        wouldst done unto you.";    //prototype
    show(s1); show(s2);
    s2++; s2++; s2++;
    show(s2);
    }
void show (char* p)
    {
    cout<<" /n";
    while (*p)
        cout<<*p++;
    }
```

The output is:

Love thy neighbour as thyself.
Do unto others as thou woudst done unto you.
unto others as thou wouldst done unto you.

Analysis

1. The prototype declares availability of a function show (char*).
2. A char type string array s1[ ] is defined and initialized.
3. Next a char type pointer is defined and initialized. Note the square brackets in the string declaration of s1 and absence of the same in the pointer declaration for s2.
4. When char pointer s2 is set up, it points to the first char "D" in the array of characters, or to s2[0] element.
5. The show( ) function is invoked to display the string in s1 and string pointed to by pointer s2.
6. See that either in the case of the array notation or pointer notation, the first address, namely s1[0], or s2 [0] is passed on to the receiving pointer variable in show( ). Thereafter incrementing the pointer "p" in show ( ), the entire string is caused to display.
7. Then s2 is incremented 3 times to point to s2 [3] and then display. That is why the last display starts with "unto ...." which is the 4th position of the s2 array.

The following program shows how to copy a string into another string array.

```
//strcpy.cpp
//string copying using strings
#include<iostream.h>
```

```
void main( )
   {
   void dup( char*, char*) ;
   char* s1 = "Leo Tolstoy said only knaves can
   succeed in life.";
   char s2[53] ;          //declaration of array
                          //s2 of 53 chars
   dup(s2, s1);
   cout << "\n"<< s2;
   }
void dup (char* d, char* s)
   {
   while (*s)
       *d++ = *s++ ;
   *d = '\0' ;
   }
```

The output:

Leo Tolstoy said only knaves can succeed in life.

Analysis

1. The prototype declares the presence of a function dup( ) with 2 char type pointers as arguments.
2. Then a char type pointer s2 is defined and initialized.
3. Next a char type array called s2, of 53 characters is declared.
4. By using dup( ) function the string pointed to by s1 is copied into the array pointed to by s2. The copying is done character by character, beginning from s1[0] upto the end of the string.
5. After the copying is over, the null character '\0' is appended to terminate the string in s2.

Aside

The function dup(char * d, char * s) is a user-defined function. This could as well be substituted by a pre-defined function strcpy( ).

For invoking the library function, the string.h header file must be included in the pre-processor directive.

```
    #include <string.h>
The function can be declared as follows:
char* strcpy( char* d, const char* s) ;
```

The "const" modifier implies that the contents pointed to by "s" remain contant.

The next program shows how to set up an array of pointers.

```
//parray.CPP
#include<iostream.h>
const int L  = 6;
void main( )
   {
   char* ptrarr[L] = { "madurai", "madras", "salem",
       "trichy", "coimbatore", "tirunelveli" };
       for ( int k = 0; k <L ; k ++)
           cout << ptrarr[k] << "\n":
   }
```

The output is:

madurai
madras
salem
trichy
coimbatorc
tirunelveli

Analysis

1. An array of pointers is defined by the statement

   `char * ptrarr[L] = { . . . . . . . . . . . . };`

2. The array pointer ptrarr[ ] points to the first location of a string such as "madurai". When the index is incremented, it points to the first location of the next element "madras" and so on.
3. Thus a string can be displayed by making the array pointer point to the first character of a string and advance until it reaches the null character in the string. This is repeated for the other strings also.

Aside

What is the advantage of an array of pointers over an array of strings?

The array of strings must be of equal length if memory space is to be used efficiently. Whereas creating an array of pointers places the strings continuously, interposed by the null character, so that there is a definite conservation of memory space.

10.7 DYNAMIC MEMORY ALLOCATION

A string array has memory space allocated only at the time of execution. No memory allocation is done at the time of declaration. This is called dynamic allocation of memory.

How exactly dynamic allocation of memory works is illustrated by the following program.

```
// newoper.cpp
// use of operator new for memory allocation
#include <iostream.h>
#include <string.h>
void main( )
   {
   char* sent = "Individuals are occasionally guided
       by reason, crowds never.";
   char* pointer;
   pointer = new char[ strlen(sent) + 1];
   strcpy(pointer, sent);
   cout << "\nThe original string is: \n"<<sent;
   cout << "\nThe copy string is: \n"<<pointer;
   delete pointer;
   }
```

The output is:

The original string is:
Individuals are occasionally guided by reason, crowds never.
The copy string is:
Individuals are occasionally guided by reason, crowds never.

Analysis

1. A pointer to a char array called "sent" is defined. It points to the first address of the string.
2. Another char type pointer called "pointer" is declared. It is used to set apart memory required to contain the string in "sent" plus a null character. The operator "new" does the task of requisitioning memory from the operating system.
3. Now we copy character by character using the two pointers:
   ```
   " pointer" as destination
   " sent" as the source
   ```
4. Both the strings pointed to by pointers "sent" and "pointer" are displayed.
5. The "delete" operater returns memory set apart for "pointer" and returns it to the operating system.

Aside

The strcpy( ) function is invoked by virtue of including the "string.h" header file. It uses source pointer "sent" to copy a character into a location pointed to by the destination pointer called "pointer".

Then both the pointers advance to the next location, and copying is repeated. This process repeats until the null character is encountered and copied into the destination location. Thereafter both pointers are made to reinitialize their positions by pointing to the first location of their respective strings. This enables the cout object to display the strings using the pointer notations.

Whenever memory is set up by the "new" operator, it is obligatory to release it by the using the "delete" operator. Hence the statement:

```
delete pointer;
```

Even otherwise when the program terminates the memory is released. But when "new" is used in functions other than the main (), and it happens to be a local variable, memory will not be released unless "delete" is specifically used. Therefore a good practice would be to use delete for every use of the new operator.

The next program illustrates the use of "new" operator in a class object. Normally string objects in a class occupy a fixed amount of memory, so that utilisation is efficient if all strings are of same size. If too short, wastage occurs; if too long system may crash. But by using the "new" operator, as illustrated in the following program, it is possible to ensure memory allocation exactly as required. This will result in effective use of memory.

```
// strclas.cpp
// new obtains memory from strings
#include <iostream.h>
#include <string.h>
class sentence
   {
   private :
       char* sent;
   public:
       sentence (char* c) //no arg constructor
       {
       sent = new char [ strlen ( c) + 1] ;
       strcpy (sent, c) ;
       }
       ~sentence ( )              // destructor
           (delete sent;)
       void show ( )
```

```
            { cout << sent ; } ;
void main ( )
    {
    sentence s1 = "Problems are opportunities/
        and there are a lot of them around.";
    cout <<"\nString is: \n";
    s1.show ( ) ;
    }
```

The output is:

Problems are opportunities and there are a lot of them around.

Analysis

1. A user-defined string type is declared in class sentence.
2. It has a one-argument constructor which uses the "new" operator to request memory to contain a string plus one null character. It returns a pointer called "sent", which points to the first address of the string of characters.
3. The strcpy( ) function uses the pointers "sent" and "c" to copy a string from "c" into 'sent'.
4. The statement

   ```
   ~sentence( ) {delete sent;}
   ```

   is called a destructor as it releases the memory set up by "new" . The operator used here is "delete". The tilde (~) before the class name "sentence" implies that it is a destructor.
5. When the "new" operator is used in a constructor, the destructor is automatically invoked to release the memory.
6. In main ( ) an object "s1" of class "sentence" is defined and initialized, using the one-argument constructor.
7. It then uses the show ( ) function to display the string.

10.8 POINTERS TO OBJECTS

When memory needs to be allocated dynamically with each creation of an object of a class, the "new" operator comes handy.

The following program illustrates its use.

```
//dynam.cpp
//pointers to objects
#include<iostream.h>
class currency
    {
```

```
    private:
        float amt;
    public:
        void fetch( )
            { cout<<"\nEnter amount: "; cin>>amt; }
        void display ( )
            { cout<<"Amount is: "<<amt; }
        };
void main()
    {
    currency c;
    c.fetch( );             //access by dot operator
    c.display( );
    currency* ptr;
    ptr = new currency;
    ptr -> fetch( );    //access by arrow operator
    ptr -> display( );
    }
```

The output is:

Enter amount: 1234.56 < ret >
Amount is: 1234.560059
Enter amount: 2345.67 < ret >
Amount is: 2345.660922

Analysis

1. The class structure has only routine declarations which does not need elaboration.
2. Examine the main( ) program. An object "c" of "currency" is defined. It access the member functions of the class using the dot or the period operator.
3. Next a pointer to an object of "currency" called "ptr" is set up.
4. The "ptr" is returned as an address pointer when we allocated memory to the class "currency" due to the following definition:

   ```
   ptr = new currency;
   ```
5. This pointer "ptr" which points to an object is used to access member functions using the arrow operator.
6. Note that the arrow operator (– >) is used with a pointer to an object, just like a dot operator is used with an object of a class.

Aside:

It is possible to set up a pointer to an object and yet "dereference" it so that the dot operator can be used to access member functions, just like the object of a class. This is shown in the next program.

The expression

```
currency& c = *(new currency)
```

sets up a pointer of an object, and uses it to reference the object "c". Therefore "c" can be used with the dot operator instead of the arrow operator.

```
// dynamic.cpp
// another use of the new operator
#include <iostream.h>
class currency
   {
   private:
       float amount;
   public
       void fetch ( )
           {cout<<"\nEnter amount: "; cin>> amount;}
       void display( )
           { cout << "\nAmount is: "<<amount;}
   };
void main( )
   {
   currency& c= *(new currency);
   c.fetch( );
   c. display( );
   }
```

The output is:

```
Enter amount: 1234.56        < ret >
Amount is: 1234.560059
```

10.9 ARRAY OF POINTERS

Creating an array of pointers to objects enables easy access to objects. This is an alternate to setting up an array of objects. The following program shows the use of this idea.

```
//ptrobj.cpp
//array of pointers to objects
#include<iostream.h>
class country
      {
      private:
          char coun[20];            //20 character string
      public:
          void fetch( )
              {cout <<"\nName country:"; cin >> coun;}
          void show( )
              { cout<<"Country is : "<<coun; }
      };
void main( )
      {
      country* counptr[20];         //20 pointers to object
      int pt = 0;
      char ne;
      do
      {
      counptr[pt}=new country;          //new allocation
      counptr[pt] -> fetch ( ) ;        //arrow operator
      counptr[pt) -> show( ) ;
      pt++;
      cout <<"\nContinue? (y/n): "; cin >>ne;
      }
      while(ne == 'y');
    }
```

The output is:

Name country: India <ret>
Contry is: India
Continue?(y/n): n <ret>

Analysis

1. The array of pointers to objects is created within main ( ) as follows:

   `country* counptr [20];`

"counptr" is an array of pointer to class "country", and can point to 20 objects.

2. The expression

```
int pt = 0;
```

sets an index to keep count of the number of objects created. It is zero at start, as it points to the first object.

3. The statement

```
counptr[pt] = new country;
```

allocates memory dynamically as each object is created. Thus each time the do-loop is executed memory is set apart for the following objects:

```
counptr[0]      for     pt = 0
counptr[1]      for     pt = 1
. . . . . .
```

There is provision to create 20 such objects.

4. The object counptr [pt] accesses the member functions of class "country" by using the arrow operator, thus:

```
counptr[pt] -> fetch( );
counptr[pt] -> show( );
```

5. The do-loop terminates when any character other than 'y' is entered.

10.10 LINKED LIST

Arrays or array of pointers handle data of constant size. This may result in inefficient use of memory space or if overflowing may lead to system crash. However linked list offers the flexibility of setting up memory exactly as needed by a block of data, by using the "new" operator. Moreover linked list enables linking of one data block to another, regardless of whatever its position in memory. The following program uses linked list.

```
#include <string.h>
//linkedlst.cpp
#include<iostream.h>
struct chain
   {
   char name[20];
   char strt [25];
   char city [10];
   float amt;
   chain* succ:
   };
class connect
```

```
{
private:
    chain* one;
public:
    connect( ) {one = NULL;}    //no arg constructor
    void nextitem(char n[ ],char s[ ], char c[ ],
    float a)    //4 arg constructor
    {
    chain* newch = new chain;
    strcpy (newch ->name, n):
    strcpy(newch ->,strt, s);
    strcpy(newch ->city, c);
    newch ->amt = a;
    newch -> succ = one;
    one = newch;
    }
void show( );
};
void connect:: show ( )
{
chain* now = one;
while(now != NULL)
    {
    cout<<"/n"<<now->name<<", "<<now->strt<<" ," ,
        <<now->city<<", "<<now->amt;
    now = now ->succ;
    }
};
void main ( )
{
connect cl, c2, c3;
cl.nextitem("R.Jayaram","Atlanta","Georgia",
123.45);
c2.nextitem("J.Vivek","Uppilipalayam","Kovai",
    234.56);
c3.nextitem("M.Suganya","Nethaji Road",
"Madurai",345.67);
    cl.show( );
```

```
        c2.show( );
        c3.show( );
        }
```

The output is:

R. Jayaram, Atlanta, Georgia, 123.45
J. Vivek, Uppilipalayam, Kovai, 234.56
M. Suganya, Nethaji Road, Madurai, 345.67

Analysis

1. A structure called "chain" is declared consisting of the following data block.

```
    char name[20];
    char strt[25];
    char city[10);
    float amt; '
    succ;
```

   This block occupies a total of 61 bytes of memory.

2. The second declaration is a class of type "connect". It has a pointer variable of structure type called "one". The "one" can be made to point to the beginning of the data block created with struct statement.
3. There is a no-argument constructor where "one" is made NULL, thereby implying that it does not point anywhere in memory.
4. The next is a 4-argument constructor. A pointer called "newch" is set up and made to point to a newly created memory block for "chain". This block consists of 4 elements of structure "chain".

```
    newch ->
        one ->  name[20]    :
                strt[25]    :
                city [10]   :   chain
                amt         :
```

5. The 4 variables are assigned values. The string variables use strcpy ( ) function to assign values. The float type element "amt" is directly assigned a float value.

   Individual members of the block are accessed by pointer "newch" using the arrow operator.
6. Then the pointer is shifted to the beginning of the next block and cause it to point to it by:

```
    newch ->succ = one;
    one = newch;
```

7. void show( ) declares the prototype for show( ) function.
8. The show( ) function has to be declared separately outside the class organization as the while–loop cannot be expanded as an inline function within a class.
9. The show( ) function is related to the "connect" type by using the scope resolution operator (: :).
10. Within the show( ) declaration another pointer to the memory block set up by struct "chain" is declared as "now" and "mode" to point to "one". Remember that "one" is the pointer to the next linked block.
11. The while loop executes so long as "one" points to some block and causes the output of the structure elements.
12. Then the "now" pointer moves to the next linked block due to the statement:

    ```
    now = now - > succ;
    ```
13. Within main( ) we define 3 objects of type "connect" cadled c1 , c2 and c3. Then using the 4-argument constructor, it is possible to assign values to the function "nextitem".
14. They are made to display by the following invocation:

    ```
    c1.show( ):  c2.show( );  c3.show( );
    ```

Aside

A class can set up a pointer to an object of its own type such as:

```
class connect
    {
    connect* ptr;
    . . . .
    };
```

However it should not contain an object of its own type with class organization.

```
class connect
    {
    connect c;
    . . . .
    };
```

10.11 ARRAY OF POINTERS TO OBJECT (CONTINUED)

This section discusses an array of pointers to objects. This can otherwise be called pointers to pointers. The array of pointers shall be used to sort names. This method of sorting is called index sorting.

```
//ptrsort . cpp
//sorts names using array of pointer
#include<iostream.h>
#include<string.h>
class inform
   {
   private:
       char n[20];
   public:
       void SN (  )
           { cout<<"Enter name : " ; cin>>n;}
       void disp( )
           ( cout<<" /n"<<n; }
       char* GN (  )
       { return n; }
   };
void main( )
   {
   void arrange (inform**, int);
   inform* ptr(20];
   int n = 0;
   char pick;
   do
       {
       ptr[n] = new inform;          //dynamic mem
                                     // allocation
       ptr[n]->SN( );
       n++;
       cout<<"Continue (y/n) ?";
       cin>>pick;
       }
   while(pick = = 'y');
   cout<<"\nOriginal list:";
   for(int k= 0; k<n; k++)
       (ptr(k]->disp( ); }
   arrange(ptr,n);
   cout<<endl; cout<<endl;
```

```
    cout <<"\nArranged list: ";
    for (int j=0; j<n; j++)
        {ptr[j]->disp( ); }
    }
void arrange(inform** i, int n)
    {
    void sort(inform**, inform**);
        int j, k;
        for(j=0; j<n - 1; j++)
            for (k=j + 1; k<n; k++)
                sort (i + j, i + k);
        }
void sort(inform** i1, inform** i2)
    {
    if(strcmp( (*i1) ->GN( ), (*i2)->GN( ) ) > 0)
        {
        inform* tp = *i1;
        *i1 = *i2;
        *i2 =tp;
        }
    }
```

The output is:

```
Enter name: Vivek            < ret >
Continue(y/n)?y              < ret >
Enter name: Tilak            < ret >
Continue(y/n)?y              < ret >
Enter name: Mahesh           < ret >
Continue(y/n)?y              < ret >
Enter name: Jayaram          < ret >
Continue(y/n)?y              < ret >
Enter name : Suganya         < ret >
Continue(y/n)?n              < ret >
Original list:
Vivek
Tilak
Mahesh
```

```
Jayaram
Suganya
Arranged list:
Jayaram
Mahesh
Suganya
Tilak
Vivek
```

Analysis

1. A class organization called "inform" is declared. A function called GN( ) is set up. This has a char type pointer. It returns the contents of "n".
2. Within main ( ) a prototype is set up for arrange( ) function. Its first argument inform** is a pointer to pointer. The second argument is type int, which specifies the size of the array.
3. Then a pointer to an array is set up by
   ```
   inform* ptr[20];
   ```
   "ptr" is the pointer to an array of pointers. It has a provision to point to 20 address elements in the array.
   ```
                   array of pointers       2000 ->       object1
   ptr: 2000 ->        2000
                       2010                 ....
                       2020                 ...
                       2030                 ...
                       2040 2200 -> object 20
                       2200
   ```
4. A counter is set up by int n=0 and initialized to zero count.
5. A char type variable "pick" is declared to accept a single character like 'y' or 'n' to decide if the process is to be continued.
6. The do-loop has its first statement
   ```
   ptr[n] = new inform;
   ```
   At start n = 0, therefore
   ```
   ptr[0] = new inform;
   ```
   dynamically assigns a memory location and causes ptr [0] to point to it.
   ```
   ptr[ ] -> object
   ```

7. The next statement

```
ptr [n] ->SN ( ) ;
```

accesses the function SN( ) of class "inform". This accepts a string through the keyboard and assigns to variable "n" or any other characters against the prompt:

```
Continue(y/n)?
```

8. The object cout then lists out the array of strings as entered by invoking the disp( ) function by means of ptr[k] and the arrow operator:

```
ptr [k] ->disp ( ) ;
```

9. The function arrange ( ) is invoked with this pointer "ptr" and the number of objects "n" to be sorted.

10. This sorted list is then displayed by the for -loop.

11. Now examine the arrange( ) function declaration

```
void arrange(inform** i, int n)
```

Recall that we invoked it with two arguments:

```
ptr [ ] and n
```

"i" which is a pointer to pointer receives the address passed by ptr [ ] and number of objects is received by "n".

12. A prototype is set up for sort ( ) with two pointers to pointer variable of type "inform".

```
void sort(inform**, inform**);
```

13. The sort( ) function is invoked as follows:

```
sort ( i +  j, i + k ) ;
```

14. The sort( ) function has two arguments which are pointers to pointers. That means two addresses are passed which again point to two addresses in the array of pointers.

15. The sort( ) function then sorts addresses pointing at starting objects lexigraphically, that is, in the alphabetical order.

```
Before Sorting:
                 array of pointers      objects of inform
ptr - >               1000                Z     <-    1000
                      1010                X     <-    1010
                      1020                E     <-    1020
                      1030                A     <-    1030
After Sorting:
                      1030                z     <-    1000
                      1020                X     <-    1010
                      1010                E     <-    1020
                      1000                A     <-    1030
```

16. Thus note that objects are held intact in their memory locations, but their pointers have been ordered according to the lexical order of the string. Now by accessing the locations pointed to by the array of pointers, an arranged list of strings can be got.

Aside

Thus note that the pointers that point to the strings have been sorted rather then the contents of the locations. Actually the strings are compared, and their addresses are swapped if necessary. What is the advantage of such sorting?

In this particular example there was only one string in the object. What if it was a structure containing several data types? It would be time consuming to move these data from one memory block to another memory block. However it would be easy to simply interchange their addresses, thus saving on the processing time.

REVIEW QUESTIONS

10.1 What does a pointer hold?

10.2 Are pointers to an int and float same?

10.3 Suppose a pointer of target type float is incremented, by how many bytes does it advance?

10.4 What is the symbol & called?

10.5 What is returned by a variable referenced as & variable?

10.6 What does a variable return if it is simply referenced by its name?

10.7 What notation implies that an address is hexadecimal?

10.8 Which way of declaring a pointer is correct?

```
* var ; int * var;
```

10.9 Can multiple pointers be defined in one line for a particular target type?

10.10 How would you set up a general purpose pointer called "point" which can point to any target type data?

10.11 Suppose you have an expression

```
ptr = array;
```

where "ptr" is a pointer to an array, to which element does it point at start?

10.12 Assume array is of target type float. If array [ ] points to location 2000, where will array [3] point to?

10.13 is passing an argument by pointer and passing by reference the same?

10.14 What do you call a statement such as:

```
void convert (float&);
```

10.15 How would you interpret a statement like

```
*a += 40;
```

10.16 What is done when a statement is written as :

```
convert (indrs);
```

10.17 Suppose "ptr" points to 1oc 2000 before the following expression is executed, where will it point after execution?

```
*ptr++ *= 31.65;
```

10.18 What is being compared by the following statement:

```
if (*n > *m)
```

address or contents?

10.19 Assume "ptr" is a pointer and m, n are integers. Then what do you call expression written as:

```
sort(ptr + m, ptr + n);
```

10.20 If "p" is a char type pointer, what do you test when you write:

```
while(*p)
```

10.21 What do d, s represent in the statement:

```
Strcpy (d, s) ;
```

10.22 What operator enables dynamic allocation of memory?

10.23 Is it always necessary to delete a pointer set up by the "new" operator?

10.24 When should operator delete be used compulsorily?

10.25 What do you call the following declaration?

```
~sentence ( ) {delete s;}
```

10.26 Suppost "ptr" is a pointer to class type currency, then how could you access a function called fetch ( )?

10.27 How a pointer to an object be set up and yet use the dot operator to access a function of class?

10.28 Suppose "country" is a class, what are we doing when we declare as:

```
country* ptr [20];
```

10.29 What do you call a declaration such as:

```
void next(char n[ ], char s; float a, int n)
{     }
```

10.30 Can a while-loop be expanded inline within a member function of a class organization?

10.31 How else should a member function of a class be expanded so that while loop can be included?

10.32 Can a class contain a pointer to an object of its own type?

10.33 Can a class contain an object of its own type within the class?

Answers

10.1 address

10.2 no

10.3 four bytes

10.4 address operator

10.5 an address

10.6 Contents of memory lacation

10.7 0x

10.8 both correct

10.9 yes

10.10 void *point

10.11 array [0]

10.12 2012

10.13 yes

10.14 a prototype

10.15 contents of loc a incremented by 40 and stored in a

10.16 invoked with argument indrs

10.17 2004

10.18 contents of loc n, m

10.19 address arithmetic

10.20 if NULL character

10.21 pointer or arrays

10.22 new

10.23 no

10.24 When new used in functions

10.25 destructor

10.26 ptr - > fetch( )

10.27 by dereferencing

10.28 20 pointers to objects of country is set up

10.29 a constructor of 4 arguments

10.30 no

10.31 using scope resolution(::) operator outside class

10.32 yes

10.33 no

Chapter 11

File Handling

Chapter 11

File Handling

OBJECTIVE

File handling by stream oriented Input/Output operations, redirection, command line arguments, overloading of insertion and extraction operators are discussed and illustrated.

KEYWORDS, FUNCTIONS AND HEADER FILES

`get( )`	`getline( )`	`read( )`	`put( )`
`write( )`	`fstream`	`friend`	`this`

11.1 INTRODUCTION

While learning about files in C++ it is good to familiarize oneself with the stream class hierarchy, which can be represented by the following graph.

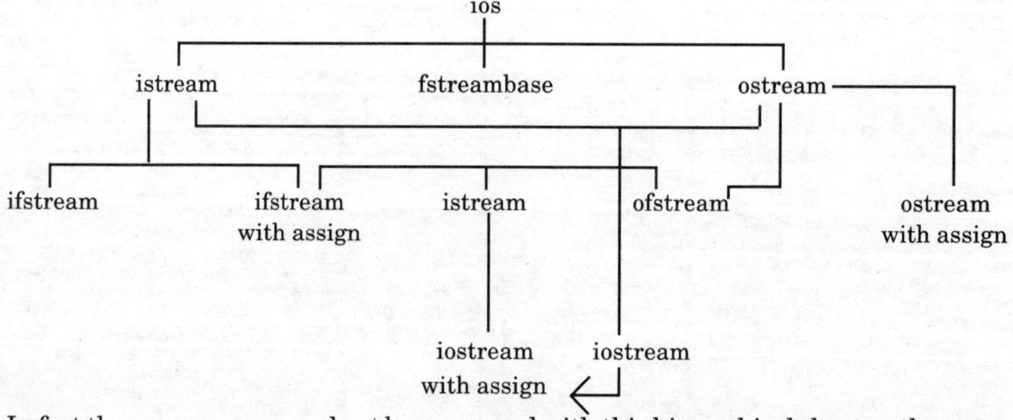

In fact the programmer need not be concerned with this hierarchical chart as the program will work anyway.

```
extraction operator > > is a member of istream
insertion operator < < is a member of ostream
cout is a predefined object of ostream with assign
cin is a predefined object of istream with assign
```

All these are derived from "iostream.h" header file. All disk file I/O are included in "fstream.h" file. Some flags such as showpoint, fixed are member functions of "ios" class. "ios" contains a pointer to "streambuf" class for processing data buffers.

get( ), getline( ), read( ), > > are member functions of istream class.

put( ), write( ), < < are member functions of ostream class.

ifstream handles input to files

ofstream handles output from files

fstream handles both output and input of files.

11.2 STRING HANDLING

The following program shows how files are read and written onto.

```
//filein.cpp
#include<fstream.h>
void main( )
{
ofstream writef ("TCE.DAT");
writef<<"Whatever your grade or position\n";
writef<<"If you know how and when to speak\n";
writef<<"and when to remain silent\n";
writef<<"your chances of real success\n";
writef<<"are proportionately increased.\n";
}
//fileout.cpp
#include<fstream.h>
void main( )
   {
   const int L = 40;
   char buf [ L];
   ifstream readf ("TCE.DAT");
   while(readf)
   {
   readf.getline(buf, L);
```

```
        cout<<" \n"<<buf;
        }
    }
```

Analysis

1. Header file fstream.h is included thereby endowing input/output capabilities to the file.
2. An object called "writef" of ofstream class is defined and initialized with the name of the file: TCE.DAT.
3. This object is used with the insertion operator (<<) to enter text into the file TCE.DAT.
4. The file closes automatically upon termination of the program.
5. In program "fileout.cpp" a buffer of size 40 characters is defined. It is called "buf".
6. An object "readf" of class ifstream is defined and initialized with the file name TCE.DAT.
7. The while-loop reads the file TCE.DAT one line at a time, until the newline character '/n' is encountered. The contents read are then put into the buffer called "buf".
8. The object cout then displays the text on the screen.

   The two programs filein.cpp and fileout.cpp are run one after another.

   The output is:

Whatever your grade or position
if you know how and when to speak
and when to remain silent
your chances of real success
are proportionately increased.

Aside

The stream object "readf" of ifstream class actually returns a pointer, which can be tested for various error conditions. So in the while statement it is tested for the true (zero value) or false (non zero value). It can also be tested for end-of-file condition, so that when the pointer reaches beyond the last line it stops reading.

11.3 set( ) AND put( ) FUNCTIONS

These two functions belong to the fstream class and can handle single character at a time. The following program shows their use.

```
//charac.cpp
#include<fstream.h>
#include<string.h>
void main ( )
    {
```

```
    char ch;
    char sent [ ] = "You maybe disapponted if you\
                    fail, but you are doomed if you\
                    don't try.";
    ofstream writef ("TCET.DAT");
    for (int k=0; k<strlen(sent); k++)
        writef.put(str[k]);
    }
    //charac1.cpp
    #include<fstream.h>
    void main ( )
        {
        char chr;
        ifstream readf ("TCET.DAT");
        while(readf)
            {
            readf.get(chr);
            cout<<chr;
            }
    }
```

The output is:

You maybe disappointed if you fail, but you are doomed if you don't try.

Analysis

1. The string.h header file is included to use the strlen ( ) function to determine the length of the string in sent [ ] in the program charac.cpp.
2. An object writef of class ofstream is defined and initialized with the filename TCET.DAT.
3. The for-loop uses the object writef and put function to write character by character of string sent [ ] into the TCET.DAT file.
4. The file closes automatically on termination of the program.
5. In the program charac1.cpp is a char type variable called "chr".
6. An object readf of class ifstream is defined and initialized with the filename TCET.DAT to be read.
7. The object readf reads character by character from TCET.DAT and send for display till the '\n' character is encountered.

11.4 WRITING AND READING OBJECTS OF DISK FILE

Turbo C++ is basically designed to handle objects of classes. Therefore in the next program it is shown how objects are written onto and read from disk files. The pre-defined functions employed here are write( ) and read( ). Another important aspect is that a single program does both writing and reading.

```
//objfile.cpp
#include<fstream.h>
class empdata
   {
   private:
       char n[15]; int e; float a;
   public:
       void fetch( )
           {
           cout<<"Name: "; cin>>n;
           cout<<"Exper: ": cin>>e;
           cout<<"Amount: "; cin>>a;
           }
       void show( )
           {
           cout<<"\nName: "<<n;
           cout<<"\nExper: "<<e;
           cout<<"\nAmount: "<<a;
           }
   };
void main ( )
   {
   empdata em;
   em.fetch( );
   ofstream writef ("EMP.DAT");
   writef.write( (char*)&em, sizeof (em));
   ifstream readf ("EMP.DAT");
   readf.read( (char*)&em, size of (em));
   em.show( );
   }
```

The output of these program are:

Name: J. Vivek < ret >

Expre: 2 < ret >

Amount: 26.57 < ret >

Name: J. Vivek

Expre: 2

Amount: 26.57

Analysis

1. Three data types are set up in the "empdata" class:

```
char n[15]; int e; float a;
```

2. The fetch ( ) function accepts relevant inputs through keyboard and assigns them to the respective variables.
3. The show( ) function causes the values stored in these variables to be displayed.
4. In main ( ) an object "em" is defined for "empdata".
5. The object is used with dot operator and fetch( ) to execute the function within class organization.
6. Next another object is defined as writef( ) of ofstream class and initializes it with the filename EMP.DAT.
7. The object writef is used with the dot operator and the write( ) function of ofstream class to write the values into disk file EMP.DAT.
8. Examine the statement that writes into the disk file:

```
writef.write( (char *)&em, size of (em);)
writef is an object of ofstream class
write( ) is a function of ofstream class
```

The function takes two arguments: the address of object "em" to be written and the length of the object in bytes as determined by sizeof(em).

9. For reading the object out of the diskfile, another object by name readf is set up.
10. The object readf of ifstream class is used in conjunction with pre-defined function of the same ifstream class, to read the EMP.DAT file. It is furnished with the address of the object "em" of type empdata and the total number of bytes to be read.
11. Then using the show( ) function the output is got as shown above .

Aside:

Data written into files can be assumed to be characters or binary values. Functions such as get ( ), put( ), < < , > > , operate on characters. Whereas the write( ) function can operate on binary values only. Therefore if DOS command "type filename" is given, it will not display file contents legibly. Whereas with characters handling functions the "type" command will give a readable output.

11.5 FILE HANDLING WITH MULTIPLE OBJECTS

The next program illustrates how to handle multiple objects in files. The program uses predefined function open( ) to create a file with different modes such as append, output and input. The program enables appending a new record each time it is executed.

```
//objmulti.cpp
#include<fstream.h>
class empdata
   {
   private:
       char n[15] ; int e; float a;
   public:
       void fetch( )
       {
       cout <<"\nName: "; cin>>n;
       cout <<"\nExper: "; cin>>e;
       cout << '\nAmojnt : "; cin >> a;
       void show( );
       }
   void show ( )
   {
   cout <<" \nName : "<<n<<"Exper : "<<e<<" Amount :
       " <<a<<"\n";
   }
} ;
void main ( )
   {
   char chr;
   empdata em;
   fstream f;
   f.open("EMP.DAT",ios::app| ios::out| ios::in);
   do
   {
   em.fetch( ) ;
   f.write (char*) &em, sizeof(em) ) ;
   cout <<"Continue ( y/n) ? "; cin >> chr;
   }
   while ( chr == 'y' ) ;
```

```
    f.seekg (0) ;
    f.read( (char* ) &em, sizeof (em) );
    while ( !f . eof( ) )
        {
        em.show( );
        f.read ( ( char* ) &em, sizeof (em) );
        }
}
```

The output is :

Name: R. Jayaram	<ret>
Exper: 5	<ret
Amount: 12.34	<ret>
Continue (y/n) ? y	<ret>
Name: J. Vivek	<ret>
Exper: 2	<ret>
Amount: 23.45	<ret>
Continue (y/n) ? n	<ret>
Name: R. Jayaram Exper: 5 Amount: 12.34	
Name J. Vivek Exper: 2 Amount : 23.45	

Analysis

1. The class structure for empdata type is exactly as in the previous program, except for the show( ) function, where a one line display is incorporated.
2. A file called "f" is created by the statement

   ```
   fstream.f;
   ```

   This gives both input and output (read or write) capabilities to the file.
3. In the next statement the file is actually opened.

   ```
   f.open("EMP.DAT", ios:: app: ios:: out :ios::in);
   ```

   The file is named EMP.DAT and is opened in 3 modes, namely: append, output, input.
4. The do-loop gets data through accessing member function. fetch( ) by use of object "em" of type empdata and writes it into the file EMP.DAT. This process repeats until we enter "n" against the prompt:

   ```
   continue(y/n)?n<RET>
   ```

5. The statement

   ```
   f.seekg();
   ```

   sets file pointer to the beginning of the file.

6. Then the first reading or "priming" reading of the file is done. The statement that reads the first record is

```
f.read( char* )&em, sizeof(em) );
```

The first argument of target type char gives the address of the object. The second argument gives the size of the object store in bytes.

7. The while (!f.eof ( )) causes the object to be displayed by

```
em.show ( ) ;
```

and goes on to read the next object. This procedure is repeated until there is no more object to be read (ie) end of file is reached.

Aside

A file is created using fstream class so as to give it input/output capabilities. seekg( ) function resets file pointer to first byte of the file. eof( ) is a member function of ios class.

11.6 POINTERS IN FILE

The discussion here is about file pointers which set up within a file to read or write data. This pointer is not the pointers used for pointing to address or location. Functions such as seekg( ), tellg( ) help to use pointer to read from file. Functions like seekp( ), tellp ( ) help to use pointer to write into file.

The seekg( ) can place the pointer anywhere in the file by use of appropriate arguments such as beg(beginning), cur(current position), end (end of file)

```
A typical use of seekg( ) is:
seekg( -12 , ios: : end) ;
```

This implies 12 bytes before end of file. The following program illustrates its use.

```
// filept.CPP
// can point to desired position in file
#include<fstream.h>
class details
  {
      private:
          char n [15]; int e; float a:
public:

   void disp( )
      {
      cout <<"\nName: "<<n;
      cout<<"Exper:"<<e;
      cout<<"Amount: "<<a;
```

```
        }
    };
void main( )
    {
    details d;
    ifstream in;
    in.open ("EMP.DAT");
    in.seekg (0, ios: :end);
    int ep = in.tellg ( );
    int m = ep/sizeof (details);
    cout<<"/nWhich numb? "; cin<<m;
    int pos = (m - 1 ) *sizeof (details);
    in.seekg (pos);
    in.read ( (char*) &d, sizeof (d) );
    d.disp ( );
    }
```

The output is:

```
Which numb? 2                                  <ret>
Name: J. Vivek Exper: 2 Amount: 23.450001
```

Analysis

1. The class organisation has been dealt with in quite detail earlier. Therefore no more discussion is done about it.
2. Within main( ) an object "d" of type "details" is defined.
3. The statement "ifstream in" creates an input file by name "in".
4. Then the already existing file EMP.DAT is opened. This file was created in a previous processing.
5. The next statement

   `in.seekg(0, ios : :end);`

   positions the file pointer in the last byte at the end of the file.
6. int ep = in.tellg ( ) helps to store the current pointer position in ep.
7. `int m = ep / sizeof (details) ;`

   actually evaluates the number of records in the file. Recall that each record of class has 3 different data types of type char, int and float. "ep" contains the total bytes to the end of the file. This divided by number of bytes per record yields number of records.
8. Then a prompt appears asking for the records to be read. When an entry is made it is stored in "m"

9. Suppose the second record is needed then 2 is entered against the prompt, thereby assigning 2 to m. Then using the equation

```
pos = (m - 1) * sizeof(details);
```

the position of the record to be read is indicated.

10. `in.seekg(pos);`

positions the file pointer at the beginning of the sought record.

11. `in.read ( ( char*) &d, sizeof(d));`

causes the pointer to read from the first address to the last address in the record.

12. d.disp( ) cause these characters to be displayed.

11.7 DISK MANIPULATIONS

This section shows how to include stream I/O operations as member functions of the class.

```
//diskio.cpp
#include<fstream.h>
struct details
   {char n[15]; int e; float a; };
class cluster
   {
   private:
       details d[30]; int c;
   public:
       cluster ( ) { c = 0 ; }
       void append( );        //add data
       void disp( );          //display from RAM
       void input( ); //write into disk file
       void output ( );       // read out of disk file
       };
void cluster : : append ( )
   {
   cout<<" \nName: " ; cin>>d[c].n;
   cout<<" Exper: "; cin>>d[c].e;
   cout<<" Amount: "; cin>>d [c].a;
   }
void cluster: :disp( )
   {
   for(int k= 0; k<c; k++)
   {
```

```
   cout<<"\nData: "<<k+1<<" Name:"<<d[k].n
       <<"Exper : "<<d[k].e<< "Amount: "<<d[k].a; }
   }
void cluster: :input( )
   {
   ifstream in:
   in.open ("CLUSTER.DAT", ios: :nocreate);
   if (in)
       in.read( (char*) this, sizeof(*this) );
   }
void cluster: :output( )
   {
   ofstream out;
   out.open ( "CLUSTER.DAT" );
   out.write ( (char*)this, sizeof(*this) );
   }
void main( )
   {
   cluster c1
   c1.input( );
   c1.disp( );
   char chr;
   do
   {
       cout <<"\nType infor: "; c1.append( );
       cout<<"More? "; cin>>chr;
   }
   while (chr == 'y') ;
   c1.disp ( ) ;
   c1 . output ( ) ;
}
```

The output is :

Type info:	< ret >
Name: J. Vivek	< ret >
Exper: 2	< ret >
Amount: 12.34	< ret >

```
More? y                                   < ret >
Type info:
Name: J. Tilak                            < ret >
Expre: 3                                  < ret >
Amount: 23.45                             < ret >
more? n                                   < ret >
```

```
Data: 1 Name: J. Vivek Exper: 2 Amount: 12.34
Data: 2 Name: J. Tilak Exper: 3 Amount: 23.450001
```

Analysis

1. There is a structure with provision for 15 characters for n [ ], an int type "e" and a float type "a". The total memory for this structure is 15 + 2 + 4 = 21 bytes.
2. The no-argument constructor sets "c" to zero.
3. The four member functions append( ), disp( ), input( ) and output( ) are declared as class members and defined outside by means of the scope resolution operator (::).
4. append( ) and disp( ) functions are quite straightforward and therefore no further explanations are given.
5. The input( ) and output( ) are member functions that are used to read out of and write into the file.
6. The input( ) function contains an object called "in". It is used to open a data file called CLUSTER.DAT in read mode.

   "nocreate" is a mode bit which implies an error when opening if file does not already exist.
7. The if( ) statement tests whether the file exists and if so reads a whole object of a specified length. "this" is the address pointer of the object to be read. It is a keyword of C++.
8. The output( ) function uses an object "out" of output file stream to open CLUSTER.DAT in the write mode. It writes whole object of a given length into the location pointed to by address "this".
9. The rest of the program is quite trivial. The output and responses are shown above.

Aside

There are several mode bits that are used with open( ) function in either read or write mode (input or output modes).

Mode bit	Operation
in	open for reading (default for ifstream)
out	open for writing (default for ofstream)
app	read/write at end of file
nocreate	error when opening if file does not exist
noreplace	error when opening for output if file already exist
binary	open file in binary mode

A file closes automatically when the function terminates. However it is also possible to use the close( ) member function as shown:

```
file.close( );
```

11.8 ERROR SITUATIONS IN FILE HANDLING

Several errors are likely to occur while handling disk files. For example opening a file in input mode when it does not exist is an error condition. Similarly naming a new file using the name of an file and also results in error. Some error indicators are tabulated by using the stream status bits.

Bit	Meaning
0x00	no error
0x01	end of file
0x02	read or write failure
0x04	invalid operation (like opening non existing file)
0x08	hard error

The following listing shows a program that gives the error or good status of a file to open. Note that several functions such as rdstate( ), good( ), eof( ), fail( ), bad( ) figure in the program that follows.

```
//ferrors.cpp
#include <fstream.h>
void main( )
     {
     ifstream f;
     f.open ("CLUSTER.DAT", ios: :nocreate);
     if( !f )
         cout<<"\nUnable to open CLUSTER.DAT";
     else
         cout<<"\nFile= "<<f<<"Error State="
         <<f.rdstate ( ) <<"good ( ) ="<<f.good ( )
         <<"eof( )="<<f.eof( )<<"fail( )="
         <<f.fail ( ) <<"bad ( ) ="<<f.bad ( );
     f.close( );
  }
```

The output is:

File = 0x4ed3ffd4 Error State = 0 good( ) = 1
eof ( )=0 fail ( )= 0 bad( ) = 0

Suppose an attempt is made to open a nonexisting file, say GROUP.DAT then the error message appears:

unable to open GROUP.DAT

Aside

When a file is opened successfully, the starting address is given as in the above case. A "0" indicates false state and a "1" a true state.

Programs such as ferrors.cpp maybe included in all file processing programs, preferably after every I/O operation.

11.9 REDIRECTION

Redirection is a technique by which the output of a program maybe written into a disk file or data retrieved from a disk file. The following program shows how C++ uses the redirection facility.

```
//redirdsk.cp
#include<iostream.h>
#include<iomanip.h>
void main( )
   {
   char chr;
   while ( !cin.eof( ) )
       {
       cin>>resetiosflags(ios: :skipws) >> chr;
       cout<<chr;
       clog<<chr ; //cerr can also be used
       }
   }
```

The output is:

Output	
the quick brown fox jumps over the lazy dog.	<ret>
the quick brown fox jumps over the lazy dog.	<–echoed
whoever coined this statement was a genius.	<ret>
whoever coined this statement was a genius.	<–echoed ^z
the quick brown fox jumps over the lazy dog.	echoed by clog
whoever coined this statement was a genius.	

Analysis

1. The while loop executes so long as the entry through the keyboard is not a EOF character (^z) or function key F6.

2. The statement

```
cin>>resetiosflags(ios : : skipws)>>Chr;
```

helps to reset the skipws flag so that blank spaces, new lines and EOF are recognized by object cout.

3. The object “clog” buffers the inputs and displays the text on screen when the program execution is terminated.

4. In the output note that as each statement is typed and entered, the object cout causes it to display immediately before another line could be typed.

Aside

“cerr” is another object which could very well substitute for “clog”. The difference is, “clog” buffers the inputs whereas “cerr” directly displays the text on the screen without buffering.

Several ios flags have been used in the previous chapters. Here a summary of all ios flags are given.

Flag	Meaning
dec	decimal conversion
fixed	fixed floating point notation
hex	hexadecimal conversion
internal	padding after syntax base indicator
left	left justify output
oct	octal expression
right	right justify output
scientific	floating point notation with E
showbase	use base indicator on output
showpoint	use decimal point in floating point output
showpos	preface pos integers with ‘+’
skipws	skip white space on input
stdio	flush stdout, stderr after insertion
unitbuf	flush all streams after insertion
uppercase	uppercase hex output

Some output/input redirections using the redirdsk.cpp program is shown.

F:\\USERS\\STAFF\\RAJARAM>redirdsk>output.fil

```
a person becomes great by shedding his ego      < ret >
and getting along well with others.             < ret >
^z
a person becomes great by shedding his ego
and getting along with others.
```

Note that the output.fil has been created. This can be verified examining the contents of this file.

F:\\USERS\\STAFF\\RAJARAM >type output.fil < ret >

and getting along well with others.

Now in another example of redirection, the input is obtained from output.fil and redirected as output to the input.fil.

F:\\USERS\\STAFF\\RAJARAM > redirdsk< output.fil > input.fil < ret >

a person becomes great by shedding his ego

and getting along well with others.

Now by examining the input.fil it will be found to have the same contents as found in output.fil.

F:\\USERS\\STAFF\\RAJARAM > type input.fil

a person becomes great by shedding his ego

and getting along well with others.

11.10 COMMAND LINE ARGUMENTS

Command line arguments enable one to specify the arguments along with the executable filename, when invoking it for execution. The following program shows how command line arguments can be used to create a file, write into it and then read it and display its contents.

```
//commline.cpp
#include<iostream.h>
#include<fstream.h>
void main ( int argc, char* argv [ ] )
    {
    fstream f ;
    f.open ( argv [ 0 ] , ios : : out) ;
    cout<<"\nNo of args = "<<arg - 1;
    for (int k=1; k<argc; k++)
        f.write( (char*) argv [k], sizeof (argv[k] );
    f.close( ) ;
    f.open(argv [ 0 ], ios::in);
    cout<<"\nContents of file:"
    cout<<"n"<<argv [ 0 ]"
    cout<<"\n" ;
    for(int j=1; j<argc; j++)
        {
```

```
        f.read( (char*) argv [ j ] , sizeof argv [ j ] );
        cout<<"      "<<argv [ j ];
        }
  f.close ( );
     cout<"/n/n";
     }
```

The output is:

F:\\USERS\STAFF\\JAYARAM>commline vivek tilak
jeya 35475 < ret >
No of args = 4
Contents of File:
F\\USERS\STAFF\\JAYARAM\\COMMLIN.EXE
:
vivek tilak jeya 35475

Analysis

1. The main ( ) function is furnished two arguments

   `int argc, char* argv [ ]`

   argc keeps count of the total number of arguments

   `argv [ ] is a pointer of char type`
2. A file with the same name as the source file is opened for write mode. The filename is pointed to by argv [0], the write mode is specified by setting the ios flag to "out".
3. The for -loop writes each argument, starting with argv [1] into the file of same name as source file, as determined by size of each string.
4. The file is closed and reopened in read mode by

   f.open (argv [ ], ios ::in);
5. The for-loop then reads the contents of the file pointed to by argv [ ] and displays only its contents in the form of each string.

Aside

Remember that argv [ ] is a string pointer, thereby implying that all data including numbers can be stored as strings only.

Another program using command line arguments for performing arithmetic is shown.

```
//comarith.cpp
#include<iostream.h>
#include<ctype.h>
#include<stdlib.h>
void main (int argc, char* argv[ ])
```

```
{
cout<<"\nNo of args ="<<argc -1;
cout<<"\noutput of file\n"<<" "
    <<argv [ ] <<" is ";
int x = atoi(argv [1] );
int y = atoi(argv [2]);
int z = atoi(argv [3]);
int w = atoi(argv [4]);
cout<<" \nAverage of:"
<<x<<", "<<y<<", "<<z<<", "<<w<<" is
"<< (x + y + z + w) /4;
cout <<"\n\n";
}
```

The output is:

F > comarith 3 5 7 9 < ret >
No. or args = 4
Output of file:
F:\\USER\\STAFF\\JAYARAM\\COMARITH.EXE is
Average of 3,5,7,9 is 6 .

Aside

atoi ( ) function converts ASCII value to interger. It's prototype is defined by stdlib.h header file.

In another illustration of use of command line argument, a useful feature is shown. The program called display.cpp behaves exactly like type command. It is possible to use the word "display" against the system prompt to display a program or file on the screen.

```
//display.cpp
#include<fstream.h>
#include<process.h>
void main (int argc, char* argv [ ])
   {
   if ( argc != 2)
      {
      cerr <<"\nFormat : otype filename";
      exit (-1) ;
      }
```

```
    char chr;
    ifstream in;
    in.open(argv[1];
    if ( !in)
        {
        cerr<<"\nUnable to open "<< argv [1];
        exit ( - 1) ;
        }
    while (in.get (chr) ! = 0)
        cout<<chr;
    }
```

The output is:

F:USERS\\STAFF\\JAYARAM>display comarith.cpp <ret>

The complete contents of file comarith.cpp is displayed on the screen. It works exactly like the type command.

Aside

In the previous section it was shown how a new command like "display" could be devised and made to act like "type", in order to send the file contents to the screen. In like manner there is a DOS command for printing. In C+ + it is possible to develop a program which will work just like the DOS print command, but with a different name.

Listed below are special file names for hardware devices connected to any computer system.

Command name	**Where connected**
CON	console
AUX,COM1	first serial port
COM2	second serial port
PRN, LPT1	first parallel port (printer)
LPT2	second parallel port (printer)
LPT3	third parallel port (printer)
NUL	dummy device

To develop the above mentioned program, the following hints maybe followed. Remove the while from display.cpp program and append the following statements. The program maybe called "print.cpp".

```
    ostream out;
    out.open("LPT1");
    while (in.get (chr)  ! = 0)
        out.put (chr);
```

This program maybe executed as follows.

```
F:print comarith.cpp
```

11.11 OVERLOADING I/O OPERATORS

This section illustrates how I/O operators like < < and > > can be overloaded so as to input or output whole objects, just like any basic data type.

```
//overldd.cpp
//operators over loading shown
#include<iostream.h>
class currency
   {
   private:
       float paise; int rupees;
   public:
       currency( ) { rupees=0; paise =0.0; }
       currency (int rs, float ps)
           {rupees = rs; paise=ps; }
       friend istream& operator >> (istream& s, currency& c);
       friend stream& operator << (ostream& s, currency& c);
   };
   istream& operator >> (istream& s, currency& c)
       {
       cout <<"\nType rupees: "; s >> c.rupees;
       cout<<"Type paise: "; s>>c.paise;
       return s;
       }
   ostream& operator << (ostream& s, currency c)
       {
       s<<"Rs."<<c.rupees<<" ps."<<c.paise;
       return s;
       }
   void main ( )
       {
       currency c1, c2;
       cout <<"\nType two currency values:";
```

```
        cin>>c1>>c2;
        currency c3(34, 67.87);
        cout<<"\nAmt1 = "<<c1<<"\nAmt2 = "<<c2;
        cout<<"\nAmt3 = "<<c3;
        cout<<" \n\n" ;
}
```

The output is:

```
Type two currency values            <ret>
Type rupees: 12                     <ret>
Type paise: 34                      <ret>
Type rupees: 23                     <ret>
Type paise: 45                      <ret>
Amt1 = Rs. 12 Ps. 34
Amt2 = Rs. 23 Ps. 45
Amt3 = Rs. 34 Ps. 67.870000
```

Analysis

1. In the class specification for "currency", there are two declarations involving the "friend" function.
2. Recall that istream and ostream are two classes of iostream. By declaring them as "friend" within "currency" class, they are enabled to access private data of "currency" class.
3. The operators > > and < < are over loaded so that they can operate on class objects treating them like basic data type.
4. "s" is an object of fstream (both istream, ostream). "c" is an object of currency. They can now access the private data of type "currency", for input (reading) or output (writing).
5. Within main ( ) program notice that the object cin operator > > being chained to get multiple inputs.
6. Similarly the object cout uses the overloaded operator < < in a chain to give multiple outputs. Whole objects are manipulated in these cases.

Aside

The "friend" function makes member functions of a class friendly to another class. This gives unrestricted access to all private and public data or member functions of the friend class. More about the friend function shall be known while studying the virtual functions in the next chapters.

REVIEW QUESTIONS

11.1 Of which class is the extraction operator > > member of ?

11.2 Of which class is insertion operator << member of ?

11.3 .... is called a predefined object of ostream - with - assign.

11.4 cin is called a predefined object of ....

11.5 In which header file are all disk file I/O operations included ?

11.6 Showpoint, fixed are member functions of .... class.

11.7 Name 3 member functions of istream class.

11.8 put ( ) and write ( ) are member functions of .... class.

11.9 What class function enables opening a file in write mode?

11.10 What class function enables opening a file in read mode?

11.11 When an object is defined such as readf, what does it imply?

11.12 What erorr conditions are tested on a file pointer?

11.13 Is it necessary to close a file explicitly by using the close ( ) function?

11.14 In the statement given, which is a function of ofstream:
writef.write((char*)& em, sizeof (em))

11.15 Can write( ) function operate on characters and binary values equally well?

11.16 What are the 3 modes in which a file can be opened?

11.17 Write a statement using an object called "file" which opens a file EMP.DAT with all 3 modes.

11.18 What capabilities are given to a file opened as follows:

```
fstream file;
```

11.19 In which position of a file is the file pointer set for f.seekg(0)?

11.20 What functions enable a file pointer to be set for read operations?

11.21 Name the functions that enable a file pointer to set it for write operation?

11.22 What does this statement imply?

```
seekg(- 4, ios: :end) ;
```

11.23 What does the tellg( ) function imply?

11.24 When is it obligatory to use close ( ) function during file processing?

11.25 What error is indicated by stream status bits 0x01 ?

11.26 Which of the objects "cerr" or "clog" buffers the input and then displays it on the screen?

11.27 Which flag when set flushes all stream after insertion?

11.28 What entry designates end of file character?

11.29 In dealing with command line argument what does argv[0] normally hold?

11.30 Does argc keep count of the filename also?

11.31 By what name is the second serial port called?

Answers

11.1 istream class

11.2 ostream class

11.3 cout

11.4 istream with assign

11.5 fstream.h

11.6 ios

11.7 get, getline, read

11.8 ostream

11.9 ofstream

11.10 ifstream

11.11 pointer
11.12 true, false, EOF condition
11.13 no
11.14 write
11.15 no, only on binary values
11.16 input, output, append
11.17 file.open("EMP.DAT ", ios::app : ios:: | out : ios::in);
11.18 read/write capabilities
11.19 beginning
11.20 seekg, tellg
11.21 seekp, tellp
11.22 position 4th byte from end
11.23 current pos of file ptr
11.24 when a file has to be opened in another mode
11.25 end of file
11.26 clog
11.27 unit buf
11.28 ^z
11.29 name of file
11.30 yes
11.31 Com2

Chapter 12

C++ Graphics

Chapter 12

C++ Graphics

SUMMARY

C++ graphics has two capabilities; text handling and regular graphics. To handle graphics special monitors such as CGA, EGA or VGA is needed for better resolution. Built-in library functions are available, fonts, size can be manipulated.

KEYWORDS, FUNCTIONS

window( ) initgraph( ) closegraph( )

12.1 INTRODUCTION TO TEXT PROCESSING

Let's straightaway get familiar with text -mode graphics functions by analysing a program. To do this we need a screen of 80-columns by 25-rows display. This program writes text to windows. Windows help program to use a graphical user interface(GUI) display in text mode.

window( ) is a library function for text mode. It is included in conio.h header file. It confines text within a rectangular area, but no borders are visible, as it merges with the background.

```
//fram.cpp
//text frame as a class
#include<string.h>
#include<conio.h>
const int L = 600;
class carton
   {
   private:
       int l, t, r, b; // left, top, right, bottom
```

```
        char str [ ];
    public:
        carton (int le, int to, int ri, int bo, char
        st [ ] )
            {
        l = le, t = to; r = ri; b = bo;
        strcpy (str, st);
        window (l, t, r, b);    //built-in fn
        cputs (str);    //built-in fn
        }
    void rub ( )
        {
        window (l, t, r, b);
        clrscr ( );
        }
    };
  void main ( );
    {
    clrscr ( );
    char st1 [ ] = "The next few lines will appear \n\r\
    as entered, because of proper parameter. \n\r\
    Note also the punctuation of each line with \n\r
    newline, ret & backslash chars. Press \n\r\
    RET key to continue.";
    char st2 [ ] = "This para will be mutilated\
    due to improper parameters to carton ( )\
    Lines haphazardly broken. Press RET.";
    carton c (25, 6, 76, 18, st1);
    getch ( );                    // wait for key press
    c.rub ( );
    carton c1 (1, 1, 28, 12, St2 );
    getch ( );
    c.rub ( );
    }
```

The output is :

F: frame <ret>

The next few line will appear
as entered, because of proper parameter.
Note also that the punctuation of each line with
new line, ret & backslash chars. Press
RET key to continue.

<ret>

This para will be mutilated
due to improper parameter
to carton ( ) Lines hapha
zardly broken. Press RET.

<ret>

F. >

Points to note

1. The window( ) function requires 4 parameters, to define its boundaries in left, top, right and bottom.
2. The string written into this window is declared by char str [L] to hold L number of characters.
3. The carton( ) function accepts the string input through keyboard and writes it into the window area.
4. The rub ( ) function rubs out the text to prepare the window for another display.
5. Within main ( ), two strings called st1 [ ] and st2 [ ] are initialized. In the first string st1 [ ] each line is terminated with a newline and a carriage return character.
6. In the second string st2 [ ], it is treated like one entry spread over several lines by a backslash character.
7. st1 [ ] is displayed in a window whose location and size is specified by
   ```
   carton c (25, 6, 76, 18, st1);
   ```
8. str2 [ ] is displayed in a window whose location and size is specified by
   ```
   carton (1,1, 28, 12, st2) ;
   ```
9. getch ( ) is a function that waits for a keyboard entry, normally any key maybe pressed.

Aside

cputs ( ) is a special function which writes text within a specified window area. Whereas cout and object < < treat the whole screen as display area.

clrscr( ) is another built-in function which clears the entire screen.

Whereas the class function rub( ) erases the contents within a specified window only.

The next program actually displays the border lines of a window. It also uses text mode colours for the window and the text.

```
//visibfr.cpp
# include<string.h>     //strcpy ( ) fn
# include<conio.h>      //window ( ), gotoxy ( ),
const int BO = 20;
const int LF = 27;
const int RI = 62;
const int TO = 8;
const int LN = 600;     //max text char
class encl
   {
   private:
       int 1, r, t, b;
       char str [LN];
       int col;
   public:
       encl( ) //no arg constructor
       {
       l=LF; t=TO; r=RI; b=BO;
       col=LIGHTBLUE;
       }
       encl (int lf, int to , int ri, int bo,
                           int c=LIGHTBLUE)
       { l = lf; t=to; r=ri; b=bo; col=c; }
   void tx (char s[ ] )
       { strcpy(str, s); }
   void sketch ( );     //sketch frame
   void rub ( )         //rub out frame
       {
       window (l, t, r, b);
       clrscr ( );
       }
   };
   void encl: :sketch ( )  //draws the window
   {
   rub ( );
```

```
window (l, t, r, b+1);
int w = r - 1 +l;   //right-
                    //left+l=window width
int h = b - t + l;  //bottom - top +
                    //l=window height
textcolor (col);
for (int k=1; k<w; k++)
    {
    gotoxy (k, 1); putch (char (205) );
    gotoxy (k, h ); putch (char (205) );
    }
    for ( k=1; k<h; k++)
    {
    gotoxy (1, k); putch (char (186) );
    gotoxy ( (w, k); putch (char (186) );
    }
    gotoxy (1, 1); putch (char (201) );
    gotoxy (w, 1); putch (char(187) ); .
    gotoxy (1, h); putch (char(200) );
    gotoxy (w, h); putch (char(188) );
    window (1 + 2, t + 1, r - 2, b - 3);
    cputs(str);
    window (1, t, r, b+1};
    gotoxy (3, h - 1);
    cputs ("Press RET key to cont: ")
    textcolor (LIGHTBLUE);
    }
void main ( )
    clrscr ( );
    encl e; //object of default window
    encl c (1, 1, 35, 15, LIGHTBLUE);
    e.tx ("\"Think,\"said the \n\r
    Mahatma,\"the whole world\n\r
    as one family, and you will \n\r
    live in peace. \" ");
    c. tx ("There are only two \n\r
    of humankind: man and woman. \n\r
    Other distinctions are merely \n\r
```

```
perceived by man himself.");
e.sketch ( ); getch ( ); e.rub ( );
c.sketch ( ); getch ( ); c.rub ( );
c.tx ("Good_bye");
c. sketch ( ); getch ( );
}
```

The output was all in lightblue colours:

8, 27 8, 62

"Think," said the
Mahatma, "the whole world
as one family, and you
will live in peace."

20, 27 Press RET key to cont: 20, 62

1,1 1, 35

There are only two
of humankind: man and woman.
Other disctinctions are merely
perceived by man himself.

15, 1 Press RET key to cont: 15, 35

1,1 1, 35

Good_bye

Press RET key to cont:

15, 1 15, 35

Analysis

1. Dimensions for a default window is specified with following coordinates:
   `bottom = 20, left = 27, right = 62, top = 8`
2. The window can contain a maximum of 600 characters.
3. The no argument constructor uses default setting for the window.
4. There is provision to set up our own window by choosing proper coordinates. This is enabled by the 5-argument constructor.
5. The other member functions are tx( ), sketch( ) and rub( ). tx( ) copies text within the window. Sketch( ) draws the border lines for the window. rub( ) erases the window.
6. Member function sketch( ) is defined outside the class organisation using the scope resolution operator (::).
7. The screen is cleared and a default window is drawn for a given width and height. The borderline colour used is specified as LIGHTBLUE.

8. The first for-loop draws top and bottom horizontal lines.
   Lines are double line, since ASCII 205 implies horizontal double line. (=).
9. The second for-loop draws the left and right vertical lines and also inserts appropriate links at the corners, by double lines.
10. cputs( ) writes appropriate text into the window. The text colour is LIGHTBLUE.
11. The main( ) function defines 2 objects e and c. e uses default window setting of the no argument constructor. c is the other object which specifies its own coordinates which is the top left area of the screen.
12. The two texts are stored in e.tx and c.tx.
13. The e and c objects then invoke member function to draw the window, write text into it, erase and prepare the screen for a new display.
14. The output is shown with window coordinates also marked. These are the authors insertion and do not appear on the screen.

Aside

1. gotoxy( ) Position cursor within text window at coordinates specified.
2. putch( ) Display 1 character at cursor position.
3. textcolour( ) Specifies color mode of text within window

   Text mode colors are as follows:

0 - black	1 - blue	2 - green	3 - cyan
4 - red	5 - magenta	6 - brown	7- lightgray
8 - darkgray	9 - lightblue	10- lightgreen	11 - lightcyan
12 - lightred	13 - lightmagenta	14 - yellow	15 - white

   high video( ) - turns on high instensity

   norm video( ) - restores original intensity

It is possible to draw windows within windows by appropriately furnishing the coordinates. The inner window has dimensions smaller than the outer window, say for example:

```
window (l, t, r, b + 1);
window (l + 2, t + 1, r - 2, b - 3);
```

Text mode enables addressing 2000 locations (80 x 25).

12.2 GRAPHICS FUNCTIONS

In graphics mode individual pixels can be addressed i.e. 640 x 480 in VGA or EGA mode. The following programs generates 5 rings slightly shifted from each other.

```
//ringd.cpp
# include<graphics.h>
# include<conio.h>
```

```
const int R = 20;
   class ring
   {
private:
   int xcent, ycent;
public:
   ring ( )
       { xcent = 0; ycent = 0; } //no arg constructor
   void init (int xc, int yc)
       { xcent=xc; ycent=yc; }
       void sketch ( )
           { circle (xcent, ycent, R); }
   };
void main ( )
   {
   int drv, mo;
   drv=DETECT;                    //best graphics mode
   initgraph (&drv, &mo, "\\tc\\bgi");
   ring r1; ring r2; ring r3; ring r4; ring r5;
   r1.init (100, 180);
   r2.init (150, 150);
   r3.init (200, 180);
   r4.init (250, 150);
   r5.init (300, 180);
   r1.sketch ( ); r2.sketch ( ); r3.sketch( );
   r4.sketch ( ); r5.sketch ( );
   getch ( );
   closegraph ( );
   }
```

The output is :

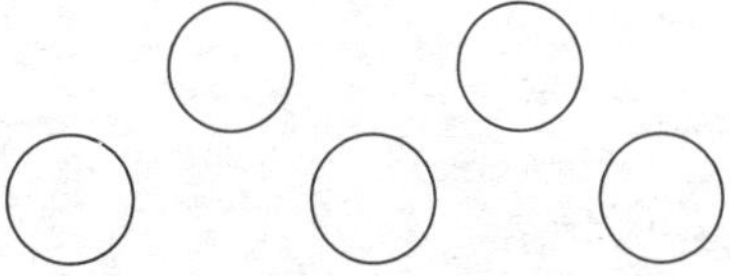

Analysis

1. Including graphics.h header file enable using all graphic functions such as initgraph( ), closegraph( ), circle( ).
2. The 2-argument constructor sets the centre coordinates for the circle.

3. The sketch( ) function draws the circle at the centre specified by 2 arg constructor with radius R.
4. The main( ) function actually sets the coordinates for centre of the circle and draws the 5 circles as depicted in the output above.

Observations

The graphic functions used in this program are initgraph( ), closegraph( ) and circle( ).

initgraph ( ) - prepares display system for graphics mode. drv = DETECT; enables the system to select its own best mode of graphic display. The programmer could also have given this information, so that the first 3 statements may as well be written as:

```
int drv = VGA;
int mo = VGHAI;
initgraph (&drv, &mo, "\\TC\\BGI");
```

There are three common display adapters:

GGA EGA VGA

Correspondingly each has an assortment of display modes. For details the student is referred to reference 1 in the References.

It is best to allow the system to decide the best display adapter and display mode. Using the address operator &, the address of these constants maybe given.

The third argument in initgraph( ) namely, "\\tc\\bgi" tells the path to graphics driver. Make sure bgi or BGI (Borland's graphics interface) files are available in the system. Or better copy them into your directory. Similarly sometimes graphics.h header file should be loaded by exercising OPTIONS menu.

closegraph( ) - restores system to video mode from text mode or graphics mode.

12.3 COLOUR OUTPUT

The next program gives colourful display for the rings that were generated in the previous program. The circles are drawn in yellow and each is filled up with different colours. Note that 3 rings are placed up and 2 down, which is slight deviation from earlier one.

```
//colring.cpp
# include<graphics.h>
# include<conio.h>
const int R=50;
class colring
  {
  private:
      int xcent, ycent;
      int lc; int fc;
```

```
    public:
        colring ( )
        {xcent=0; ycent=0: lc=WHITE; fc = WHITE; }
    void init (int xc, int yc, int lco, int fco)
        { xcent=xc; ycent=yc; lc=lco; fc=fco;)
    void sketch ( )
        {
        setcolor (lc);
        setlinestyle (SOLID_LINE,0, THICK_WIDTH);
        circle (xcent, ycent, R);
        setfillstyle (SOLID_FILL, fc):
        floodfill (xcent, ycent, lc):
        } };
void main( )
        {
    int drv, mo;
    drv = DETECT;
    initgraph (&drv,&mo, "\\tc\\bgi"); colring r1, r2, r3, r4,r5;
    r1.init (100, 150, YELLOW, RED);
    r2.init (150, 180, YELLOW, GREEN);
    r3.init (200, 150, YELLOW, BLUE);
    r4.init (250, 180, YELLOW, LIGHTBLUE);
    r5.init (300, 150, YELLOW, BROWN);
    r1.sketch ( ); r2.sketch ( ); r3.sketch ( );
    r4.sketch ( ); r5.sketch ( );
    getch ( ); closegraph( );
    }
```

The output is :

Observations

Let's examine closely some of the graphic functions used in the above program. These are:

```
setcolor ( )        setlinestyle ( )
setfillstyle ( )    floodfill ( )
```

setcolor( ) - sets colour of outlines used in drawing circles, rectangles, lines etc. 16 colour options are available for EGA/VGA similar to textcolor( ) function.

setlinestyle( ) - specifies thickness of lines for circles. The following options of line styles are available for drawing lines:

```
    0 - SOLID_LINE       1 - DOTTED_LINE
    2 - CENTER_LINE      3 - DASHED_LINE
    4 - USERBIT_LINE
setlinestyle (SOLID_LINE, 0, THICK_WIDTH
                             |       |
                             |       |
                     user-defined    |
                         style,0     3-pixel width
Linewidth options are:
    0 - NORM WIDTH 3 - THICK_WIDTH
    (1 pixel default)
    setfillstyle ( ) - fill interior of figures/shapes
                setfill style (SOLID_FILL, color);
                         |                  |
                         |                  |
            to fill whole space - same option as
        inside figure              setcolor ( )
floodfill ( ) -  fill interior of circles. Color and pattern
                 specified by setfillstyle. Expands from x, y
                 coordinates of centre of circle and goes outwards.
                 floodfill (x, y, colour);
                 This function fails with EGA monitor.
                 Therefore make sure VGA monitor is used.
```

There are a total of 12 patterns of which SOLID_FILL is the second. The other are listed for sake of completion. But for other details reader may refer to reference 1 in the References.

```
EMPTY_FILL        SOLID_FILL        LINE_FILL
LTSLASH_FILL      SLASH_FILL        BKSLASH_FILL
LTBKSLASH_FILL    HATCH_FILL        XHATCH_FILL
INTELEAVE-FILL    WIDE_DOT_FILL     CLOSE_DOT_FILL
USER_FILL
```

12.4 STRAIGHT LINE SHAPES

The next program draws rectangles and lines. The functions that help to draw them are rectangle ( ) and line ( ) with appropriate coordinate specifications.

```
rectangle (left, top, right, bottom);
                                        //edges specified
line (x1, y1, x2, y2);                  //start & end
                                        //coordinates given
//boxdiag.cpp
#include<graphics.h>
#include<conio.h>
const int w = 25;
class box
   {
   private:
       int xcent, ycent;
       int lc; int fc;
   public:
   box ( )
       {xcent=0; ycent=0;lc=WHITE; fc=WHITE;}
   void init (int x, int y, int l, int f)
       {xcent=x; ycent=y; lc=l; fc=f;}
   void sketch ( )
       {
       setcolor ( lc);
       setlinestyle (SOLID_LINE, 0, THICK_WIDTH);
       rectangle (xcent-w, ycent-w,xcent+w, ycent+w);
       setfillstyle (SOLID_FILL, fc);
       floodfill (xcent, ycent, lc);
       line (xcent-w, ycent-w, xcent+w, ycent+w);
       }
   };
void main ( )
   {
   int drv, mo;
   drv=DETECT;
   initgraph (&drv, & mo, ""\\tc\\bgi");
   box b1; box b2; box b3; box b4; box b5;
```

```
b1.init (100, 100, YELLOW, GREEN);
b2.init (100, 150, YELLOW, LIGHTBLUE);
b3.init (100, 150, YELLOW, LIGHTGREEN);
b4.init (50, 150, YELLOW, CYAN);
b5.init (150, 150, YELLOW, RED); ;
b1.sketch ( ); b2.sketch ( ); b3.sketch ( );
b4.sketch ( ); b5.sketch ( );
getch ( ); closegraph ( );
}
```

The output is:

12.5 DERIVED CLASSES FOR POLYGONS

This section illustrates the concept of derived class or inheritance, to display assorted shapes like a ring, box and triangle, each in different colour.

The following descriptions pertain to the program to follow.

"figure" is the base class.

Other classes like "triang", "box" and "ring" are derived from this base class "figure".

Thus it is said that the derived classes inherit the right to access the member functions of the base class "figure".

In the following program which shows these concepts, the only new function is:

```
fillpoly ( 3, tridet );
```

This is for drawing the triangle. The first argument 3 specifies the 3 coordinates where the triangle is located. The next argument "tridet" specifies the address of the array.

Similarly fillpoly( ) function can be used to draw any shape such as square, rectangle, hexagon, etc, provided the array contain relevant coordinates from start to end point.

Suppose it is required to draw a hexagon like:

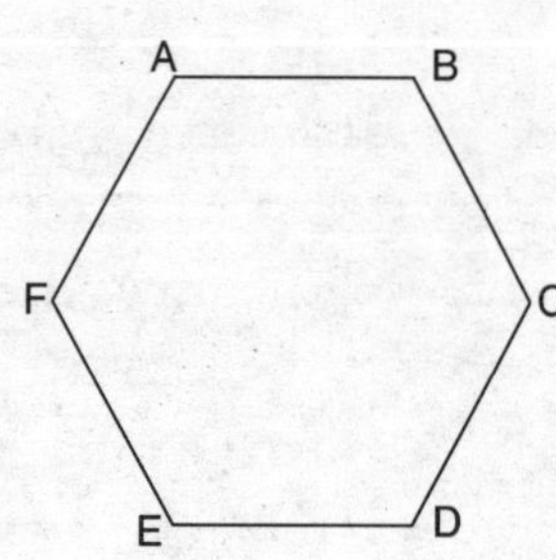

Then the function to do this can be stated as

```
fillpoly (6, hexarray);
```

where 6 specifies the six corners of the hexagon. "hexarray" is the address of an array which gives the x-y coordinates for points A, B, C, D, E, F.

The hexagon will be drawn starting from the first point, proceed to the second, then to the third and so on, until the whole figure is drawn. The path followed will be:

```
A -> B -> C -> D -> E -> F
```

```
//assort.cpp
# include<graphics.h>
# include<conio.h>
const int W = 58; //58 pixels
class figure
     {
     protected:
          int xcent, ycent;
          int lc; int fc;
   public:
     figure ( )
          {xcent=0; ycent=0; lc=WHITE; fc=WHITE;)
     void init (int x, int y, int 1, int f)
          {xcent=x; ycent=y; lc=1; fc=f;}
     void sketch ( )
     {
     setcolor (lc);
     setlinestyle (SOLID_WIDTH, 0 , THICK_WIDTH);
     setfillstyle (SOLID_FILL, fc);
     }
   };
class triang : public figure
   {
   public:
     triang ( ) : figure ( ) {          }
     void init (int x, int y, int 1, int f)
          {figure: :init (x, y, 1, f );}
     void sketch ( )
          {
          int tridet [ ] = { xcent, ycent - W,
                                      xcent + W, ycent + W,
                                      xcent- W, ycent +W };
          figure: :sketch ( );
```

```
            fillpoly (3, tridet);
        }
    };
class box: public figure
    {
    public:
        box ( ) : figure ( ) {   }
        void init (int x, int y, int 1, int f)
             {figure: :init (x, y, 1, f);}
        void sketch ( )
            {
            figure: : sketch ( );
            rectangle ( xcent-W, ycent-W, xcent +W, ycent +W);
            floodfill (xcent, ycent, 1c);
            moveto (xcent-W, ycent +W);
            lineto (xcent-W, ycent-W);
            }
    };
class ring:public figure
    {
    public:
        ring ( ) : figure ( ) {   }
        void init (int x, int y, int 1, int f)
            {figure : : init (x, y, 1, f); }
        void sketch ( )
            {
                figure: :sketch ( );
                circle (xcent, ycent, W);
                floodfill (xcent, ycent, 1c):
            }
    };
void main ( )
    {
    char ch;
    int drv, mo;
    drv=DETECT;
    initgraph (& drv, & mo, "\\tc\\bgi");
    ring r1; box b1; triang t1;
```

```
ring r2; box b2; triang t2;
r1.init (150, 119,YELLOW, RED );
b1.init (175, 240, YELLOW, GREEN);
t1.init (250, 100, YELLOW, BLUE);
r2.init (150, 160, YELLOW, BROWN);
b2.init (125, 160, YELLOW, CYAN);
t2.init (350, 130, YELLOW, WHITE);
r1.sketch ( ); b1.sketch ( ) ; t1.sketch ( );
r2.sketch ( ); b2.sketch ( ); t2.sketch ( );
getch ( ); closegraph ( );
}
```

The output is:

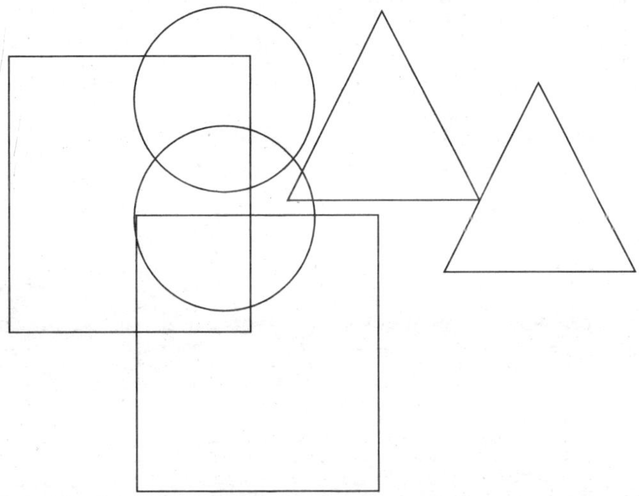

12.6 ANIMATED SHAPES

The program in this section creates 3 windows with a slot in each. The colour of each slot keep changing in random fashion and accompanied by sound. The windows are arranged vertically. Finally when the program stops each slot may have some random colour.

The program is designed with several derived classes and derived-derived classes (interitance of inherited class)

"figure" is the base class.

"ring", "box", "cone", "nonent", "round" are all derived from "figure".

"neem", "wine" are derived from "ring", "nonent";

"eqside" is derived from "box", "nonent".

"soilcone" is derived from "cone", "nonent"

"round" is defined outside round class, using scope resolution operator.

Some C++ library functions are unique to this program.

They are:

sound( ) delay( ) nosound( )

sound( ) turns ON and sets sound generator to specified frequency in cycles/sec.

nosound( ) turns OFF the sound generator.

delay( ) determines time duration of sound generator.

It takes time in milliseconds as argument.

The output is shown at the end of the program. During a particular run, the slots had the colours indicated. For another run, the colours may be different, varying among red, blue or yellow.

```
//sonetlum.cpp
#include<graphics.h>
#include<stdlib.h>                  // rand ( ), ramdomize ( )
#include<time.h>
#include<conio.h>
#include<dos.h>                     //delay (0, sound( ),
                                //nosound ( )
const int W = 25;
const int M = 20;
   class figure
   {
   protected:
       int xcent; int ycent; int 1c; int fc;
   public:
       figure ( ){ xcent=0;ycent=0;fc=WHITE; 1c=WHITE; }
   void init (int x, int y, int 1, int f)
       {xcent=x; ycent=y; 1c=1; fc=f; }
   void sketch ( )
       {
       setcolor (1c);
       setfillstyle (SOLID_FILL, fc);
   };
class ring : public figure
   {
```

```
    public:
        ring ( ) : figure ( ) { }
        void init (int x, int y, int 1, int f)
            { figure: :init (x, y, 1, f); }
        void sketch ( )
            {
            figure: :sketch ( );
            circle (xcent, ycent, W);
            floodfill (xcent, ycent, 1c);
            }
        };
class box : public figure
    {
    public:
        box ( ) : figure ( ) { }
        void init (int x, int y, int 1, int f)
            {figure: :init (x, y, 1, f); }
        void sketch ( )
        {
        figure: :sketch ( );
        rectangle (xcent-W, ycent-W, xcent+W, ycent+W);
        floodfill (xcent, ycent, 1c);
        moveto (xcent-W, ycent+W);
        lineto (xcent+W, ycent-W);
        }
    };
class cone : public figure
    {
    public:
        cone ( ):figure( ) { }
        void init (int x, int y, int 1, int f )
            {figure: :init (x, y, 1, f); }
        void sketch ( )
            {int conearr [ ] = { xcent, ycent-W,
                                 xcent+W, ycent+W,
                                 xcent-W, ycent+W };
            figure: :sketch( );
```

```
            fillpoly (3, conearr);
            }
        };
class nonent : public figure
    {
    public :
        void rub ( )
            {
            int bound [ ] =
            {   xcent-W-M, ycent-W-M,
                xcent+W+M, ycent-W-M.
                xcent+W+M, ycent+W+M,
                xcent-W-M, ycent+W+M };
            setfillstyle (SOLID_FILL, DARKGRAY);
            fillpoly (4, bound);
            }
        };
class neem : public ring, public nonent
    {
    public:
        neem ( ) : ring ( ) { }
    void init ( int x, int y)
        {
        ring: :init (x, y, WHITE, RED);
        nonent: :init (x, y, WHITE, RED);
        }
    void sketch ( )
        {rub ( ); ring: :sketch ( ); }
    };
class wine : public ring, public nonent
    {
    public:
        wine ( ) : ring ( ) { }
        void init (int x, int y)
        {
        ring: : init (x, y, WHITE, YELLOW);
    nonent: :init (x, y, WHITE, YELLOW);
        }
```

```
void sketch ( )
   {rub ( ); ring: :sketch ( ); }
   };
class eqside : public box, public nonent
   {
   public:
   eqside ( ) : box ( ) {       }
   void init (int x, int y )
       {
       box: : init (x, y, WHITE, GREEN);
       nonent: :init (x, y, WHITE, GREEN);
       }
   void sketch ( )
       { rub ( ) ; box: :sketch ( ); }
   };
class solcone : public cone, public nonent
       {
       public:
           solcone ( ) : cone ( ) { }
       void init (int x, int y)
           {
       cone: :init (x, y, WHITE, GREEN);
       nonent: :init (x, y, WHITE, GREEN);
       }
   void sketch( )
       { rub ( ); cone: :sketch ( ); }
   };
class round : public figure
   {
   private:
       neem nm; wine wi; eqside eq; solcone so;
   public:
       round ( ) { xcent = 0; ycent = 0; }
       void init (int x, int y)
       xcent = x; ycent = y;
       nm.init (xcent, ycent);
       wi.init (xcent, ycent);
```

```
        eq.init (xcent, ycent);
        so.init (xcent, ycent);
        }
    void sketch ( );
    };
void round : sketch ( )
    {
    setcolor (WHITE);
    rectangle (xcent-W-M, ycent-W-M,xcent+W+M,
        ycent+W+M);
    switch (random (4))
        {
        case 0: nm.sketch ( ); break;
        case 1: wi.sketch ( ); break;
        case 2: eq.sketch ( ); break;
        case 3: so.sketch ( ); break;
        }
    };
void main( )
    {
    const int N=20:
    int drv, mo;
    drv=DETECT;
    initgraph (&drv, &mo, "\\tc\\bgi");
    randomize ( );
    round r1, r2, r3;
    r1.init (320, 50);
    r2.init (320, 150);
    r3.init (320, 250);
    for (int k=0; k<N; k++)
        {
        r2. sketch ( ); r3.sketch( );
        r1. sketch ( );
        sound (125); delay (25); nosound ( );
        }
    getch ( );
    closegraph ( );
    }
```

The output is:

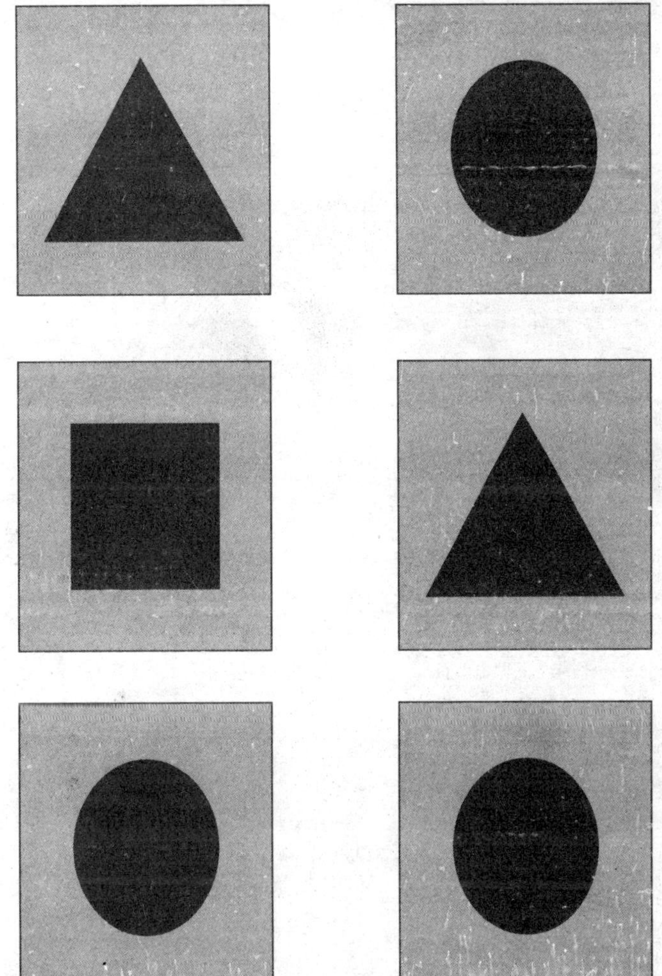

12.7 TEXT IN GRAPHICS MODE

Generating text in graphics mode affords great flexibility. Height, width, size, direction, color, font and style of letter can be easily specified.

The program defines one class called textgraph with its private data and public functions.

Most parameters have default values set. Generally the BGI files and specific font files (CHR) must be included in the user directory to run this program successfully. This program uses the GOTHIC_FONT and DEFAULT_FONT only in sample runs.

Other options are discussed at the end of the program. The output is a text display "T.C.E" given in Gothic font and "Tirupparankundram" in default font. Due to large font size the second string goes out of the screen, and therefore only 10 characters are displayed.

```
//txtgrph.cpp
#include<graphics.h>
#include<conio.h>
#include<string.h>
   class txtgrph
   {
   private:
       char string [ 100 ]; int xcent, ycent;
       int font; int dir; int sz; int col;
       int hrj; int vrj;
       int mux, dx; int muy, dy;
   public:
       txtgrph ( )
           {
           string [0] = '0';
           xcent =0; ycent =0;
           font = GOTHIC_FONT;
           dir = HORIZ_DIR;
           sz = 6;
           col = YELLOW:
           hrj = LEFT_TEXT;
           vrj = TOP TEXT;
           mux = 1; dx = 1; muy = 1; dy = 1;
           }
       void sktxt ( )
           {
           moveto (xcent, ycent );
           settextstyle (font, dir, sz);
           setcolor (col);
           settextjustify (hrj, vrj);
           setusercharsize (mux, dx, muy, dy);
           outtext (string);
           }
       void stxt (char s [ ] )
           {strcpy (string, s); }
       void spos (int x, int y)
           {xcent = x; ycent = y; }
       void sfon (int f)
           {font = f;}
```

```
        void sdir (int d)
            {dir = d; }
        void ssz (int s)
            {sz = s;)
        void scol (int c)
            {col = c; }
        void shj (int h)
            {hrj =h; }
        void svj (int v)
            {vrj = v ;}
        void shs (int m, int d)
            {sz = 0; mux = m; dx =d;}
        void svs (int m, int d)
            {sz = 0; muy =m; dy =d;}
        };
    void main ( )
        {
        int drv, mo;
        drv=DETECT;
        initgraph (&drv, & mo, "\\tc\\bgi");
        txtgraph t1, t2;
        t1.stxt (" T.C.E.");
        t2.stxt ("Tirupparankundram");
        t1.sfon (DEFAULT_FONT);
        t2.spos (5, 90 );
        t1.sktxt ( );
        t2.sktxt ( );
        getch ( );
        closegraph ( );
        }
```

The output is:

T.C.E.

Tirupparankundram

Analysis

Note the five C++ library functions figuring in the program.

They are:

```
moveto ( )              settextstyle ( ) settextjustify ( )
setusercharsize ( ) outtext ( )
```

moveto( ) - sets cursor position to x, y coordinates furnished as arguments. Default position is upper left corner

settextstyle - sets font, direction and character size of letters. Font options available in TC or BC are:

```
DEFAULT_FONT     TRIPLEX_FONT SMALL_FONT
SANSERIF_FONT    GOTHIC_FONT
```

Appropriate font file must be present in the current working directory by specifying the path argument to initgraph ( ).

There are two directions like:

HORIZ_DIR   VERT_DIR

character size 1 smallest followed by 2, 3, 4, etc. Note 6 has been used in the above program.

settextjustify ( ) - specifies position with respect to cursor position, where text is displayed.

Horizontal justification:

LEFT_TEXT   CENTER_TEXT   RIGHT_TEXT

Vertical justification:

TOP_TEXT   CENTER_TEXT   BOTTOM_TEXT

setusercharsize ( ) - sets width and height of letters or characters. For this to be effective, size in settextstyle ( ) must be made 0, so that a default font size 4 is used.

Now 4 arguments used in this function are:

mux dx muy dy

Therefore width = (mux/dx) *4, height = (muy/dy)*4

outtext ( ) - This works like object cout or < < and displays the string furnished as argument.

REVIEW QUESTIONS

12.1 For graphic display what screen size is needed?

12.2 In which header file is library function window ( ) included?

12.3 What 4 arguments must be furnished in the window ( ) function?

12.4 What does getch ( ) function do ?

12.5 Which function writes text within a specified window area?

12.6 Which function positions cursor within text window ( )?

12.7 What is the ASCII code for horizontal double line (=)?

12.8 What is the ASCII code for symbol which is the corner character of a window?

12.9 Which function displays a single character at the cursor position?

12.10 Which function specifies the colour of text within window?

12.11 What number implies the text mode colour lightgreen?

12.12 Which function turns on high intensity?

12.13 How can you set the driver so that it selects the best mode for graphic display?

12.14 Which display mode has the highest resolution and how many colours are available?

12.15 How can you specify the outline colours of different figures like circle, lines, etc.?

12.16 What is the number of pixels when we specify THICK_WIDTH in setlinestyle ( )?

12.17 How do you specify a 1 pixel width for line width?

12.18 In what type of monitor will floodfill ( ) function work successfully?

12.19 How many arguments are specified to draw a rectangle?

12.20 How many arguments are specified to draw a straight line?

12.21 What number should be specified in setlinestyle ( ) to draw dashed line?

12.22 What function draws a triangle?

12.23 What should be the first numeric argument of fillpoly ( ) to draw a octagon?

12.24 Which function set the characteristics of letters such as font, direction and size?

12.25 Name the function which specifies the position with respect to cursor position?

12.26 Name the function which specifies the width and height of letter or characters?

12.27 What function causes strings to be displayed when furnished as arguments?

Answers

12.1 80 col x 25 rows

12.2 conio.h

12.3 left, top, right, bottom

12.4 awaits a key press

12.5 cputs ( )

12.6 gotoxy ( )

12.7 205

12.8 200

12.9 putch ( )

12.10 textcolor ( )

12.11 10

12.12 highvideo ( )

12.13 DETECT

12.14 640 x 480, 16 colours

12.15 setcolor ( )

12.16 3 pixels

12.17 NORM_WIDTH

12.18 VGA monitor

12.19 4

12.20 4

12.21 3

12.22 fillpoly ( )

12.23 8

12.24 settextsytle ( )

12.25 settextjustify ( )

12.26 setusercharsize ( )

12.27 outtext ( )

Chapter 13

Advanced Topics in C++

Chapter 13

Advanced Topics in C++

OBJECTIVE

This chapter discusses some non-essential but widely used features of C++. These features are virtual functions, friend functions, static functions, overloaded operator, copy constructor and "this" pointer. The advantage of studying these features is to gain more insight into C++ programming and may come in handy for some users.

KEYWORDS

virtual this static friend

13.1 INTRODUCTION TO VIRTUAL FUNCTIONS

A person lost in a vast hot desert becomes very thirsty. His mind begins to conjure up visions of date palms and plenty of fresh cool water. He walks towards this mental scenery called "mirage" and but does not appear to reach it. It recedes further away from him as he trudges towards it. Thus are virtual functions. A virtual function appears to exist but does not exist in reality.

A virtual function is defined and declared in the base class. It is then used by several derived functions by setting up pointers.

For example the best application of virtual function is found in graphics, where several shapes are to be drawn. Suppose it is required to sketch different figures like circle, rectangle, square, triangle etc., then a separate derived class can be defined containing member functions which generate these figures. Then a common sketch( ) function defined and declared as virtual function in the base class can be invoked to perform the sketching in the derived class.

All that is now required is to set up an array of pointers, and make each of these pointers point to a particular derived class. Then by means of the arrow operator, the object of the derived class can be associated with the sketch( ) function to draw the required figure.

One rule must however be adhered to. The pointers to objects of a derived class should be type-compatible with pointers to objects of the base class.

13.2 ILLUSTRATING VIRTUAL MEMBER FUNCTIONS

Before embarking on study of the concept of virtual function, let's briefly see what non-virtual function imply. A nonvirtual pointer set up in any derived class always points to the member function in a base class only. Whereas when virtual functions are defined, the virtual pointers point to member functions of the derived class.

The following notations are associated with virtual functions.

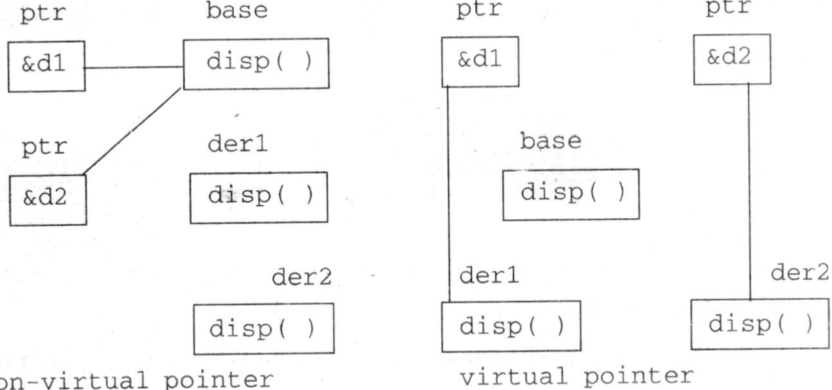

Now study the following program which uses virtual functions and virtual pointers to access the virtual function in the respective derived classes.

```
//virt.cpp
#include<iostream.h>
class base
   {
   public:
       virtual void disp ( )
       {cout <<"\n This is base";}
   };
class der1 : public base
   {
   public:
       void disp( )
           {cout <<"\nThis is der1"; }
   };
class der2 : public base
   {
```

```
    public:
    void disp( )
    { cout<<"\nThis is der2";}
};
void main( )
    {
    der1 d1; der2 d2; base* ptr;
    ptr = &d1; ptr->disp( );
    ptr = &d2; ptr->disp( );
    }
```

The output is:

This is der1
This is der2

Analysis

1. Two objects d1 and d2 are defined for derived class der1 and der2 respectively.
2. The pointer "ptr" belongs to the base class.
3. However the pointer "ptr" of base class maybe made to point to the object d1 or d2 of the derived class.
4. The pointer "ptr" can then be caused to execute disp( ) function defined in the respective derived classes.

13.3 BODYLESS VIRTUAL FUNCTION

A bodyless virtual function is otherwise called a pure virtual function. In the previous program the virtual function in base class has a body of its own as shown :

```
virtual void disp( )
    {cout <<"\nThis is base";}
```

This can be made a pure or bodyless virtual function by removing the statement within the curly braces and equating the declarative to zero as:

```
virtual void disp( ) = 0;
```

The following program illustrates the concept of pure or bodyless virtual function. It works exactly like the previous program with identical output.

```
//purevirt.cpp
#include<iostream.h>
class base
```

```
    {
    public:
        virtual void disp( ) = 0;\\pure virtual fn
    };
class der1 : public base
    {
    public:
        void disp( ) { cout <<"\nThis is der1"; }
    };
class der2 : public base
    {
    public:
        void disp( ) {cout <<"\nThis is der2"; }
    };
void main ( )
    {
    base* ptr[2]; //arry of pointers
    der1 d1; der2 d2; //objects to drived class
    ptr[0] = &d1; ptr [1] = &d2;
    ptr[0]->disp( ); ptr[1]->disp( );
    }
```

The output is:

This is der1
This is der2

13.4 GRAPHICS USING VIRTUAL FUNCTIONS

The following program defines sketch ( ) as a virtual function in base class. There are 3 derived classes called round, box and cone, which declare a circle, rectangle and triangle. Note that the fix( ) function, which fixes the coordinates of different shapes, is associated with each derived class by means of the scope resolution operator (::).

In the main( ) a pointer array, ptr [3], of 3 elements is defined. Each pointer points to an object of the derived class and is then used to invoke the sketch( ) function to sketch the figures.

By suitably choosing the coordinates, the following shape is displayed, by executing the program.

output of virtgrap. cpp program

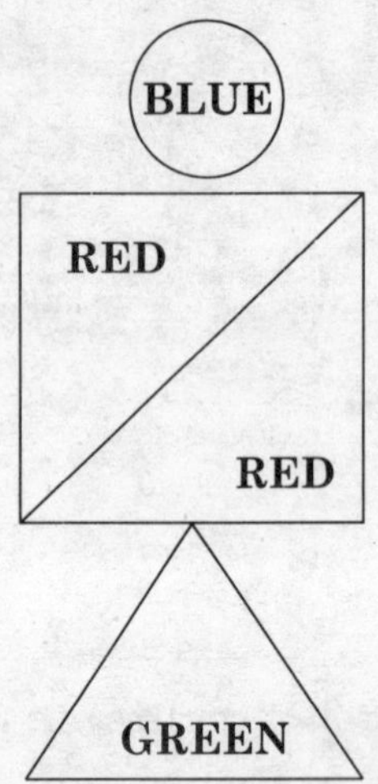


```
//virtgrap.cpp
#include<graphics.h>
#include<conio.h>
const int B = 50;
class base
   {
   protected:
       int xcent, ycent; int lc; int fc;
   public:
       base( )
           {xcent =0; ycent =0; lc=WHITE; fc=WHITE;}
       void fix(int h, int v, int l, int f)
           {xcent=h; ycent=v; lc=l; fc=f;}
       void paint
           {
           setcolor(lc);
           setlinestyle(SOLID_LINE,0, THICK_WIDTH);
           setfillstyle(SOLID_FILL, fc);
           virtual void sketch( ) = 0;
                                       //pure virtual fn
           }:
       class round : public base
       {
       public:
```

```
        round ( ) : base ( ) { }
        void fix (int h, int v, int 1,int f)
            {
            base: :fix(h, v, 1, f);}
        void sketch( )
            {
            paint ( ) ;
            circle(xcent, ycent, 1c);
            floodfill (xcent, ycent, 1c);
            }
    };
  class box:public base
    {
    public:
        box ( ) : base ( ) { }
        void fix(int h, int v, int 1, int f)
            {base : : fix(h, v, 1, f);}
        void sketch( )
        {
        paint( );
        rectangle (xcent-B, ycent - B,
            xcent+B, ycent+B) ;
        floodfill (xcent, ycent, 1c) ;
        moveto (xcent -B, ycent+B);
        lineto (xcent+B, ycent - B);
        }
    };
class cone : public base
   {
   public:
       cone ( ) : base ( ) {  }
void fix( int h, int v, int 1, int f )
   { base : : fix(h, v, 1, f  ); }
void sketch( )
   {
   paint ( );
   int conedet [ ] = { xcent, ycent - B,
                       xcent+B, ycent+B,
```

```
                              xcent -B, ycent+B };
        fillpoly (3, conedet );
        }
    };
void main ( )
    {
    int drv, mo;
    drv = DETECT;
    initgraph (&drv, &mo, "\\borlandc\\bgi");
    base* ptrmat[3];
    round r1; box b1; cone c1;
    r1.fix(100, 100, WHITE, BLUE );
    b1.fix(100, 200, WHITE RED );
    c1.fix(100, 300, WHITE, GREEN );
    ptrmat[0] = &r1;
    ptrmat[1] = &b1;
    ptrmat[2] = &c1;
        for(int k=0; k<3; k++ )
            ptrmat[k] ->sketch ( );
    getch( );
    closegraph( );
    }
```

Caution

The above program demands that all .bgi (.BGI) files and graphics header files be included in the current working directory. In such case find the path for. bgi files and copy them in the current working directory. In case error message appears about initgraph( ) function, then select OPTIONS menu and set the graphics mode by entering "X" against it. The above guidelines are exercised only if the include < > directive fail.

13.5 FRIEND FUNCTIONS

Friend functions tend to violate ideas of encapsulation and data hiding, by permitting unrestricted access to private and protected data. Use of friend function should be done only in unavoidable circumstances and not as a general practice.

Friend functions can operate on objects of totally different and unrelated classes. The following program shows its use.

```
//friend.cpp
#include<iostream.h>
   class curr
   {
   private:
       float rupees;
public:
   curr( ) {rupees = 0.0;}
   curr(float rs) {rupees = rs;}
   void disp ( ) {cout<<"Rs."<<rupees; }
   friend curr operator + (curr c1, curr c2)
       {
       float r = c1.rupees + c2.rupees;
       return curr(r) ;
       }
   };
void main( )
   {
   curr c1 = 123.45; curr c2 = 234.56;
   curr c3;,
   cout <<"\nAmt1 = "; c1.disp( );
   cout <<"\nAmt2 = "; c2.disp( );
   c3 = c1 + c2 ;
   cout<<"\nAmt+3 =";
   c3.disp ( ) ;
   }
```

The output is:

```
Amt1 = Rs. 123.449997
Amt2 = Rs.234:559998
Amt3 = Rs.358.01001
```

Observations

The friend function overloads the + sign, so that it is able to accept two objects as simple arguments and perform addition on them.

In order to complete the discussion of friend function, one more example is given.

```
//message.cp
#include<iostream.h>
class base
   {
   private:
       char* mess1;
   public:
       base( ) { mess1 = "Hello"; }
       friend class derv;
   };
class derv
   {
   public:
       void str1(base b) {cout <<"\nMess1
       is "<<b.mess1; }
       void str2 (base b) {cout<<"\nMess2 is "<<
           "<<b.mess1; }
   };
void main( )
   {
   base b; derv d;
   d.str1(b) ; d.str2(b) ;
   }
```

The output is:

Mess1 is Hello
Mess2 is Hello

Observation

Here class "derv" is made a friend of class "base", so that it is able to access the private data of class "base".

13.6 ASSIGNMENT AND DUPLICATION

If two objects are associated by the assignment operator (=), then data of one object is copied, member-by-member, into the other. An example of assignment is:

```
d1 = d2;
```

data of d1 is copied member-by-member into d2. Similarly a statement such as:

```
madurai m3 (m1 ) ;
```

creates an object m3 and initializes each member of m1 into corresponding member of m3. This is a process of duplication. This is also known as copy constructor.

What are shown above are the default operations performed by the assignment operator and the process of duplication. However, it is possible to overload the assignment operator to perform complex tasks.

The following program overloads the assignment (=) operator:

```
//overequ.cpp
#include<iostream.h>
   class madurai
   {
   private:
       int inform;
   public:
       madurai( ) { }
       madurai(int i) {inform = i;}
       void output( ) { cout <<inform;}
       madurai operator=(madurai& m)
                               //overloading
       {
       inform = m.inform;
       cout<<"\n= sign is called here";
       return madurai(inform) ;
                               //return copy of madurai
       }
   };
void main( )
   {
   madurai m1(99); madurai m2;
   m2 = m1;                    //= sign invoked
   cout << "\n value m2 = "; m2.output( );
   madurai m3 = m2; // copy initialization
   cout<<"\nValue m3 = "; m3.output( );
   }
The output is:
= sign is called here
value m2 = 99
value m3 = 99
```

Observations

Note the assignment done on objects by using = operator.

m2 = m1;

This invoked the overloaded = operator; value of m1 assigned to m2.

Whereas duplication or copy initialization is done for:

madurai m3 = m2;

or

madurai m3(m2);

Note that a member data maybe copied from one object to another due to the overloaded = operator as

inform = m.inform;

where "inform" is the lone member data.

Argument to operator = ( ) is passed by reference which results in saving of memory. Whereas passing by value would have resulted in wastage of memory.

Similarly returning by reference conserves memory. It returns only the address of the data being returned.

13.7 DUPLICATION OR COPY CONSTRUCTOR OVERLOADED

By overloading the duplicator or copy constructor, it is possible to create new objects and perform member-by-member copying from one object to another.

The following program shows this feature.

```
//overeqq.cpp
#include<iostream.h>
class madurai
   {
   private:
       int inform;
   public:
       madurai( ) { }
       madurai(int i) { inform = i; }
       madurai(madurai& m)
          {
          inform = m.inform;
          cout< <"\nDuplicating feature called";
          }
       void output( ) { cout < <inform; }
```

```
    void operator = (madurai& m )
        {
        inform = m.inform;
        cout<<"\n = sign called";
        }
    };
void main( )
    {
    madurai m1 (99);
    madurai m2;
    m2 = m1;          //overloaded = sign invoked
    cout< <"\nValue m2 ="; m2.output ( );
    madurai m3(m2);           //duplicator invoked
    cout< <"\nValue m3 = "; m3.output( );
    }
```

The output is:

= sign is called
Value m2 = 99
Duplicating feature called
Value m3 = 99

Observations

The copy constructor

```
madurai (madurai& m)
```

takes one argument, which is passed by reference.

The statements

```
madurai m3(m1); or madurai m3 = m1;
```

are both different forms of the copy constructor.

13.8 POINTERS TO STRING CLASS

By using pointers to string class, it is possible to save memory usage. The following program has provision to keep count of the number of pointers to a string. Any number of pointers maybe caused to point to a string. This number is stored in a object of a new separate class, as is shown in the following program.

```
//stringcl.cpp
#include<iostream.h>
#include<string.h>
class number            //counts unique string
   {
   private:
       int numb; char* rope;
       friend class thread;         //friend function
   public:
       number(char*n )              //constructor
       {
       int l = strlen (n) ;
       rope = new char[l + 1];
                                    //allocate memory
       strcpy(rope, n) ;
       numb = 1;                    //set count to 1
       }
       number ( ) {delete rope ; }
   } ;
class thread
   {
   private:
       number* ptr;             //pointer to number
   public:
       thread ( ) (ptr= new number("NULL");}
       thread(char* r) {ptr new number(r); }
                                //constructor
       thread (thread& t)
           {
           ptr = t.ptr;
           (ptr->numb)++;
           }
           ~thread( )           //destructor
           {
           if(ptr->numb==1)
               delete ptr;
           else
               (ptr->numb)--;
```

```
        }
    void output ( )
        {
        cout< <ptr->rope;
        cout< <"(location = "< <ptr< < ")";
        }
    void operator = (thread& t)
                                    //assign string
        {
        delete ptr;
        ptr = t.ptr;
        (ptr ->numb)++;
        }
    };
void main( )
    {
    thread t3 = "\nLook upon God,\
    when man lets down. ";
    t3.output( );
    thread t1;
    t1 = t3;
    t1.output( );         //output after
                          //assignment
    thread t2(t3);  //copy constructor
    t2.output ( ) ;
    }
```

The output is:

Look upon God, when man lets down. (location = 0x04d150d1e)
Look upon God, when man lets down. (location = 0x4d150d1e)
Look upon God, when man lets down. (location = 0x4d150d1e)

Observations

Three objects called t1, t2 and t3 are set up for "thread". t3 contains the string

`"Look upon God, when man lets down".`

Then the assignment operator (=) is invoked to assign contents of t3 to t1. Thereafter the copy constructor is invoked to copy the contents of t3 to t2.

The number class has the pointer n, which keeps count of class objects to the string. The constructor accepts n as argument and sets up memory for the string. Then it copies the string in this memory and set numb to 1. Thereafter the destructor releases the memory allocated earlier.

The thread class has 3 constructors. These have provision to set up new objects when new strings are created and also keep count of such objects which point to each string area.

13.9 "this" POINTER

"this" is a pointer to an object of extraordinary capability. It points to the object itself. Using "this" any member function can find out the address of an object of which it is a member.

Accessing member data with "this" pointer is quite common and easy. However in the ensuing program it is shown how to return value using "this" pointer. This enables returning by reference an object of which a function is a member.

```
//this.cpp
#include<iostream.h>
class madurai
  {
  private:
      int inform:
  public:
      madurai( ) { }
      madurai(int i) { inform = i; }
      void output( ) { cout << inform; }
      madurai& operator = ( madurai& m)
         {
         inform = m.inform ;
         cout<<"\n=sign operator called here";
      return *this; //returns copy of madurai
      }
  };
void main ( )
  {
  madurai m1(99);
  madurai m2, m3;
  m3 = m2 = m1; //invokes overloaded=sign
  cout < <" \nValue m2 = "; m2.output ( ) ;
  cout < <"\nValue m3 ="; m3.output ( );
  }
```

The output is:

```
= sign operator called here
= sign operator called here
Value m2 = 99
Value m3 = 99
```

Observations

The declaration

```
madurai& operator = (madurai& m)
```

enables return by reference, unlike the declaration

```
madurai operator = (madurai& m)
```

which returns by value. Thus

```
return *this;
```

points to the object, and therefore is said to return by reference.

13.10 STATIC FUNCTIONS

It has already been seen that member data item is shared or accessed by all objects of a class. In the following section it is shown what static function imply.

A static member function can easily access a static member data by using the class name. The following program shows the organisation of the statements, involving static member data and static function.

```
//static.cpp
#include<iostream.h>
class stat
  {
  private:
      static int n;
  public:
      stat ( ) { n++; }  //constructor without arg
      stat( ) {n--; }
      static void disp( )
          {cout < < n; }
  } ;
int stat: :n=0;
void main ( )
  {
```

```
    stat: : disp ( );
            //invoking static data by static fn
    }
```

The lone statement in main ( ) accesses the entire class. Note that the static function disp( ) is accessed by using only the class name "stat" associated with the scope resolution operator(::).

Static variable must be initialized before main( ) using scope resolution operator (::) to avoid linker error.

REVIEW QUESTIONS

13.1 In which class should a virtual function be declared and defined?

13.2 How can a derived function use a virtual function?

13.3 Should a dot or an arrow operator be associated with the object of a derived function to invoke a member function?

13.4 What rule should pointers to objects of derived class satisfy with respect to pointers to objects of base class?

13.5 Can nontrivial pointers point to member functions of a derived class?

13.6 What type of pointers can be made to point to member functions of derived class?

13.7 Can a virtual function be declared in a derived class?

13.8 How can you indicate or declare a pure virtual function?

13.9 Which operator helps to invoke a member function of a base class in a derived class?

13.10 Which files must be present in your working directory to use initgraph function?

13.11 Do friend functions honour idea of encapsulation and data hiding?

13.12 What is the impact of relating two objects by the = sign?

13.13 What is the task involved in the following statement?

```
madurai m3 (m1) ;
```

13.14 Does this declaration return by value or by reference

```
madurai operator = (madurai & m)
```

13.15 Which uses up more memory? passing by value or passing by reference.

13.16 What does this statement do?

```
rope = new char (l + 1];?
```

13.17 How do you brand the following member function?

```
~thread ( ) {        }
```

13.18 "this" pointer returns by value or by reference?

Answers

13.1 base class

13.2 by a pointer

13.3 arrow operator

13.4 type compatible

13.5 no

13.6 virtual pointers

13.7 no, only in base class

13.8 setting declarative = 0

13.9 scope resolution operator

13.10 bgi or .h files

13.11 no

13.12 data copied member by member

13.13 initialization

13.14 by value

13.15 by value

13.16 set up l + 1 bytes of memory

13.17 destructor

13.18 by reference

Chapter 14

Exception Handling

Chapter 14

Exception Handling

Exception means out of the ordinary or deviating from the normal course. In using computer languages to solve problems, we come across many instances which are out of the ordinary or deviating from the normal course. These may cause the program to terminate abruptly or give wrong answers. Some such instances which may raise an exception are listed as follows:

- Trying to open a non existent file.
- Requesting more memory, when memory is short.
- Arithmetic operations which give unreasonable result, (eg) divide by zero.

There are many more instances which raise exceptions.

C++ has powerful mechanisms to handle such exceptions.

The keywords used in handling exceptions are try, throw and catch.

When we know that a particular action is likely to cause an exception, we put this statement within the try block. Within the same block, we can identify the exception and use the throw statement to throw it out of the try block to the catch block.

The catch block may be suitably devised to handle the exception or to overcome the exception. Thus the C++ language uses try, throw and catch keywords to handle exception.

We shall illustrate the use of these keywords by a very simple program. This program called "prog1.cpp" accepts two values called a and b. It tests whether a is greater than b, and if true, it creates an integer called k, and assigns 0 to it. If the test is false, that is, if a is not greater than b, then k is assigned 1. In the normal course, when a is greater than b, there is no exception, and the program runs to completion. On the other hand, when a is not greater than b, there is an exception, and the exception is thrown to the catch block. The catch block catches the exception and is made to deliver a message. Now study the program is detail.

```
//prog1.cpp
#include<iostream.h>
int main()
```

```
{
    int a,b;
    cout<<"Enter a, b values \n";
    cin>>a>>b;
    int k = a > b ? 0 : 1;
    try
        {
        if (k==0)
            cout<<"a > b by "<< a - b<<"\n";
        else
    throw(k);
    }
    catch(int j)
    {
        cout<<"Exception : since a !> b, j="<<j<<" is false \n";
    }
    return 0;
    }
```

The above program was compiled and run in Debian Linux environment. Students who are not familiar with Debian Linux may get a hands on practice before attempting to run these programs. You may also try Turbo C++ environment, if you have access to it. Alternatively the program may be compiled and run in any UNIX environment.

On running the program the following result is got.

```
hdcse:~# ./a.out
Enter a, b values
11 9
a > b by 2
hdcse:~# ./a.out
Enter a, b values
9 11
Exception : since a !> b, j=1 is false
hdcse:~#
```

That was a simple program using one try block and one catch block. We shall extend the program to include multiple catch blocks. The next program called 'prog2.cpp' illustrates the use of 3 catch blocks.

```
//prog2.cpp
#include<iostream.h>
void entry(int val)
{
   try
   {
       if(val > 0) throw 'c';
       else
   if(val < 0) throw .0;
       else
           if(val == 0) throw val;
   }
   catch(double f)
   {
       cout<<"Entry is negative \n";
   }
   catch(char d)
   {
       cout<<"Entry is a char value \n";
   }
   catch(int k)
   {
       cout<<"Entry is a pos value \n";
   }
}
int main()
{
   entry(6);
   entry(-7);
   entry(0);
   return 0;
}
```

The output of this program is:

```
hdcse:~# ./a.out
Entry is a char value
Entry is negative
Entry is a pos value
```

The above programs do not pose a challenge to C++ programmers. The real challenge lies in using the exception handling mechanism to handle sophisticated issues like stack overflow and stack underflow. The following program called 'prog3.cpp' illustrates how to handle stack overflow and underflow exceptions.

```
//prog3.cpp
#include<iostream.h>
#include<stdlib.h>
#include<string.h>
const int ST_SZ = 50;
class stack{
   public:
       stack(void);
       void push(const int val);
       int pop(void);
   protected:
       int c;
   private:
       int d[ST_SZ];
};
inline stack::stack(void)
{
   c = 0;
}
inline void stack::push(const int val)
{
   d[c] = val;
   c++;
   }

inline int stack::pop(void)
{
   c--;
   return (d[c]);
}

const int E_MSG = 60;
class limit_err{
```

```
    public:
        char cause[E_MSG];
        limit_err(char *_max) {
        if(strlen(_max) < (E_MSG -1))
            strcpy(cause, _max);
    else
        strcpy(cause, "error: _max is too large");
    }
};

class lim_stack: public stack {
    public:
        void push(const int val) throw(limit_err);
        int pop(void)throw(limit_err);
    };

inline void lim_stack::push(const int val) throw(limit_err)
{
    if(c >= ST_SZ) {
        limit_err overflow("Stack overflows");
        throw overflow;
        }
        stack::push(val);
    }

inline int lim_stack::pop(void) throw(limit_err)
{
    if(c <= 0) {
        throw limit_err("Stack underflows");
    }
    return(stack::pop());
}

lim_stack check;
void push_value(void) {
    int k;
    for(k = 0; k < 1000; k++) {
        check.push(k);
```

```
    }
}

main()
{
    try{
        push_value();
    }
    catch(limit_err &error) {
        cerr<<"Error: Stack limit exceeded\n";
        cerr<<"Cause: "<< error.cause<<"\n";
        exit(8);
    }
    catch(...) {
        cerr<<"Error: Unanticipated exception occurred\n";
        exit(8);
    }
    return 0;
}
```

This program gives an output as follows:

```
hdcse:~# ./a.out
Error: Stack limit exceeded
Cause: Stack overflows
```

That was quite a heavy dose to swallow. However one has somehow to bear with such twists occasionally. Next, to end up this chapter, let us dabble with some mathematical solution in 'prog4.cpp'..

```
//prog4.cpp
#include<iostream.h>
#include<math.h>
double harmonicmean(double x, double y) throw (const char *);
double geometricmean(double x, double y) throw (const char *);
int main()
{
    double a,b,c;
    cout<<"Enter values for a and b  \n";
    try{
```

```
        while(cin>>a>>b)
    {
        c = harmonicmean(a,b);
        cout<<"Harmonic mean of "<<a<<" and "<<b<<" is "<<c<<"\n";
            cout<<"Geometric mean of "<<a<<" and "<<b<<" is
                                        "<<geometricmean(a,b)<<"\n";
        cout<<"\nEnter next set a b values or q for quit \n";
    }
}
catch(const char * e)
    {
        cout<<e<<"\n";
        cout<<"Program terminated\n";
        }
    return 0;
}

double harmonicmean(double x, double y) throw(const char *)
{
    if(x == -y)
        throw "Harmonic mean cannot be evaluated\n ";
    return 2.0 * x * y /(x + y);
}
double geometricmean(double x, double y) throw(const char *)
{
    if(x < 0 || y < 0)
        throw "Geometric mean cannot be evaluated \n";
    return sqrt(x*y);
}
```

The output is as follows:

```
hdcse:~# ./a.out
Enter values for a and b
15 150
Harmonic mean of 15 and 150 is 27.2727
Geometricmean of 15 and 150 is 47.4342
Enter next set a b values or q for quit
15 -12
```

```
Harmonic mean of 15 and -12 is -120
Geometric mean cannot be evaluated
Program terminated
hdcse:~#
```

We could have terminated the program by typing q against the prompt. That should be sufficient to give a idea about how exceptions are handled in C++.

Chapter 15

Templates and Standard Template Library

Chapter 15

Templates and Standard Template Library

The dictionary meaning of template is,

"A pattern or gauge, such as a thin metal plate with a cut pattern, used as a guide in making something accurately, as in woodworking or the carving of architectural profiles."

In computer science we can define template as a document or file having a preset format, used as a starting point for a particular application so that the format does not have to be recreated each time it is used.

Templates are now a standard part of ANSI C++. Templates provide what is called Generic programming by defining Generic classes. Generic means belonging to a class or an entire group. When we say generic data types, it implies a variety of data types such as int,float, char, double. Thus a function that works for all C++ data types is called a generic function.

Templates enable the programmer to declare a group of functions or classes. For example we can create a template for a function called square(), which can evaluate the square of any data type such as int, float, long or double. Template for classes are called class templates and those for functions are called function templates.

Let us straightaway develop a program to learn the use of template. Our program sets up a function called maximum to determine the larger of two values, which may be integer, character, float, long. The program 'prog5.cpp' is given:

```
//prog5.cpp
#include<iostream.h>
#include<string.h>
template<class type>
type max(type d1, type d2) {
   if (d1 > d2)
       return (d1);
   return(d2);
```

```
}
char *max(char *d1, char *d2) {
    if(strcmp(d1,d2) > 0)
        return(d1);
    return(d2);
    }
main()
    {
    cout<<"max(3,7) " <<max(3,7) <<"\n";
    cout<<"max(7,3) " <<max(7,3) <<"\n";
    cout<<"max(\"ananthan\",\"baskaran\")"<<max
                                ("ananthan","baskaran")<<"\n";
    cout<<"max(\"baskaran\",\"ananthan\")
                                "<<max("baskaran","ananthan")<<"\n";
    return 0;
}
```

On running the program in debian linux environment it gives the following output:

```
hdcse:~# ./a.out
max(3,7) 7
max(7,3) 7
max(<<ananthan>>, <<baskaran>>) ananthan
max("baskaran","ananthan") ananthan
hdcse:~#
```

In the above program, we have used two types of data, namely int and char. The generic function did not specify the type of data. Whereas for handling string data we have to write a specific string function.

The next program 'prog6.cpp' uses a template to push a value onto the top of a stack, and then pop out the value from the top of the stack. Here again the template does not specify the particular data type.

```
#include<stdlib.h>
#include<iostream.h>
const int ST_SZ = 100;
template<class type>
class stack {
  private:
     int c;
```

```
    type d[ST_SZ];
  public:
    stack(void)
  {
      c =0;
    }
  void push(const type val)
{
     d[c] = val;
      ++c;
      }
  type pop()
  {
     --c;
     return(d[c]);
      }
  };
  int main()
  {
    stack<int> obj;
    obj.push(6);
    cout<<"A value has been pushed into stack;\n";
    int x=obj.pop();
    cout<<"value popped out is x = "<<x<<endl;
  }
```

The program gives an output as follows:

```
hdcse:~# ./a.out
A value has been pushed into stack;
value popped out is x = 6
hdcse:~#
```

One word of caution needs to be mentioned here. Though the function is generic, 'main' is designed to return an int. The student is encouraged to try other return types for the 'main'.

Before we take up the next program, let us be introduced to the Standard Template Library or the STL as it is popularly called. The STL is a collection of templates representing containers, iterators, function objects and algorithms.

Container is a data structure that holds a number of objects of the same type or class.

Algorithms are instructions to do certain tasks, such as sorting an array, finding a particular value in a list,etc.

Iterators are like pointers that enable one to move through an array.

Function objects act like functions; they can be either class objects or function pointers.

Thus using the STL we can construct an assortment of containers, including arrays, queues and lists. We can then perform various operations like searching, sorting and randomizing .

Now a word about the term vector. This term has nothing to do with the vector of mathematics. Instead the vector holds a set of indexes that enable us to access any element in an array randomly. It is possible to create a vector object, assign one vector object to another, and use the access operator [ ] to access any vector element.

Armed with these terminologies, now read through the program 'prog7.cpp' carefully and if possible, try to run it in the Debian Linux environment.

```
//prog7.cpp
#include<iostream.h>
#include<string.h>
#include<vector.h>
using namespace std;
const int GRAD = 4;
int main()
{
  vector<char> grades(GRAD);
  vector<string> names(GRAD);
  cout<<"Enter the names and grades(A to D) of\n"
      <<GRAD<<" students \n";

  int j;
  for(j=0; j< GRAD;j++)
    {
      cout<<"Enter student name "<<j+1<<":.";
      getline(cin,names[j]);
      cout<<"Enter the grade (A to D): ";
      cin>>grades[j];
      cin.get();
    }
  cout<<"The rank list is as follows:\n"
```

```
        <<"Grade\tStudent Name\n";
    for(j=0;j<GRAD;j++)
    {
      cout<<grades[j]<<"\t"<<names[j]<<endl;
    }
    return 0;
}
```

The program gives an output as follows:

```
hdcse:~#./a.out
Enter the names and grades(A to D) of
4 students
Enter student name 1:.ramar
Enter the grade (A to D): B
Enter student name 2:.sundar
Enter the grade (A to D): C
Enter student name 3:.arasu
Enter the grade (A to D): A
Enter student name 4:.baskar
Enter the grade (A to D): D
The rank list is as follows:
Grade  Student Name
B      ramar
C      sundar
A      arasu
D      baskar
hdcse:~#
```

The vector template that was illustrated above was a simple application. However it can do much more as we shall see in the next program. The STL containers have certain basic methods such as size(), swap(), begin() and end().

size() - returns the number of elements in a container.

swap() -exchanges contents of two containers.

begin() - returns a pointer (iterator) to the first element of the container.

end() - returns a pointer (iterator) to the last element of the container.

using namespace std;-

All the elements of the standard C++ library are declared within what is called a namespace, the namespace with the name *std*.

The next program 'prog8.cpp' uses all these features of the container:

```
//prog8.cpp
#include<iostream.h>
#include<string.h>
#include<vector.h>
using namespace std;
struct Assess {
  string name;
  int grade;
};
bool FAssess(Assess & dd);
void SAssess(const Assess & dd);
int main()
{
  vector<Assess> students;
  Assess temp;
  while(FAssess(temp))
    students.push back(temp);
  cout<<"The list is as follows:\n"
       <<"grade\tname\n";
  int num = students.size();
  for (int i=0;i<num;i++)
     SAssess(students[i]);
  cout<<"Reproducing:\n"
      <<"Ranking\tName\n";
  vector<Assess>::iterator pr;
  for(pr = students.begin(); pr != students.end(); pr++)
     SAssess(*pr);
  vector<Assess> oldlist(students);
  if(num > 3)
  {
     students.erase(students.begin()+1, students.begin()+3);
     cout<<"After deletion:\n";
     for(pr = students.begin(); pr != students.end(); pr++)
           SAssess(*pr);
     students.insert(students.begin(), oldlist.begin()+1,
           oldlist.begin()+2);
```

```
        cout<<"After addition:\n";
        for(pr = students.begin(); pr != students.end(); pr++)
            SAssess(*pr);
    }
    students.swap(oldlist);
    cout<<"Swapping oldlist with students:\n";
    for(pr = students.begin(); pr != students.end(); pr++)
        SAssess(*pr);
    return 0;
}
bool FAssess(Assess & dd)
{
    cout<<"Enter name of student (type 'q' for quit): ";
    getline(cin,dd.name);
    if(dd.name == "q")
        return false;
    cout<<"Enter student grade(1-10): ";
    cin>>dd.grade;
    if(!cin)
        return false;
    cin.get();
    return true;
}
 void SAssess(const Assess & dd)
{
    cout<<dd.grade<<"\t"<<dd.name<<endl;
}
```

The program gives as output as follows:

`hdcse:~# ./a.out`

Enter name of student (type 'q' for quit): raman

Enter student grade(1–10): 5

Enter name of student (type 'q' for quit): venkat

Enter student grade(1–10): 8

Enter name of student (type 'q' for quit): suruli

Enter student grade(1–10): 6

Enter name of student (type 'q' for quit): badri

Enter student grade(1–10): 7

Enter name of student (type 'q' for quit): q

The list is as follows:

grade	name
5	raman
8	venkat
6	suruli
7	badri

Reproducing:

Ranking	Name
5	raman
8	venkat
6	suruli
7	badri

After deletion:

5	raman
7	badri

After addition:

8	venkat
5	raman
7	badri

Swapping oldlist with students:

5	raman
8	venkat
6	suruli
7	badri

```
hdcse:~#
```

The above program is now shown with more functions such as sort and random shuffling. The program called 'prog9.cpp" is listed.

```
//prog9.cpp
#include<iostream.h>
#include<string.h>
#include<vector.h>
using namespace std;
struct Assess {
  string name;
  int grade;
```

```
};
bool operator<(const Assess & d1, const Assess & d2);
bool inferior(const Assess & d1, const Assess & d2);
bool FAssess(Assess & dd);
void SAssess(const Assess & dd);
int main()
{
  vector<Assess> students;
  Assess temp;
  while(FAssess(temp))
    students.push_back(temp);
  cout<<"The list is as follows:"
      << students.size() << "grade; \n"
       << "Grade\tname\n";
  for_each(students.begin(), students.end(), SAssess);
  sort(students.begin(), students.end());
  cout<<"Sorted by name:\nGrade\tname\n";
  for_each(students.begin(), students.end(), SAssess);
  sort(students.begin(),students.end(),inferior);
  cout<<"Sorted by grade\nGrade\tname\n";
  for_each(students.begin(), students.end(),SAssess);
  random_shuffle(students.begin(), students.end());
  cout<<"After scrambling:\nGrade\tname\n";
  for_each(students.begin(), students.end(), SAssess);
  cout<<"Bye!\n";
  return 0;
}
bool operator<(const Assess & d1, const Assess & d2)
{
   if(d1.name < d2.name)
       return true;
   else  if(d1.name == d2.name && d1.grade < d2.grade)
     return true;
   else
   return false;
}
```

```
bool inferior(const Assess & d1, const Assess & d2)
{
  if(d1.grade < d2.grade)
    return true;
  else
    return false;
}
bool FAssess(Assess & dd)
{
  cout<<"Enter name (q to quit): ";
  getline(cin,dd.name);
  if(dd.name  == "q")
    return false;
  cout<<"Enter grade: ";
  cin>> dd.grade;
  if(!cin)
    return false;
  cin.get();
  return true;
}
void SAssess(const Assess & dd)
{
  cout<<dd.grade <<"\t" << dd.name << endl;
}
```

This program gives as output as follows:

```
hdcse:~# ./a.out
Enter name (q to quit): ramar
Enter grade: 6
Enter name (q to quit): mohan
Enter grade: 9
Enter name (q to quit): arumugam
Enter grade: 4
Enter name (q to quit): john
Enter grade: 7
Enter name (q to quit): q
```

The list is as follows: 4grade;

Grade	name
6	ramar
9	mohan
4	arumugam
7	john

Sorted by name:

Grade	name
4	arumugam
7	john
9	mohan
6	ramar

Sorted by grade

Grade	name
4	arumugam
6	ramar
7	john
9	mohan

After scrambling:

Grade	name
6	ramar
4	arumugam
7	john
9	mohan

Bye!

hdcse:~#

That was a sample of what templates and STL could do. This is an ocean. We have not fathomed the depths sufficiently. The student is encouraged to use the Google search engine to know more about these features.

Additional Programs for testing

Sorting Strings

```
#include<iostream.h>
#include<conio.h>
#include<stdio.h>
#include<string.h>
```

```
#define MAX 5
#define ML 100
#define SIZE 100
class sortString
{
   public:
       char *lp[MAX];
       char buf[SIZE];
       char *acp;
   private:
       char *temp;
       char *p,sen[ML];
       int i,extr;
       int len,nl;
       int k,j;
   public:
       sortString()
       {
           acp=buf;
       }
       int read(char *lp[],int nl);
       void write(char *lp[],int nl);
       void qsort(char *lp[],int l,int r);
       int fetch(char st[],int high);
       char* alloc(int n);
       void swap(char *ar[],int m,int n);
};
int sortString::fetch(char st[],int high)
{
   for(j=0;j<high-1 && (k=getchar())!=EOF && k!='\n';++j)
   {
       st[j]=k;
   }
   if(k=='\n')
   {
       st[j]=k;
       ++j;
   }
```

```
    st[j]='\0';
    return j;
}
int sortString::read(char *lp[],int m1)
{
    while((len==fetch(sen,m1))>0)
        if(n1>=m1 || (p=alloc(len))==NULL)
            return -1;
        else
        {
            sen[len-1]='\0';
            strcpy(p,sen);
            lp[n1++]=p;
        }
    return m1;
}
char* sortString::alloc(int n)
{
    if(buf+SIZE-acp>=n)
    {
        acp+=n;
        return acp-n;
    }
    else
        return 0;
}
void sortString::write(char *lp[],int n1)
{
    cout<<"\nThe lines are arranged as follows\n";
    for(i=0;i<n1;i++)
        cout<<"\n"<<lp[i];
}
void sortString::qsort(char *ar[],int l,int r)
{
    if(l>=r)
        return;
    swap(ar,l,(l+r)/2);
    extr=l;
```

```
    for(i=i+1;i<=r;i++)
        if(strcmp(ar[i],ar[l])<0)
            swap(ar,++extr,i);
    swap(ar,l,extr);
    qsort(ar,l,extr-1);
    qsort(ar,extr+1,r);
}
void sortString::swap(char *ar[],int m,int n)
{
    temp=ar[m];
    ar[m]=ar[n];
    ar[n]=temp;
}
main()
{
    sortString st;
    int n1;
    cout<<"\nEnter only 5 Lines each < 100 Characters";
    cout<<"\nAfter 5th Line terminate by ^Z \n";
    if((n1=st.read(st.lp,MAX))>=0)
    {
        st.qsort(st.lp,0,n1-1);
        st.write(st.lp,n1);
        return 0;
    }
    else
    {
        cout<<"\nError : Large input not sortable\n";
        return 1;
    }
}
```

Output:

C:>1_SORTSTRING.exe

Enter only 5 lines each less than 100 characters

After 5th line terminate by ^Z

the quick

jumps over

```
brown fox
the
the lazy dog
^Z
The lines are arranged as follows:
brown fox jumps over lazy dog the the quick
```

Echoes the String

```
#include<iostream.h>
#include<conio.h>
#include <stdio.h>
#include <string.h>
#define MAX 500
class EchoString
{
   int k,j;
public:
   int fetch(char *line,int max);
};

int EchoString::fetch(char st[],int high)
{
   for(j=0;j<high-1 && (k=getchar())!=EOF && k!='\n';++j)
       st[j]=k;
   if(k=='\n')
   {
       st[j]=k;
       ++j;
   }
   st[j]='\0';
   return j;
}
main(int argc,char **argv)
{
   char line[MAX];
   long lineno=0;
   int c,except=0,number=0,found=0;
```

```
    EchoString f;
    while(--argc>0 && (*++argv)[0]=='-')
    {
        while(c=*++argv[0])
        {
            switch(c)
            {
                case 'x':
                    except=1;break;
                case 'n':
                    number=1;break;
                default:
                    cout<<"\nFind illegal option "<<c;
                    argc=0;
                    found=-1;
                    break;
            }
        }
    }
    if(argc!=1)
        cout<<"\nUsage : Find -x -n pattern \n";
    else
        while(f.fetch(line,MAX)>0)
        {
            lineno++;
            if((strstr(line,*argv)!=NULL)!=except)
            {
                if(number)
                    cout<<"\n"<<lineno;
                cout<<"\n"<<line;
                found++;
            }
        }
    return found;
}
```

Output

> EchoString.exe –x –n "the quick brown fox jumps over the lazy dog"
quick
fox
jumps
over
^Z
line:
1
quick
line:
2
fox
line:
3
jumps
line:
4
over

Count number of occurrence of file

```
#include <iostream.h>
#include <ctype.h>
#include <stdio.h>
#include <string.h>
#define MAX 100
#define NWORDS 12
struct Word
{
    char *word;
    int count;
};
struct Word wordtab[] =
{
   "ant",0,
   "bat",0,
```

```
    "cat",0,
    "dog",0,
    "elephant",0,
    "fox",0,
    "gorilla",0,
    "hyena",0,
    "jackal",0,
    "kangaroo",0,
    "lamb",0,
    "monkey",0
};
class CWord
{
    int chek,c;
    int min,max,cen;
    char *w;
public:
    char buf[100];
    int bufp;
public:
    CWord()
    {
        min=0;
        bufp=0;
    }
    int searchword(char *word,struct Word tab[],int n);
    int fetch(char *word,int lim);
    void ungetch(int c);
    int getch(void);
};
int CWord::searchword(char *word,Word tab[],int n)
{
    max=n-1;
    while(min<=max)
    {
        cen=(min+max)/2;
        if((chek=strcmp(word,tab[cen].word))<0)
            max=cen-1;
```

```
        else if (chek>0)
            min=cen+1;
        else
            return cen;
    }
    return -1;
}
int CWord::fetch(char *word,int lim)
{
    w=word;
    while(isspace(c=getch()));
    if(c!=EOF)
        *w++=c;
    if(!isalpha(c))
    {
        *w='\0';
        return c;
    }
    for(;--lim>0;w++)
      if(!isalnum(*w=getch()))
        {
            ungetch(*w);
            break;
        }
        *w='\0';
  return word[0];
}
int CWord::getch (void)
{
    return (bufp>0)?buf[--bufp]:getchar();
}
void CWord::ungetch(int c)
{
    if(bufp>=100)
        cout<<"ungetch too many chars\n";
    else
        buf[bufp++]=c;
```

```
}
main()
{
   int n;
   char word[MAX];
   CWord c;
    printf("Enter some words\n");
   fflush(stdout);
   while(c.fetch(word,MAX) !=EOF)
       if(isalpha(word[0]))
           if((n=c.searchword(word,wordtab,NWORDS))>=0)
               wordtab[n].count++;
   for (n=0;n<NWORDS;n++)
       if(wordtab[n].count >0)
           cout<<"Keywords:"<<wordtab[n].word<<" Occurs:
                            "<<wordtab[n].count<<" times";
   return 0;
}
```

Output

C:> 3_CountWord.exe

Enter some words

cat cat

^Z

Keywords:cat Occurs: 2 times

Displays number of times a phrase occurs in a string

```
#include <stdio.h>
#include <ctype.h>
#include <stdlib.h>
#include <string.h>
#include <iostream.h>
#define MAX 100
struct node
{
   char *phrase;
   int count;
```

```
    struct node *llink;
    struct node *rlink;
};

class NoPhrase
{
    int cond;
    int c;
    char *w;
public:
    struct node* addnode(struct node*,char *);
    void disp(struct node*);
    int fetch(char *,int);
    struct node* nalloc(void);
};

struct node* NoPhrase::addnode(struct node* p,char *w)
{
    if(p==NULL)
    {
        p=nalloc();
        p->phrase=strdup(w);
        p->count = 1;
        p->llink=p->rlink=NULL;
    }
    else if((cond=strcmp(w,p->phrase ))==0)
        p->count ++;
    else if(cond<0)
        p->llink = addnode(p->llink ,w);
    else
        p->rlink = addnode(p->rlink ,w);
    return p;
}
void NoPhrase::disp(struct node* p)
{
    if(p!=NULL)
    {
```

```
        disp(p->llink );
        if(p->count ==1)
            cout<<"the phrase "<<p->phrase<<" occurs once.\n";
        else
            cout<<"the phrase "<<p->phrase <<"occurs
                                        "<<p->count<<" times\n";
        disp(p->rlink );
    }
}
struct node* NoPhrase::nalloc()
{
    return (struct node*)malloc(sizeof(struct node));
}
int NoPhrase::fetch(char *phrase,int lim)
{
    w=phrase;
    while(isspace(c=getc(stdin)));
    if(c!=EOF)
        *w++-c;
    if(!isalpha(c))
    {
        *w='\0';
        return c;
    }
    for(;--lim>0;w++)
        if(!isalnum(*w=getc(stdin)))
        {
            ungetc(*w,stdin);
            break;
        }
        *w='\0';
    return phrase[0];
}

main()
{
    struct node *origin;
    char phrase[MAX];
```

```
    NoPhrase p;
    origin=NULL;
    printf("Enter phrases and terminate with ^Z \n");
    while(p.fetch(phrase,MAX)!=EOF)
        if(isalpha(phrase[0]))
            origin=p.addnode(origin,phrase);
    p.disp(origin);
    return 0;
}
```

Output

C:> 4_NoPhrase.exe
Enter phrases and terminate with ^Z
the tce mdu
^Z
the phrase mdu occurs once.
the phrase tce occurs once.
the phrase the occurs once.

Simulates a Calculator

```
#include <stdio.h>
#include <iostream.h>
#include <stdlib.h>
#include <ctype.h>
#define DECPT '.'
typedef enum
{
   IN_ERR,
   OP_ERR,
   OPER_ERR,
   TYPE_ERR
}ERROR_STYPE_ERR;

class Calci
{
   int n,i,count,c;
   double val,fraction;
```

```
public:
   Calci()
   {
       count=0;
       val=0;
   }
   double readnumb();
   double compute(double oper1,char symbol,double oper2);
   //double compute(double op1,int oper,double op2);
   void avoid_spc();
   void disp_error(ERROR_STYPE_ERR);
};

void Calci::disp_error(ERROR_STYPE_ERR ec)
{
   switch(ec)
   {
   case IN_ERR:
       cout<<"Error: invalid input.";
       break;
   case OP_ERR:
       cout<<"Error: Wrong operand.";
       break;
   case OPER_ERR:
       cout<<"Error: stray operator.";
       break;
   case TYPE_ERR:
       cout<<"Error: data mismatch.";
       break;
   default:
       cout<<"Error: Wrong error code="<<ec;
       break;
   }
}
double Calci::compute (double oper1,char symbol,double oper2)
{
   switch(symbol)
   {
```

```
    case '+':
        return oper1+oper2;
    case '-':
        return oper1-oper2;
    case '*':
        return oper1*oper2;
    case '/':
        return oper1/oper2;
    default:
        disp_error(OPER_ERR);
        exit(1);
    }
}
double Calci::readnumb ()
{
    val=0;
    while(isdigit(n=getchar()))
    {
        val=val*10;
        val=val+(n-'0');
    }
    if(n==DECPT)
        while(isdigit(n=getchar()))
        {
            ++count;
            fraction=n-'0';
            for(i=0;i<count;++i)
                fraction=fraction/10;
            val=val+fraction;
        }
    ungetc(n,stdin);
return val;
}
void Calci::avoid_spc ()
{
    while(isspace(c=getchar()));
    ungetc(c,stdin);
}
```

```
main()
{
   double op1,op2,res;
   char oper;
   Calci c;
   printf("Enter <n1> <symb> <n2> : \n");
   c.avoid_spc();
   op1=c.readnumb();
   c.avoid_spc();
   oper=getchar();
   c.avoid_spc();
   op2=c.readnumb();
   res=c.compute(op1,oper,op2);
   cout<<op1<<" "<<oper<<" "<<op2<<" = "<<res;
   return 0;
}
```

Output:

C:> 5_Calculator.exe

Enter <n1> <symb> <n2> :

12.3 * 3

12.3 * 3 = 36.9

Separates the integer part from a float type number

```
#include<iostream.h>
#include<stdio.h>
#include<ctype.h>
#include<conio.h>
#define DECPT '.'
class sep
{
 public:
   float value;
void cal(void);
float readnumb(void);
};
void sep::cal()
{
```

```
     value=readnumb();
       cout<<"\nThe whole number is ";
 cout<<value;
 }
 float sep::readnumb()
 {
    int i,n,count=0;
    float val=0,fraction;
 cout<<"Now enter a float type value :\n";
 while(isdigit(n=getchar()))
 {
     val=val*10;
 val=val+(n-'0');
 }
 cout<<"The integral part is "<<val;
 if(n==DECPT)
    while(isdigit(n=getchar()))
      {
    ++count;
     fraction=n-'0';
  for(i=0;i<count;i++)
   fraction=fraction/10;
 val=val+fraction;
 }
 ungetc(n,stdin);
 return val;
 }
 void main()
 {
    sep j;
    clrscr();
 j.cal();
 }
```

Output:

Now enter a float type value:

12.3

The integral part is 12

The whole number is 12.3

Sort integers in an array

```
#include<stdio.h>
#define MAX  10
#include<iostream.h>
#include<conio.h>
class sort
{
    public:
           int i,array[MAX];
    void ip(void);
void sor(int array [],int array_size);

};

void sort::ip()
{
 cout<<"Enter the values for the array :\n";
    for(i=0;i<MAX;i++)
           cin>>array[i];
sor(array,sizeof(array)/sizeof(array[0]));
cout<<"\nThe sorted array is :\n";
for(i=0;i<MAX;i++)
       cout<<array[i]<<" ";
}
void sort::sor(int array[],int array_size)
{
int i,j,temp,order=0;
while(!order)
{
   order=1;
       for(j=0;j<array_size-1;j++)
           {
    if(array[j]>array[j+1])
{
       order=0;
temp=array[j];
array[j]=array[j+1];
```

```
array[j+1]=temp;
}
}
}
}
void main()
{
clrscr();
   sort d;
d.ip();
}
```

Output:

Enter the values for the array :

12 0 -5 67 56 123 4 34 76 99

The sorted array is :

-5 0 4 12 34 56 67 76 99 123

Stack Operation

```
#include<iostream.h>
#include<conio.h>
class stack
{
  public:
   int i;float d;
int sp;
float val[5];
void push(float );
float pop(void);
void ip(void);
void op(void);
};
void stack::ip()
{      sp=0;
cout<<"Enter the values to store in stack :\n";
for(i=0;i<5;++i)
{
```

```
   cin>>d;
  push(d);
  }

  }
  void stack::op()
  {
     push(99);
      cout<<"The values in the stack are :\n";
  for(i=0;i<5;i++)
     cout<<pop()<<"\n";
     pop();
  }
  void stack::push(float d)
  {
     if(sp<5)
         val [sp++]=d;
  else
     cout<<"Stack is full. Cannot push "<<d<<"\n";
  }
  float stack::pop()
  {
  if(sp>0)
      return val[--sp];
  else
   cout<<"Too many pops!";
  }
  void main()
  {
      stack si;
      clrscr();
  si.ip();
  si.op();
  }
```

Output

Enter the values to store in stack :

123

234

456

567

678

stack is full. cannot push 99

The values in the stack are :

678

567

456

234

123

Too many pops!

Evaluates trigonometric values

```
#include<iostream.h>
#include<math.h>
#include<conio.h>
typedef struct
{
  double sineval,cosineval,tanval;
}TRIGNO;
TRIGNO* fetch(double angle)
{
static TRIGNO output;
output.sineval=sin(angle);
output.cosineval=cos(angle);
output.tanval=tan(angle);
return &output;
}
void main()
{
    static TRIGNO res;
double trigval;
clrscr();
cout<<"Enter a trignometric value in degrees :";
cin>>trigval;
res=*fetch(trigval*22/(180*7));
cout<<"\nsineval value is "<<res.sineval;
```

```
cout<<"\ncosineval value is "<<res.cosineval;
cout<<"\ntanval value is "<<res.tanval;
}
```

Output

Enter a trignometric value in degrees :45

sineval value is 0.70733

cosineval value is 0.706883

tanval value is 1.00632

Command line argument for calculation

```
#include<iostream.h>
#include<math.h>
void main(int argc,char *argv[])
{
   float n,m;
   if(argc<3 || argc>3)
   {
      cout<<"\nEnter correct number of parameters :";
   }
   n=atof(*++argv);
   m=atof(*++argv);
   cout<<"\n"<<n<<"^"<<m<<" is "<<pow(n,m);
}
```

Output

d:\TC\BIN>cmdlinea 3 4

3 ^ 4 is 81

Converts String to number

```
#include<iostream.h>
#include<stdio.h>
#include<ctype.h>
#include<conio.h>
class ston
{
public:
   char st[10];
```

```
long numb;
void ip(void);
void op(void);
long atoi(char st[]);
};
void ston::ip()
{
cout<<"Enter numeric string";
cin>>st;
numb=atoi(st);
}
long ston::atoi(char st[])
{
  int ind,res,si;
for(ind=0;isspace(st[ind]);ind++)
    si=1;
if(st[ind]=='+'||st[ind]=='-')
  ind++;
for(res=0;isdigit(st[ind]);ind++)
  res=res*10+(st[ind]-'0');
return si*res;
}
void ston::op()
{
   cout<<"The converted number is"<<"\n";
cout<<numb;
}
void main()
{
 ston a;
 clrscr();
a.ip();
a.op();
getch();
}
```

Output

Enter numeric string

-12345 <>

The converted number is

31400

Finds Common elements in two strings

```
#include<iostream.h>
#include<stdio.h>
#include<conio.h>
class fc
{  public:
   char s1[10],s2[10];
int n;
void ip(void);
int trace(char st1[],char st2[]);
};
void fc::ip()
{
 cout<<"Enter the first string :";
cin>>s1;
cout<<"Enter the second string :";
cin>>s2;
n=trace(s1,s2);
if(n==0)
   cout<<"No common elements found.";
else
   cout<<"Number of common elements is "<<n;
}
int fc::trace(char st1[10],char st2[10])
{
    int  i,j,k;
k=0;
for(i=0;i<10;i++)
    for(j=0;j<10;j++)
        if(st1[i]!='\0' && st1[i]==st2[j])
    {
```

```
    k++;
  }
 return k;
 }
 void main()
 {
   clrscr();
  fc g;
 g.ip();
 }
```

Output:

Enter the first string :Trichy

Enter the second string :Madras

No. of common elements = 1

Enter the first string :Adcd

Enter the second string :Efgh

No common elements found.

Finds a target word

```
#include <iostream.h>
#include <conio.h>
#include <stdio.h>
#define MAX 500
class findtarg
{
   public:
       char sen[MAX],pat[10];int got;
   void ip();
   int fetch(char[],int);
   int match(char[],char[]);
};
void findtarg::ip()
{
   got=0;
   cout<<"Enter word to match :";
   cin>>pat;
```

```
   cout<<"\nEnter the sentences : \n";
   while(fetch(sen,MAX)>0)
   {
       if(match(sen,pat)>=0)
       {
           cout<<"\nThere is a match:"<<sen<<"\n";
           got++;
       }

   }

}
int findtarg::fetch(char st[],int high)
{
   int i,j;
   j=0;
   while(--high>0 && (i=getchar())!=EOF && i!='\n')
       st[j++]=i;
   if(i=='\n')
       st[j++]=i;
       st[j]='\0';
   return j;
}
int findtarg::match(char orig[],char targ[])
{
   int i,j,k;
   for(i=0;orig[i]!='\0';i++)
   {
       for(j=i,k=0;targ[k]!='\0' && orig[j]==targ[k];j++,k++)
       if(k>0 && targ[k]=='\0')
           return i;
   }
   return -1;
}
void main()
{
```

```
    findtarg f;
    clrscr();
    f.ip();
}
```

Output:

Enter word to match: Madurai <>

Enter the sentences:

Thiagarajar college of engineering<>

Madurai tirupparankundram<>

There is a match:Madurai

^Z

Quick Sort algorithm

```
#include<iostream.h>
#include<conio.h>
class qsort
{
  public:
   int ar[10],i,e,w;
void swap(int arr[] ,int i ,int j );
void qqsort(int arr[] ,int l ,int r );
void op(void);
void ip(void);
};
void qsort::ip(void)
{
  cout<<"Enter your values :";
e=0;w=9;
for(i=0;i<10;i++)
{
  cin>>ar[i];
}
qqsort(ar,e,w);
}
void qsort::qqsort(int arr[],int l,int r)
{
```

```
    int j,last;
   if(l>=r)
     return;
swap(arr,l,(l+r)/2);
last=l;
for(j=l+1;j<=r;j++)
   if(arr[j]<arr[l])
swap(arr,++last,j);
swap(arr,l,last);
qqsort(arr,l,last-1);
qqsort(arr,last+1,r);
}
void qsort::swap(int arr[],int i,int j)
{
   int temp;
temp=arr[i];
arr[i]=arr[j];
arr[j]=temp;
}
void qsort::op()
{
    cout<<"the sorted array is";
for(i=0;i<10;i++)
 {
   cout<<ar[i];
cout<<"\n";
}
}
void main()
{
     qsort a;
     clrscr();
a.ip();
a.op();
getch();
}
```

Output:

Enter your values :

65

76

12

0

54

65

13

86

32

22

The sorted array is

0

12

13

22

32

54

65

65

76

86

Identifies largest sentence

```
#include<iostream.h>
#include<conio.h>
#include<stdio.h>
#define MAX 500
class id
{
 public:
     int linelen;
int nowmax;
char line[MAX];
char large[MAX];
```

```
int fetchline(char line[],int largeline);
void preserve(char des[],char src[]);
void ip(void);
};
void id:: ip(void)
{
    nowmax=0;
    cout<<"Enter some lines of text ending with a newline.";
while((linelen=fetchline(line,MAX))>0 )
   if(linelen>nowmax)
{
    nowmax=linelen;
preserve(large,line);
}
cout<<"The largest sentence so far is \n";
if(nowmax>0)
   cout<<large;
}
int id::fetchline(char x[],int size)
{
  int ch,j;
 for(j=0;j<size-1&&(ch=getchar())!=EOF&&ch!='\n';++j)
   x[j]=ch;
if(ch=='\n')
 {
 x[j]=ch;
++j;
}
x[j]='\0';
return j;
}
void id::preserve(char des[],char src[])
{
   int j;
j=0;
while((des[j]=src[j])!='\0')
++j;
}
```

```
void main()
{
    id f;
    clrscr();
   f.ip();
}
```

Output:

Enter some lines of text ending with a newline :
thiagarajar college of engg
the quick brown fox jumps over the lazy dog
madrai
^Z
The largest sentence so far is
the quick brown fox jumps over the lazy dog

Counts words,Spaces,Chars

```
#include<iostream.h>
#include<stdio.h>
#include<conio.h>
class count
{
  public:
       int i,wsp,cha;
int ch;
        int digit[10];
void ip(void);
void op(void);
void cal(void);
};
void count::ip()
{
   wsp=cha=0;
    for(i=0;i<10;++i)
    digit[i]=0;
}
void count::op()
{
```

```
            cout<<"\nOutput : ";
    for(i=0;i<10;i++)
            cout<<digit[i]<<" ";
    cout<<"\nWhite space : ";
    cout<<wsp<<"\nOther characters :"<<cha;
    }
    void count::cal()
    {
       while((ch=getchar())!=EOF)
    {
       if(ch>'0'&&ch<='9')
       {
            //cout<<"Number :";
           ++digit[ch-'0'];
       }
     else if(ch==' '||ch=='\n'||ch=='\t')
         ++wsp;
    else
           ++cha;
    }
    }
    void main()
    {
        count ab;
        clrscr();
    ab.ip();
    ab.cal();
    ab.op();
    }
```

Output

thiagarajar college of engineering

madurai - 625015

tamilnadu phone 882242

^Z

Output : 0 1 4 0 1 2 1 0 2 0

White space : 10

Other characters : 54

Counts words,Spaces,Chars

```
#include<stdio.h>
#include<iostream.h>
#include<conio.h>
class count
{
   public:
    int ch,i,nw,no,nd[10];
void cal(void);
void ip(void);
void op(void);
};
void count::ip()
{
   nw=no=0;
   for(i=0;i<10;++i)
       nd[i]=0;
}
void count::cal()
{
cout<<"Enter a few lines of code :\n";
while((ch=getchar())!=EOF)
{
switch(ch)
{
    case'0': case '1': case '2':
case'3': case '4':case'5':case '6':
case '7': case '8':case '9':
nd[ch-'0']++;
break;
case' ': case '\n': case '\t':
nw++;
break;
default:
    no++;
break;
}
```

```
}
}
void count::op()
{
cout<<"Digits = ";
 for(i=0;i<10;i++)
   cout<<nd[i]<<" ";
cout<<"White space = "<<nw;
cout<<"Others are = "<<no;
}
void main()
{
   clrscr();
  count d;
d.ip();
d.cal();
d.op();
}
```

Output:

Enter a few lines of code :
thiagarajar college of engineering
madurai 625015
phone 882242
^Z
digits = 1 1 4 0 1 2 1 0 2 0 White space = 8 Others = 43

Numbers to String conversion

```
#include<iostream.h>
#include<conio.h>
#include<string.h>
class nm
{
 public:
    long i;
char st[10];
void ip(void);
void itoa(long n,char st[]);
```

```
 void rev(char st[]);
};
void nm::ip(void)
{
   cout<<"Enter an integer number :";
    cin>>i;
cout<<"\nThe number is "<<i;
itoa(i,st);
cout<<"\nThe converted string is "<<st;
}
void nm::itoa(long n,char s[])
{
    int i;long sign;
 if((sign=n)<0)
  n=-n;
i=0;
do
{
    s[i++]=n%10+'0';
}while((n/=10)>0);
if(sign<0)
       s[i++]='-';
 s[i]='\0';
rev(s);
}
void nm::rev(char str[])
{
   int i,j;
char ch;
for(i=0,j=(strlen(str))-1;i<j;i++,j--)
{
    ch=str[i];
 str[i]=str[j];
str[j]=ch;
}
}
void main()
{
```

```
 clrscr();
 nm h;
h.ip();
getch();
}
```

Output:

Enter an integer number -56789

The number is -56789

The converted string is -56789

Inverting string

```
#include<iostream.h>
#include<string.h>
#include<conio.h>
class st
{
   public:
    char str[10];
int i;
void rev(char str[]);
void ip(void);
void op(void);
};
void st::ip(void)
{
    cout<<"Enter ten values for the str[10]:\n";
    for(i=0;i<10;i++)
    cin>>str[i];
       cout<<"\nThe original string is :\n";
    for(i=0;i<10;++i)
   cout<<str[i];
       rev(str);
}
void st::rev(char str[])
{
   int i,j;
char ch;
```

```
for(i=0,j=(strlen(str))-1;i<j;i++,j--)
{
    ch=str[i];
 str[i]=str[j];
str[j]=ch;
}
}
void st::op(void)
{
   cout<<"\nThe reverse string is :\n";
    for(i=0;i<10;i++)
   cout<<str[i];
}
void main()
{
 st f;
 clrscr();
f.ip();
f.op();
}
```

Output:

Enter ten values for str[10]:

thirupparnkunram

The original string is:

thiruppara

The reverse string is:

arappuriht

Sorting an Array

```
#include <iostream.h>
#include <conio.h>

class sort
{
   public:
   int  arr[10];
       int elem,i;
```

```
        void ip();
        void shellsort(int[],int);
};
void sort::ip()
{
    elem=10;
    cout<<"\nEnter the strings for arr[10] with space :\n";
    for(i=0;i<10;++i)
        cin>>arr[i];
    cout<<"The original strings are :\n";
    for(i=0;i<10;++i)
        cout<<arr[i]<<" ";
    shellsort(arr,elem);
    cout<<"\nThe sorted array is : \n";
    for(i=0;i<10;++i)
        cout<<arr[i]<<" ";
}
void sort::shellsort(int ar[],int n)
{
    int spc,i,j;
    int temp;
    for(spc=n/2;spc>0;spc/=2)
        for(i=spc;i<n;++i)
                for(j=i-spc;j>=0&&ar[j]>ar[j+spc];j-=spc)
                {
                    temp=ar[j];
                    ar[j]=ar[j+spc];
                    ar[j+spc]=temp;
                }
}
void main()
{
    sort s;
    clrscr();
    s.ip();
}
```

Output:

```
Enter values for arr[10] with space:
77 43 90 12 -9 44 21 65 85 9
The original array is :
77 43 90 12 -9 44 21 65 85 9
The sorted array is :
-9 9 12 21 43 44 65 77 85 90
```

Appendix

Appendix

MARKLIST PROCESSING EXAMPLE

```
#include<fstream.h>
#include<iostream.h>
#include<conio.h>
#include<string.h>
const int MAX =10;
class person
   {
protected:
   char name[30];
   int sub[3] [2];
public:
   person( ) { }
   void getdata( );
   void showdata( );
   };
void person: :getdata( )
   {
   int j;
   cout < <"\n Enter name: "; cin > >name;
       for (j=0; j<=2; j++) {
           sti:cout < <"Enter internal Marks for
           Subject #"; cout< <j+l;cout
           <<" : "; cin>>sub [j]
```

```
        if (sub [ j ] [ 0 ] >25) {cout<<"Please
            Re_enter:\a\n";goto sti;}
                    /*Validation of Input
        ste:cout< <"Enter External Marks for
        Subject #"; cout<<j+1: cout<<" : "; cin>> sub[j]
            if(sub[ j ] [1 ]>75){cout< <"Please
                Re_enter:\a\n";goto ste; }
                                    / /*Validation of E
        }
    }
void person: : showdata( )
    {
    int j;
    int subtotal [ 3 ] = {0,0,0};
        cout < <" \n Name :  \t "< <name;
        cout< <"\n -----------------------------\n";
        cout< <"Subject:     Int Ext Total P/F|n";
        cout< <"-----------------------------\n";
        for ( j=0; j<=2; j++)
            {subtotal [ j ]=sub [ j ] [ 0 ] + sub [ j ] [ 1 ];
            cout< <"\n Subject #"; cout<<j+1; cout<<"\t\t\t\t:";
            cout<<" "; cout<<sub [ j ] [ 0 ];
            cout<<" "; cout<<sub [ j ] [ 1 ];
            cout<<" "; cout<<subtotal [ j ];
        /* Catagorize as Pass/Fail */
            if (subtotal [ j ] <50 | | sub [ j ] [ 1 ] < 30) cout
            <<"FAIL";
                    else cout< <" PASS";
            }
    cout<<"\n----------------------------\n";
    cout <<"Total Marks: \t\t\t\t\t ||
    "<<subtotal [0]+ subtotal [ 1 ] + subtotal [ 2 ];
    cout <<"\n";
        }
    void main (void)
        {
        person pers;
```

```
     fstream file;
     int select, num;
     rep:
         clrscr ( );
         cout << "\n1. To create the file";
         cout << "\n2. To process";
         cout << "\n3. quit\n";
         cin >>select;
     /*open the file for writing */
     switch(select) {
     case 1 :
         cout <<"Enter the number of students";
         cin >>num;
         file.open ("STU.DAT", ios::out);
             for (int j=0; j<num;j++)
             {
             cout <<\nEnter person's data: ";
             pers.getdata( );
             file.write( (char*)&pers, sizeof(pers) );
             }
             file.close( );
             goto rep;

             break;
case 2:
/* open the file for Reading */
file.open("STU.DAT",ios: :in );
if (!file) cout < <"Can't find...";
file.read( (char*)&pers, sizeof(pers) );
    while (!file.eof ( ) ) {
    clrscr( );
    pers.showdata( );
    file.read( (char*)&pers, sizeof (pers) );
    getch ( );
    }
file.close ( );
goto rep;
break;
```

```
case 3:
   break;
} }
```

To run the above program, create mark.exe file by compiling it with Tubro C++ compiler. Then run it by entering the name "mark" against the C > prompt.

C > mark < ret >

1. To create the file

2. To process

3. quit

1. < ret >

Enter the number of students 2 < ret >

Enter person's data:

Enter name: J. Vivek < ret >

Enter internal marks for Subject #1:25 < ret >

Enter External marks for Subject #1:46 < ret >

Enter internal marks for Subject #2:24 < ret >

Enter External marks for Subject #2:56 < ret >

Enter internal marks for Subject #3:22 < ret >

Enter External marks for Subject #3:58 < ret >

Enter person's data:

Enter name: V. Ramprakash < ret >

Enter internal marks for Subject #1:24 < ret >

Enter External marks for Subject#1:36 < ret >

Enter External marks for Subject #2:25 < ret >

Enter External marks for Subject #2:45 < ret >

Enter internal marks for Subject #3:22 < ret >

Enter External marks for Subject #3:54 < ret >

1. To create the file

2. To process

3. quit

2. < ret >

Name: J.Vivek

Subject	Int	Ext	Total	P/F
Subject #1	: 25	46	71	PASS
Subject #2	: 24	56	80	PASS
Subject #3	: 22	58	80	PASS
Total Marks			231	< ret >

Name: V. Ramprakash

Subject	Int	Ext	Total	P/F
Subject #1	: 24	36	60	PASS
Subject #2	: 25	45	70	PASS
Subject #3	: 22	54	76	PASS

Total Marks 206

<ret>

C>

Payroll Processing Example

```
#include<fstream.h>     //fstream prototype
#include<process.h>     //exit prototype
#include<conio.h>       //clrscr prototype
#include<stdio.h>       //getchar prototype
#include<io.h>
class employee

   private:
       char name[20];
       int num;
       char desig[20];
       int basic;
   public:
       void getdata( );
       void showdata( );
       void updata( );
       void payslip( );
       int checkkey (int);
   };
void employee: :getdata( )
   {
   cout < <"\n\t            NAME        :";
   cin>> name;
   cout < <"\n\t            NUMBER      :";
   cin>>num;
   cout< <"\n\t             DESIGNATION :";
   cin>>desig;                          :";
```

```
    cout<< "\n\t              BASICPAY    :";
    cin >> basic;
    }
void employee: :showdata ( )
    {
    cout < <" \n    1:NAME            :\t "< < name;
    cout < <"\n     2:NUMBER          :\t "<<num;
    cout < <"\n     3:DESIGNATION     :\t "< <desig;
    cout < < "\n    4 : BASICPAY      :\ t "< <basic;
void employee::updata( )
    {
    int fld;
    char ans;
    up: showdata( );
        cout< <" \n \n Enter the field number
    you want to change \n";
        cin > >fld;
        switch (fld)
        {
    case 1:
        cout <<"\n NAME: \t " < <name;
        cout <<"\n\n NAME:\t";
        cin <<name;
        break;
    case 2:
        cout <<"\ n NUMBER: \t " < <num;
        cout <<"\n\n NUMBER: \t ";
        cin >>num;
        break;
    case 3:
        cout <<"\n DESIGNATION:\t"<<desig;
        cout <<" \n\n DESIGNATION: \t";
        cin > >desig;
        break;
    case 4:
        cout < <" \n BASICPAY : \t " < <basic;
        cout < <"\n\n BASICPAY : \t";
        cin > >basic;
```

```
        break;
    default:
        cout <<"\ n WRONG CHOICE";
    }
    cout < <" \n \n You want to change some more?";
    cin > > ans;
    clrscr ( );
        if (ans == 'y' || ans == 'Y') goto up;
    }
void employee: :payslip( )
    {
    float da, hra, ada, lic, gis, spt, it, gross, ded;
    cout < <"n\t\t\t ABC COMPANY\n" ;
    cout < <"\n\t\t PAY SLIP FOR THE MONTH OF MAY \n\n\n";
    cout < <"\t\t\t —— ------------\n\n";
    cout <<"\t NAME      : "< <name;
    cout <<" \t\t\t NUMBER: "<<num<<endl<<endl
<<endl;
    cout <<"\t BASIC     : "<<basic;
    lic=0.05*basic;
    cout <<"\t LIC       : "<<lic< <endl;
    da = 0.9*basic;
    cout <<" \t DA       : "<<da;
    it = 0.2*basic;
    cout <<" \t I.T      : "<<it< <endl;
    hra = 0.3*basic;
    cout <<" \t H.R.A.  :"<<hra;
    spf = 0. 1*basic;
    cout <<" \t Sp. F    : "<<spf< <endl;
    ada = 0. 2*basic;
    cout <<" \t Addl.DA : "<<ada;
    gis=20;
    cout <<" \t G.I.S    : "<<gis<<endl<endl;
    gross = basic + da+hra+ada;
    cout <<" \t GROSS         : "<<gross;
    ded = lic+it+spf+gis;
    cout <<" \t DEDUCTIONS  : "<<ded<end 1<endl;
```

```
cout  <<"\t\t\t NET PAY : "< <gross-ded;
}
int employee: :checkkey(int k )
{
if (k == num)
return ( 0 );
else return (1);
}
void main (void)
{
char ans;
int count;
int key;
    int choice;
employee person;
fstream file;
up:
clrscr ( );
cout < <" \ t1 : CREATE \n";
cout < <" \ t2 : APPEND\n";
cout < <" \ t3 :. UPDATE\n";
cout < <" \ t4 : PAYSLIP \n"; ;
cout < <" \ t5 : SHOW \n";
cout < <" \ t6 : QUIT \n";
cout < <" \n\n\t ENTER CHOICE:";
cin > >choice;
switch (choice)
{
case 1:
    file.open ("person.dat",ios:: out);
    do
    clrscr( );
    person.getdata( );
    file.write ((char *)&person, sizeof
    (person) );
    cout <<" \n\n Do you want to add more?\t";
    cin >> ans;
    }
```

```
    while (ans =='y' || ans =='Y'); file.close( );
    break ;
case 2:
    file.open ("person.dat", ios :: app);
    do
    {
    clrscr( );
    person.getdata( );
    file.write((char *)&person, sizeof
    (person));
    cout<<" \nDo you want to add more?\t";
    cin >>ans;
    }
    while(ans == 'y' || ans == 'Y');.
    file.close ( );
    break;
case 3:
    file.open ("person.dat",ios :: out | ios ::in );
    do
    {
    cout <<"\n \t ENTER NUM:";
    cin >>key;
    clrscr( ); file.seekg(0); count = 0;
        do
        {
    file.read ( (char *)&person, size of
    (person));
    count + =1;
        if(person.checkkey (key) == 0)
            {
            person.updata ( );
            file.seekg ((count-1)*sizeof (person ));
            file.write ((char*)&person, sizeof(person));
        break;
            }
        } while (!file.eof( ));
    cout <<" \n \n Do you want to update more?\t";
    cin > >ans;
```

```
        } while (ans == 'y' || ans == 'Y');
        file.close( );
    break;
case 4:
    file.open("person.dat", ios: :in );
    do
        {
        cout < <"\n \t ENTER NUM : ";
        cin > >key;
        clrscr( );
        file.seekg(0);
        while ( !file.eof( ) )
            {
            file.read (( char *)&person, size of (person )) ;
            if (person.checkkey(key) == 0)
                {
                person.payslip( );
                break;
                }
            }
        cout <<"\n\n\tDo you want to prepare more?\t";
        cin > >ans;
        } while (ans = = 'y' || ans = = 'Y' );
        file.close ( );
        break;
        case 5:
            file.open("person.dat", ios: :in);
            file.seekg(0);
            if(!file) cout <<"can't find ....";
            else
            file.read ((char*)&person, sizeof (person));
            while (!file.eof( ))
            {
            clrscr( );
            person.showdata( );
            getch( );
            file.read ( ( char*)&person, size of (person ));
            }}
```

```
            file.close ( );
            break;
        case 6:
            exit ( 0 );
    goto up;
    }
```

A Sample run:

1. CREATE
2. APPEND
3. UPDATE
4. PAYSLIP
5. SHOW
6. QUIT

ENTER CHOICE:1

ENTER NAME :	R. Raman
ENTER NUMBER :	1200
ENTER DESIGNATION :	Asst. Professor
ENTER BASICPAY :	5000
Do you want to add more :	Y
ENTER NAME :	R. Murugan
ENTERNUMBER :	1300
ENTER DESIGNATION :	Lecturer
ENTER BASICPAY :	2200
Do you want to add more :	N

1. CREATE
2. APPEND
3. UPDATE
4. PAYSLIP
5. SHOW
6. QUIT

ENTER CHOICE : 5

1. NAME	: R. Raman
2. NUMBER	: 1200
3. DESIGNATION	: Asst. Professor
4. BASICPAY	: 5000

1. NAME : R. Murugan
2. NUMBER : 1300
3. DESIGNATION : Lecturer
4. BASICPAY : 2200
1. CREATE
2. APPEND
3. UPDATE
4. PAYSLIP
5. SHOW
6. QUIT

ENTER CHOICE : 4

ABC COMPANY

PAYSLIP FOR THE MONTH OF MAY

NAME: R. Raman		0	NUMBER : 1200
BASIC	: 5000	LIC	250
DA	: 4500	I.T.	1000
H.R.A.	: 1500	Sp.F	500
Addl. DA	: 1000	G.I.S	20
GROSS	: 12000	DEDUCTIONS: 1770	

NET PAY : 10230

Do you want to prepare more? y

ABC COMPANY

PAYSLIP FOR THE MONTH OF MAY

NAME	R. Raman	Number	1200
BASIC	: 2200	LIC	110
DA	: 1980	I.T.	440
H.R.A.	: 660	Sp.F	220
Addl. DA	: 440	G.I.S	20
GROSS 5280		DEDUCTIONS : 790	

NET PAY : 4490

Do you want to prepare more? n

1. CREATE
2. APPEND
3. UPDATE
4. PAYSLIP

```
5. SHOW
6. QUIT
ENTER CHOICE : 3
ENTER NUM: 1200
     1. NAME                  : R. Raman
     2. NUMBER                : 1200
     3. DESIGNATION           : Asst. Professor
     4. BASICPAY              : 5000
Enter the Field number you want to change : 4
     BASICPAY         : 5000
     BASICPAY         : 6000
You want to change some more ? n
Do you want to update more ? n
1. CREATE
2. APPEND
3. UPDATE
4. PAYSLIP
5. SHOW
6. QUITE
ENTER CHOICE : 6
C:>
```

EXERCISE

CHAPTER 2

2.1 Develop a program which accepts degree in Fahrenheit through the keyboard and converts it into Celcius.

2.2 Develop a program to determine the volume of a sphere given vol= (4/3)*pi*r*r*r.

2.3 Write a program which accepts a number like 70000 through the keyboard using data types such as int, unsigned, long and arrange to display it in all forms.

2.4 Write a program involving the sqrt ( ) predefined function to evaluate the square root of a double type number 9876.0.

CHAPTER 3

3.1 Write a program that raises the number 7 to the power of 4. Use a while statement to test whether the exponent is positive.

3.2 Develop a program using the do.while structure to determine the sum of a series of real numbers and then evaluate its average.

3.3 Develop a program using the concept of nesting an if statement within a for statement to decide the number of males and females out of a total of 100 people arriving at a function and maintain a count of each category.

3.4 Write a program which uses the if.. else structure to add the marks of 6 subjects of a student and decide his pass or fail status. Evolve you own startegy to declare pass or fail.

3.5 Develop a program using the else if construction to determine if an employee in a company is a manager, an assistant, casher or a worker. Evolve your own code to identify these persons.

3.6 Write a program using the switch statement to determine the nature of account a customer has in a bank.

CHAPTER 4

4.1 Develop a program incorporating a structure called student containing his particulars of marks in various subjects, name and register number. The program should use this structure, process his marks and declare him qualified or otherwise.

4.2 Rewrite the program in question 4.1 using the concept of structure within a structure; the first structure contains the name and register number, and the second structure contain marks and fee particulars.

4.3 Write a program using the enumerated data type to enter the Roman calendar months in sequence and determine if a particular month entered through the keyboard figures before or after June.

CHAPTER 5

5.1 Develop a program which accepts US $ through the keyboard and uses a user-defined function to convert it into Indian Rupees and Paise. Evolve a structure to declare the US currency and pass the structure variable to the processing function.

5.2 Develop a program which creates a structure to define the Indian currency. Write a function which adds two Indian currencies and converts it into US $. Develop another function which could display this result.

5.3 Develop a program which has a structure defining Indian currency, a structure variable and overloaded functions to display Indian currency in Rs. Ps. and whole Rs. only.

5.4 Develop an inline function to convert US $ into Indian rupees.

CHAPTER 6

6.1 Write a program which declares a class called student with its private data and public functions. The data pertains to the student's particulars like name, register number, marks in subjects. The public functions should elicit the student's particulars and arrange to display them on the VDU monitor.

6.2 Develop a class called currency with its private data and public functions. Define a constructor which receives two objects from the main ( ) function and adds them and displays the sum of the two objects of currency.

CHAPTER 7

7.1 Write a program using a 2 dimensional array which gives the sales figures on region-wise month-wise basis. Your program should determine the salesman who did the largest sales and applaud him.

7.2 Develop a program which uses an array of structures for an inventory control program. On giving the code number of the product, your program should show its current stock, price, re-order level and net sales amount.

7.3 Develop a program which creates a string array to store a poem of your choice and copy it in the most elegant way into another string array.

7.4 Write a program which treats string as a member of a class called student. The program should receive the marks obtained by the student in various subjects and assess his performance.

CHAPTER 8

8.1 Write a program which overloads the unary operator + + so that it manipulates a counter to count the marks attained by students in a quiz contest.

8.2 Develop a program which overloads the binary + operator so that two objects of a class called currency can be added and the resulting sum displayed.

8.3 Write a program which overloads the binary + operator so that two strings can be concatenated and displayed as a, single string.

8.4 Develop a class called currency containing a conversion function which converts basic data type to user-defined type and vice versa. The program should convert US $ into Indian rupees.

CHAPTER 9

9.1 Develop a class called employees for a company having various categories of employees like manager, clerk, accountant and worker. Define your own base class for employees and other classes should be derived from it. Display the particulars of all employees.

9.2 Develop a program which uses multiple inheritance for an institution having different levels of employees. Get their personal particulars through the keyboard and arrange to display them.

9.3 Develop a program which illustrates the concept of containership. Your program should convert US $ into Indian currency using appropriate class specifications and public functions.

CHAPTER 10

10.1 Develop a program which uses pointers to sort the contents of a multidimensional array containing a series of strings. Your program should arrange the strings in alphabetical order.

10.2 Write a program which allocates memory dynamically using the new operator to store strings in a multidimensional string array.

10.3 Write a program which uses an array of pointers to objects and sort them in the alphabetical sequence.

CHAPTER 11

11.1 Write a program to create a disk file to contain student particulars pertinent to his studies. The program should then read the file and process the results and prepare the marklist.

11.2 Develop a program which uses the concept of redirection to read data from an existing file, process it and arrange for both display in the VDU and storage in another disk file.

11.3 Write a program using the idea of command line argument to execute a program by mentioning its name and furnishing two arguments to be multiplied and display the result.

CHAPTER 12

12.1 Develop a program to create a window and insert your favourite nursery rhyme in it.

12.2 Develop a program to draw the International Olympic symbol. The outline should be in yellow and the inset colours should be assorted colours.

12.3 Develop a graphics program which positions a box at the base, a sphere on it and a cone over it in vertical position. The three objects should be in three different colours.

CHAPTER 13

13.1 Develop a program using the idea of virtual function to draw a box and a cone adjacent to each other in two different colours. You may define a base function and derive two other functions to do the task.

13.2 Develop a friend function and overload the binary + operator to add two objects and display result.

13.3 Develop a program to illustrate a copy constructor so that a string maybe duplicated into another variable either by assignment or copying.

10.2 Write a program which [illegible] in ascending order.

12.1 Develop a program to draw [illegible] on the screen [illegible].

[illegible] Develop a program to [illegible] string [illegible].

Index

A

B

C

D